IMPROVING VOCABULARY SKILLS

SECOND EDITION

IMPROVING VOCABULARY SKILLS *SECOND EDITION*

SHERRIE L. NIST
UNIVERSITY OF GEORGIA

CAROLE MOHR

TOWNSEND PRESS   Marlton, NJ 08053

Books in the Townsend Press Vocabulary Series:

GROUNDWORK FOR A BETTER VOCABULARY, 2/e
BUILDING VOCABULARY SKILLS, 2/e
IMPROVING VOCABULARY SKILLS, 2/e
ADVANCING VOCABULARY SKILLS, 2/e
BUILDING VOCABULARY SKILLS, SHORT VERSION, 2/e
IMPROVING VOCABULARY SKILLS, SHORT VERSION, 2/e
ADVANCING VOCABULARY SKILLS, SHORT VERSION, 2/e

Books in the Townsend Press Reading Series:

GROUNDWORK FOR COLLEGE READING, 2/e
KEYS TO BETTER COLLEGE READING
TEN STEPS TO BUILDING COLLEGE READING SKILLS, FORM A, 2/e
TEN STEPS TO BUILDING COLLEGE READING SKILLS, FORM B, 2/e
TEN STEPS TO IMPROVING COLLEGE READING SKILLS, 2/e
IMPROVING READING COMPREHENSION SKILLS
TEN STEPS TO ADVANCING COLLEGE READING SKILLS, 2/e

Supplements Available for Most Books:

Instructor's Edition
Instructor's Manual, Test Bank, and Computer Guide
Set of Computer Disks (IBM or Macintosh)

Copyright © 1997 by Townsend Press, Inc.
Printed in the United States of America
ISBN 0-944210-33-3
9 8 7 6 5

Send book orders to:
Townsend Press
1038 Industrial Drive
West Berlin, New Jersey 08091

For even faster service, call us at our toll-free number:
1-800-772-6410

Or FAX your request to:
1-609-753-0649

ISBN 0-944210-33-3

Contents

Note: Twenty-six of the chapters present ten words apiece. The other four chapters each cover ten word parts and are so marked. For ease of reference, the title of the selection that closes each chapter is included.

Preface

The problem is all too familiar: *students just don't know enough words*. Reading, writing, and content teachers agree that many students' vocabularies are inadequate for the demands of courses. Weak vocabularies limit students' understanding of what they read and the clarity and depth of what they write.

The purpose of *Improving Vocabulary Skills* and the other books in the Townsend Press vocabulary series is to provide a solid, workable answer to the vocabulary problem. In the course of 30 chapters, *Improving Vocabulary Skills* teaches 260 important words and 40 common word parts. Here are the book's distinctive features:

1 **An intensive words-in-context approach.** Studies show that students learn words best by reading them repeatedly in different contexts, not through rote memorization. The book gives students an intensive in-context experience by presenting each word in six different contexts. Each chapter takes students through a productive sequence of steps:

- Students infer the meaning of each word by considering two sentences in which it appears and then choosing from multiple-choice options.
- On the basis of their inferences, students identify each word's meaning in a matching test. They are then in a solid position to deepen their knowledge of a word.
- Finally, they strengthen their understanding of a word by applying it three times: in two sentence practices and in a selection practice.

Each encounter with a word brings it closer to becoming part of the student's permanent word bank.

2 **Abundant practice.** Along with extensive practice in each chapter, there are a crossword puzzle and a set of unit tests at the end of every six-chapter unit. The puzzle and tests reinforce students' knowledge of the words in each chapter. In addition, most chapters reuse several words from earlier chapters (such repeated words are marked with small circles), allowing for more reinforcement. Last, there are supplementary tests in the *Test Bank* and the computer disks that accompany the book. All this practice means that students learn in the surest possible way: by working closely and repeatedly with each word.

3 **Controlled feedback.** The opening activity in each chapter gives students three multiple-choice options to help them decide on the meaning of a given word. The multiple-choice options also help students to complete the matching test that is the second activity of each chapter. A limited answer key at the back of the book then provides answers for the third activity in the chapter. All these features enable students to take an active role in their own learning.

4 **Focus on essential words.** A good deal of time and research went into selecting the 260 words and 40 word parts featured in the book. Word frequency lists were consulted, along with lists in a wide range of vocabulary books. In addition, the authors and editors each prepared their own lists. A computer was used to help in the consolidation of the many word lists. A long process of group discussion then led to final decisions about the words and word parts that would be most helpful for students on a basic reading level.

5 **Appealing content.** Dull practice materials work against learning. On the other hand, meaningful, lively, and at times even funny sentences and selections can spark students' attention and thus enhance their grasp of the material. For this reason, a great deal of effort was put into creating sentences and selections with both widespread appeal and solid context support. We have tried throughout to make the practice materials truly enjoyable for teachers and students alike. Look, for example, at the selection on page 27 that closes the fifth chapter of this book.

6 **Clear format.** The book has been designed so that its very format contributes to the learning process. Each chapter consists of two two-page spreads. In the first two-page spread (the first such spread is on pages 8–9), students can easily refer to all ten words in context while working on the matching test, which provides a clear meaning for each word. In the second two-page spread, students can refer to a box that shows all ten words while they work through the fill-in activities on these pages.

7 **Supplementary materials.**

a A convenient *Instructor's Edition* is available at no charge to instructors using the book. It is identical to the student book except that it contains answers to all of the activities and tests.

b A combined *Instructor's Manual and Test Bank* is also offered at no charge to instructors who have adopted the book. This booklet contains a general vocabulary placement test as well as a pretest and a posttest for the book and for each of the five units in the text. It also includes teaching guidelines, suggested syllabi, an answer key, and an additional mastery test for each chapter.

c A *comprehensive series of computer disks* also accompanies the book. Free to adopters of 200 or more copies, these disks provide up to four tests for each vocabulary chapter in the book. The disks include a number of user- and instructor-friendly features: brief explanations of answers, a sound option, frequent mention of the user's first name, a running score at the bottom of the screen, a record-keeping file, and (in the case of the Macintosh disks) actual pronunciation of each word.

Probably in no other area of reading instruction is the computer more useful than in reinforcing vocabulary. This vocabulary program takes full advantage of the computer's unique capabilities and motivational appeal. Here's how the program works:

• Students are tested on the ten words in a chapter, with each word in a sentence context different from any in the book itself.

• After students answer each question, they receive immediate feedback: The computer tells if a student is right or wrong and why, frequently using the student's first name and providing a running score.

• When the test is over, the computer supplies a test score and—this especially is what is unique about this program—a chance to retest on the specific words the student got wrong. For example, if a student misses four items on a test, the retest provides four different sentences that test just those four words. Students then receive a score for this special retest. What is so valuable about this, of course, is that the computer gives students added practice in the words they most need to review.

• In addition, the computer offers a second, more challenging test in which students must identify the meanings of the chapter words without benefit of context. This test is a final check that students have really learned the words. And, again, there is the option of a retest, tailor-made to recheck only those words missed on the first definition test.

By the end of this program, students' knowledge of each word in the chapter will have been carefully reinforced. And this reinforcement will be the more effective for having occurred in an electronic medium that especially engages today's students.

To obtain a copy of any of the above materials, instructors may write to the Reading Editor, Townsend Press, Pavilions at Greentree—408, Marlton, NJ 08053. Alternatively, instructors may call our toll-free number: 1-800-772-6410.

8 **Realistic pricing.** As with the first edition, the goal has been to offer the highest possible quality at the best possible price. While *Improving Vocabulary Skills* is comprehensive enough to serve as a primary text, its modest price also makes it an inexpensive supplement.

9 **One in a sequence of books.** The most basic book in the Townsend Press vocabulary series is *Groundwork for a Better Vocabulary*. It is followed by the three main books in the series: *Building Vocabulary Skills* (also a basic text), *Improving Vocabulary Skills* (an intermediate text), and *Advancing Vocabulary Skills* (a more advanced text). There are also short versions of these three books. Suggested grade levels for the books are included in the *Instructor's Manual*. Together, the books can help create a vocabulary foundation that will make any student a better reader, writer, and thinker.

NOTES ON THE SECOND EDITION

A number of changes have been made to the book.

- Instead of an opening preview, each chapter now begins with a new format that uses a multiple-choice question to get students interacting immediately with each word. Teachers' and students' responses to this change have been extremely favorable.

- For ease of grading, including the use of Scantron machines, answer spaces can now be marked either with the letter or number of the word or with the word itself.

- The print in the book has been enlarged, a pronunication key now appears on the inside front cover, a crossword puzzle has been added as a unit review, and the introduction to the book has been expanded. In addition, hundreds of changes have been made throughout the book to make each practice item work as clearly and effectively as possible.

- Thanks to feedback from reviewers and users, many of the words in each chapter are now repeated in context in later chapters (and marked with small circles). Such repetition provides students with even more review and reinforcement.

ACKNOWLEDGMENTS

We are grateful for the enthusiastic comments provided by users of the Townsend Press vocabulary books over the life of the first edition. Particular thanks go to the following reviewers for their many helpful suggestions: Barbara Brennan Culhane, Nassau Community College; Carol Dietrick, Miami-Dade Community College; Larry Falxa, Ventura College; Jacquelin Hanselman, Hillsborough Community College; Shiela P. Kerr, Florida Community College at Jacksonville; John M. Kopec, Boston University; Belinda E. Smith, Wake Technical Community College; Daniel Snook, Montcalm Community College; and William Walcott, Montgomery College. We appreciate as well the editing work of Eliza Comodromos and the design, editing, and proofreading skills of the multi-talented Janet M. Goldstein. Finally, we dedicate this book to the memory of our computer programmer, Terry Hutchison.

Sherrie L. Nist   *Carole Mohr*

Introduction

You have probably often heard it said, "Building vocabulary is important." Maybe you've politely nodded in agreement and then forgotten the matter. But it would be fair for you to ask, "*Why* is vocabulary development important? Provide some evidence." Here are four compelling kinds of evidence.

1 Common sense tells you what many research studies have shown as well: vocabulary is a basic part of reading comprehension. Simply put, if you don't know enough words, you are going to have trouble understanding what you read. An occasional word may not stop you, but if there are too many words you don't know, comprehension will suffer. The content of textbooks is often challenge enough; you don't want to work as well on understanding the words that express that content.

2 Vocabulary is a major part of almost every standardized test, including reading achievement tests, college entrance exams, and armed forces and vocational placement tests. Test developers know that vocabulary is a key measure of both one's learning and one's ability to learn. It is for this reason that they include a separate vocabulary section as well as a reading comprehension section. The more words you know, then, the better you are likely to do on such important tests.

3 Studies have indicated that students with strong vocabularies are more successful in school. And one widely known study found that a good vocabulary, more than any other factor, was common to people enjoying successful careers in life. Words are in fact the tools not just of better reading, but of better writing, speaking, listening, and thinking as well. The more words you have at your command, the more effective your communication can be, and the more influence you can have on the people around you.

4 In today's world, a good vocabulary counts more than ever. Far fewer people work on farms or in factories. Far more are in jobs that provide services or process information. More than ever, words are the tools of our trade: words we use in reading, writing, listening, and speaking. Furthermore, experts say that workers of tomorrow will be called on to change jobs and learn new skills at an ever-increasing pace. The keys to survival and success will be the abilities to communicate skillfully and learn quickly. A solid vocabulary is essential for both of these skills.

Clearly, the evidence is overwhelming that building vocabulary is crucial. The question then becomes, "What is the best way of going about it?"

WORDS IN CONTEXT: THE KEY TO VOCABULARY DEVELOPMENT

Memorizing lists of words is a traditional method of vocabulary development. However, a person is likely to forget such memorized lists quickly. Studies show that to master a word (or a word part), you must see and use it in various contexts. By working actively and repeatedly with a word, you greatly increase the chance of really learning it.

The following activity will make clear how this book is organized and how it uses a words-in-context approach. Answer the questions or fill in the missing words in the spaces provided.

Inside Front Cover and Contents

Turn to the inside front cover.

- The inside front cover provides a _____ that will help you pronounce all the vocabulary words in the book.

Now turn to the table of contents on pages v-vi.

- How many chapters are in the book? _____

- Most chapters present vocabulary words. How many chapters present word parts? _____

- Three short sections follow the last chapter. The first of these sections provides a limited answer key, the second gives helpful information on using _____, and the third is an index of the 260 words and 40 word parts in the book.

Vocabulary Chapters

Turn to Chapter 1 on pages 8–11. This chapter, like all the others, consists of five parts:

- The *first part* of the chapter, on pages 8–9, is titled _____.

    The left-hand column lists the ten words. Under each **boldfaced** word is its _____ (in parentheses). For example, the pronunciation of *absolve* is _____. For a guide to pronunciation, see the inside front cover as well as "Dictionary Use" on page 179.

    Below the pronunciation guide for each word is its part of speech. The part of speech shown for *absolve* is _____. The vocabulary words in this book are mostly nouns, adjectives, and verbs. **Nouns** are words used to name something—a person, place, thing, or idea. Familiar nouns include *boyfriend, city, hat,* and *truth.* **Adjectives** are words that describe nouns, as in the following word pairs: *former* boyfriend, *large* city, *red* hat, *whole* truth. All of the **verbs** in this book express an action of some sort. They tell what someone or something is doing. Common verbs include *sing, separate, support,* and *imagine.*

    To the right of each word are two sentences that will help you understand its meaning. In each sentence, the **context**—the words surrounding the boldfaced word—provides clues you can use to figure out the definition. There are four common types of context clues: examples, synonyms, antonyms, and the general sense of the sentence. Each is briefly described below.

    1 Examples

    A sentence may include examples that reveal what an unfamiliar word means. For instance, take a look at the following sentence from Chapter 1 for the word *eccentric*:

    > Bruce is quite **eccentric**. For example, he lives in a circular house and rides to work on a motorcycle, in a three-piece suit.

    The sentences provide two examples of what makes Bruce eccentric. The first is that he lives in a circular house. The second is that he rides to work on a motorcycle while wearing a three-piece suit. What do these two examples have in common? The answer to that question will tell you what *eccentric* means. Look at the answer choices below, and in the answer space provided, write the letter of the one you feel is correct.

___ *Eccentric* means   a. ordinary.   b. odd.   c. careful.

Both of the examples given in the sentences about Bruce tell us that he is unusual, or odd. So if you wrote *b*, you chose the correct answer.

2 *Synonyms*

Synonyms are words that mean the same or almost the same as another word. For example, the words *joyful, happy*, and *delighted* are synonyms—they all mean about the same thing. Synonyms serve as context clues by providing the meaning of an unknown word that is nearby. The sentence below from Chapter 2 provides a synonym clue for *irate*.

If Kate got angry only occasionally, I could take her more seriously, but she's always **irate** about something or other.

Instead of using *irate* twice, the author used a synonym in the first part of the sentence. Find that synonym, and then choose the letter of the correct answer from the choices below.

___ *Irate* means   a. thrilled.   b. selfish.   c. furious.

The author uses two words to discuss one of Kate's qualities: *angry* and *irate*. This tells us that *irate* must be another way of saying *angry*. (The author could have written, "but she's always *angry* about something or other.") Since *angry* can also mean *furious*, the correct answer is *c*.

3 *Antonyms*

Antonyms are words with opposite meanings. For example, *help* and *harm* are antonyms, as are *work* and *rest*. Antonyms serve as context clues by providing the opposite meaning of an unknown word. For instance, the sentence below from Chapter 1 provides an antonym clue for the word *antagonist*.

In the ring, the two boxers were **antagonists**, but in their private lives they were good friends.

The author is contrasting the boxers' two different relationships, so we can assume that *antagonists* and *good friends* have opposite, or contrasting, meanings. Using that contrast as a clue, write the letter of the answer that you think best defines *antagonist*.

___ *Antagonist* means   a. a supporter.   b. an enemy.   c. an example.

The correct answer is *b*. Because *antagonist* is the opposite of *friend*, it must mean "enemy."

4 *General Sense of the Sentence*

Even when there is no example, synonym, or antonym clue in a sentence, you can still deduce the meaning of an unfamiliar word. For example, look at the sentence from Chapter 1 for the word *malign*.

That vicious Hollywood reporter often **maligns** movie stars, forever damaging their public images.

After studying the context carefully, you should be able to figure out what the reporter does to movie stars. That will be the meaning of *malign*. Write the letter of your choice.

___ *Malign* means   a. to praise.   b. to recognize.   c. to speak ill of.

Since the sentence calls the reporter "vicious" and says she damages public images, it is logical to conclude that she says negative things about movie stars. Thus answer *c* is correct.

By looking closely at the pair of sentences provided for each word, as well as the answer choices, you should be able to decide on the meaning of a word. As you figure out each meaning, you are working actively with the word. You are creating the groundwork you need to understand and to remember the word. *Getting involved with the word and developing a feel for it, based upon its use in context, is the key to word mastery.*

It is with good reason, then, that the directions at the top of page 8 tell you to use the context to figure out each word's _____. Doing so deepens your sense of the word and prepares you for the next activity.

• The *second part* of the chapter, on page 9, is titled _____.

According to research, it is not enough to see a word in context. At a certain point, it is helpful as well to see the meaning of a word. The matching test provides that meaning, but it also makes you look for and think about that meaning. In other words, it continues the active learning that is your surest route to learning and remembering a word.

Note the caution that follows the test. Do not proceed any further until you are sure that you know the correct meaning of each word as used in context.

Keep in mind that a word may have more than one meaning. In fact, some words have quite a few meanings. (If you doubt it, try looking up in a dictionary, for example, the word *make* or *draw*.) In this book, you will focus on one common meaning for each vocabulary word. However, many of the words have additional meanings. For example, in Chapter 13, you will learn that *devastate* means "to upset deeply," as in the sentence "The parents were devastated when they learned that their son had been arrested." If you then look up *devastate* in the dictionary, you will discover that it has another meaning—"to destroy," as in "The hurricane devastated much of Florida." After you learn one common meaning of a word, you will find yourself gradually learning its other meanings in the course of your school and personal reading.

• The *third part* of the chapter, on page 10, is titled _____.

Here are ten sentences that give you an opportunity to apply your understanding of the ten words. After inserting the words, check your answers in the limited key at the back of the book. Be sure to use the answer key as a learning tool only. Doing so will help you to master the words and to prepare for the last two activities and the unit tests, for which answers are not provided.

• The *fourth and fifth parts* of the chapter, on pages 10–11, are titled _____ and _____.

Each practice tests you on all ten words, giving you two more chances to deepen your mastery. In the fifth part, you have the context of an entire passage in which you can practice applying the words.

At the bottom of the last page of this chapter is a box where you can enter your score for the final two checks. These scores should also be entered into the vocabulary performance chart located on the inside back page of the book. To get your score, take 10% off for each item wrong. For example, 0 wrong = 100%, 1 wrong = 90%, 2 wrong = 80%, 3 wrong = 70%, 4 wrong = 60%, and so on.

Word Parts Chapters

Word parts are building blocks used in many English words. Learning word parts can help you to spell and pronounce words, unlock the meanings of unfamiliar words, and remember new words.

This book covers forty word parts—prefixes, suffixes, and roots. **Prefixes** are word parts that are put at the beginning of words. When written separately, a prefix is followed by a hyphen to show that something follows it. For example, the prefix *non* is written like this: *non-*. One common meaning of *non-* is "not," as in the words *nontoxic* and *nonfiction*.

Suffixes are word parts that are added to the end of words. To show that something always comes before a suffix, a hyphen is placed at the beginning. For instance, the suffix *ly* is written like this: *-ly*. A common meaning of *-ly* is "in a certain manner," as in the words *easily* and *proudly*.

Finally, **roots** are word parts that carry the basic meaning of a word. Roots cannot be used alone. To make a complete word, a root must be combined with at least one other word part. Roots are written without hyphens. One common root is *cycl*, which means "circle," as in the words *motorcycle* and *cyclone*.

Each of the four chapters on word parts follows the same sequence as the chapters on vocabulary do. Keep the following guidelines in mind as well. To find the meaning of a word part, you should do two things.

1 First decide on the meaning of each **boldfaced** word in "Ten Word Parts in Context." If you don't know a meaning, use context clues to find it. For example, consider the two sentences and the answer options for the word part *quart* or *quadr-* in Chapter 6. Write the letter of your choice.

> Let's cut the apple into **quarters** so all four of us can have a piece.
>
> The ad said I would **quadruple** my money in two months. But instead of making four times as much money, I lost what I had invested.
>
> ___ The word part *quart* or *quadr-* means   a. overly.   b. two.   c. four.

You can conclude that if four people will be sharing one apple, *quarters* means "four parts." You can also determine that *quadruple* means "to multiply by four."

2 Then decide on the meaning each pair of boldfaced words has in common. This will also be the meaning of the word part they share. In the case of the two sentences above, both words include the idea of something multiplied or divided by four. Thus *quart* or *quadr-* must mean _____.

You now know, in a nutshell, how to proceed with the words in each chapter. Make sure that you do each page very carefully. *Remember that as you work through the activities, you are learning the words.*

How many times in all will you use each word? If you look, you'll see that each chapter gives you the opportunity to work with each word six times. Each "impression" adds to the likelihood that the word will become part of your active vocabulary. You will have further opportunities to use the word in the crossword puzzle and unit tests that end each unit and on the computer disks that are available with the book.

In addition, many of the words are repeated in context in later chapters of the book. Such repeated words are marked with small circles. For example, which words from Chapter 1 are repeated in the Final Check on page 15 of Chapter 2?

_____   _____

A FINAL THOUGHT

The facts are in. A strong vocabulary is a source of power. Words can make you a better reader, writer, speaker, thinker, and learner. They can dramatically increase your chances of success in school and in your job.

But words will not come automatically. They must be learned in a program of regular study. If you commit yourself to learning words, and you work actively and honestly with the chapters in this book, you will not only enrich your vocabulary—you will enrich your life as well.

Unit One

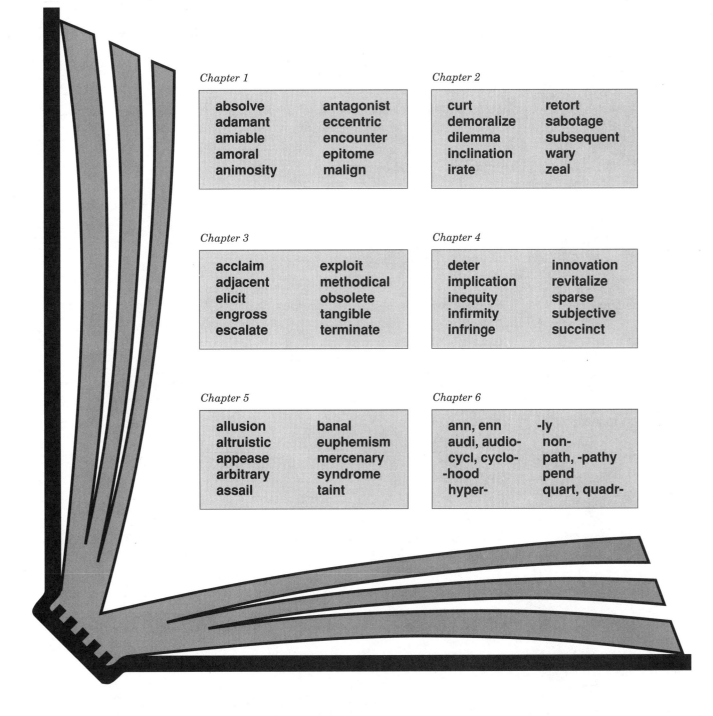

Chapter 1

absolve	antagonist
adamant	eccentric
amiable	encounter
amoral	epitome
animosity	malign

Chapter 2

curt	retort
demoralize	sabotage
dilemma	subsequent
inclination	wary
irate	zeal

Chapter 3

acclaim	exploit
adjacent	methodical
elicit	obsolete
engross	tangible
escalate	terminate

Chapter 4

deter	innovation
implication	revitalize
inequity	sparse
infirmity	subjective
infringe	succinct

Chapter 5

allusion	banal
altruistic	euphemism
appease	mercenary
arbitrary	syndrome
assail	taint

Chapter 6

ann, enn	-ly
audi, audio-	non-
cycl, cyclo-	path, -pathy
-hood	pend
hyper-	quart, quadr-

absolve	antagonist
adamant	eccentric
amiable	encounter
amoral	epitome
animosity	malign

Ten Words in Context

In the space provided, write the letter of the meaning closest to that of each **boldfaced** word. Use the context of the sentences to help you figure out each word's meaning.

1 **absolve**
(ăb-zŏlv′)
-verb

- Having insufficient evidence of his guilt, the jury had to **absolve** Mr. Melman of the murder.
- Accused of taking bribes, the mayor said, "In the end, I'll clear my name and be **absolved** of any wrongdoing."

__ *Absolve* means   a. to accuse.   b. to clear of guilt.   c. to inform.

2 **adamant**
(ăd′ə-mənt)
-adjective

- Ron is **adamant** about not changing plans. He insists we still camp out even though the weather report now says it will be cold and rainy.
- **Adamant** in his support of gun control, Senator Keen won't give in to pressure from powerful opponents.

__ *Adamant* means   a. firm.   b. uncertain.   c. flexible.

3 **amiable**
(ā′mē-ə-bəl)
-adjective

- My **amiable** dog greets both strangers and old friends with a happy yip and energetic tail-wagging.
- At first, our history teacher doesn't seem very friendly, but once you get to know her, she shows her **amiable** side.

__ *Amiable* means   a. intelligent.   b. uncaring.   c. good-natured.

4 **amoral**
(ā-mŏr′əl)
-adjective

- Jerry is almost totally **amoral**. He cares only about making money and having fun and couldn't care less about right or wrong.
- A former president of Uganda, Idi Amin, was truly **amoral**. He jailed, tortured, and killed innocent opponents without the slightest feeling of guilt.

__ *Amoral* means   a. cowardly.   b. lazy.   c. lacking ethical principles.

5 **animosity**
(ăn′ə-mŏs′ə-tē)
-noun

- I was shocked when Sandy said she hated Lionel. I'd never realized she felt such **animosity** toward him.
- Ill will between the two families goes back so many generations that nobody remembers what originally caused the **animosity**.

__ *Animosity* means   a. strong dislike.   b. admiration.   c. great fear.

6 **antagonist**
(ăn-tăg′ə-nĭst)
-noun

- At the divorce hearing, the husband and wife were such bitter **antagonists** that it was hard to believe they had once loved each other.
- In the ring, the two boxers were **antagonists**, but in their private lives they were good friends.

__ *Antagonist* means   a. a supporter.   b. an enemy.   c. an example.

7. **eccentric**
(ĭk-sĕn′trĭk)
-adjective

- Bruce is quite **eccentric**. For example, he lives in a circular house and rides to work on a motorcycle, in a three-piece suit.
- Florence Nightingale, the famous nursing reformer, had the **eccentric** habit of carrying a pet owl around in one of her pockets.

___ *Eccentric* means   a. ordinary.   b. odd.   c. careful.

8. **encounter**
(ĕn-koun′tər)
-verb

- I was surprised to **encounter** Matt in a supermarket in Los Angeles, since I thought he still lived in Chicago.
- I dislike returning to my small hometown, where I am likely to **encounter** people who knew me as a troubled kid.

___ *Encounter* means   a. to think of.   b. to forget.   c. to meet.

9. **epitome**
(ĭ-pĭt′ə-mē)
-noun

- To many, the **epitome** of cuteness is a furry, round-eyed puppy.
- The great ballplayer and civil rights leader Jackie Robinson was the **epitome** of both physical and moral strength.

___ *Epitome* means   a. a perfect model.   b. an opposite.   c. a main cause.

10. **malign**
(mə′līn)
-verb

- Stacy continually **maligns** her ex-husband. The way she describes him, you'd think he was a cross between a blockhead and a mass murderer.
- That vicious Hollywood reporter often **maligns** movie stars, forever damaging their public images.

___ *Malign* means   a. to praise.   b. to recognize.   c. to speak ill of.

Matching Words with Definitions

Following are definitions of the ten words. Clearly write or print each word next to its definition. The sentences above and on the previous page will help you decide on the meaning of each word.

1. _____ Not giving in; stubborn

2. _____ Lacking a moral sense; without principles

3. _____ Differing from what is customary; odd

4. _____ To find innocent or blameless

5. _____ To meet unexpectedly; come upon

6. _____ A perfect or typical example of a general quality or type

7. _____ An opponent; one who opposes or competes

8. _____ Bitter hostility

9. _____ To make evil and often untrue statements about; speak evil of

10. _____ Good-natured; friendly and pleasant

CAUTION: Do not go any further until you are sure the above answers are correct. Then you can use the definitions to help you in the following practices. Your goal is eventually to know the words well enough so that you don't need to check the definitions at all.

➣ *Sentence Check 1*

Using the answer line provided, complete each item below with the correct word from the box. Use each word once.

a. absolve	b. adamant	c. amiable	d. amoral	e. animosity
f. antagonist	g. eccentric	h. encounter	i. epitome	j. malign

_____ 1. Lilly was ___ in her belief that Sam was faithful. Even lipstick on his cheek didn't weaken her trust in him.

_____ 2. My brothers had planned to meet in the restaurant, but they ___(e)d each other in the parking lot.

_____ 3. I'm tired of hearing the two candidates for governor ___ each other with stupid insults.

_____ 4. Because he doesn't want to lose a sale, Mac remains polite and ___ even when he's annoyed with a customer.

_____ 5. Some criminals are truly ___—they don't see that some actions are right and that others are wrong.

_____ 6. The ___ of refreshment is drinking an ice-cold lemonade on a sizzling hot day.

_____ 7. Jed was ___(e)d of stealing money from the company, but the damage the accusation did to his reputation remained.

_____ 8. The owners of the department store were always competing with each other. They acted more like ____s than partners.

_____ 9. I avoid serious discussions with my sister because she shows great ___ toward me if I don't share her opinion.

_____ 10. Today it's not odd for females to learn carpentry, but when my mother went to high school, girls who took wood shop were considered ___.

NOTE: Now check your answers to these questions by turning to page 175. Going over the answers carefully will help you prepare for the next two practices, for which answers are not given.

➣ *Sentence Check 2*

Using the answer lines provided, complete each item below with **two** words from the box. Use each word once.

_____
_____ 1–2. The ___ millionaire dressed so shabbily that anyone who ___(e)d him thought he was poor.

_____
_____ 3–4. Hector feels such ___ toward his sister that he never says a single kind thing about her; he only ___s her.

_____   5–6. Since the congresswoman was ___ in opposing the nuclear power
_____   plant, the plant's owners regarded her as their toughest ___.

_____   7–8. Wayne is so ___ that he doesn't even have the desire to be ___(e)d of
_____   guilt for all the times he has lied, cheated, and stolen.

_____   9–10. With his friendly air, good-natured laugh and generosity, Santa Claus is
_____   the ___ of the ___ grandfather.

➤ *Final Check:* **Joseph Palmer**

Here is a final opportunity for you to strengthen your knowledge of the ten words. First read the following selection carefully. Then fill in each blank with a word from the box at the top of the previous page. (Context clues will help you figure out which word goes in which blank.) Use each word once.

In 1830, a Massachusetts farmer named Joseph Palmer moved to the city, only to find that people continually reacted to him with anger and hatred. Why? Palmer certainly wasn't a(n) (1)_____ man—no, he had a strong sense of right and wrong. He was a friendly and (2)_____ person as well. And on the whole, Palmer was the (3)_____ of a normal citizen, living a typical life with his family. Yet his neighbors crossed to the other side of the street when they (4)_____(e)d him. Children insulted Palmer and sometimes threw stones at him. Grown men hurled rocks through the windows of his house. Even the local minister (5)_____(e)d Palmer, telling the congregation that Palmer admired only himself.

One day, four men carrying scissors and a razor attacked Palmer and threw him to the ground. Pulling out a pocketknife, Palmer fought back, slashing at their legs. His (6)_____s fled. Afterward, Palmer was the one arrested and jailed. While in jail he was attacked two more times. Both times, he fought his way free. After a year—although his accusers still wouldn't (7)_____ him of guilt—he was released.

Palmer had won. The cause of all the (8)_____ and abuse had been his long, flowing beard. Palmer, (9)_____ to the end, had refused to shave.

Thirty years after Palmer's difficulties, it was no longer (10)_____ to wear whiskers. Among the many who wore beards then was the President of the United States, Abraham Lincoln.

Scores   Sentence Check 2 _____%   Final Check _____%

Enter your scores above and in the vocabulary performance chart on the inside back cover of the book.

CHAPTER 2

curt	retort
demoralize	sabotage
dilemma	subsequent
inclination	wary
irate	zeal

Ten Words in Context

In the space provided, write the letter of the meaning closest to that of each **boldfaced** word. Use the context of the sentences to help you figure out each word's meaning.

1 curt
(kûrt)
-adjective

- The fast-food manager trained workers to give polite, full answers to customers, not **curt** responses.
- Betsy doesn't mean to be **curt**. She seems rudely brief with people because she's so shy.

__ *Curt* means   a. cautious.   b. courteous.   c. abrupt.

2 demoralize
(dĭ-môr'ə-līz')
-verb

- Cara's refusal to date my brother **demoralized** him to the point that for months he lacked the confidence to ask another woman out.
- When Bonita gained a pound during her diet, it so **demoralized** her that she ate a banana split.

__ *Demoralize* means   a. to cheat.   b. to discourage.   c. to excite.

3 dilemma
(dĭ-lĕm'ə)
-noun

- The store manager faced a **dilemma**: either having an elderly, needy man arrested or ignoring store rules about shoplifters.
- In old romantic movies, the heroine's **dilemma** often involves choosing between a rich boyfriend and the poor man she really loves.

__ *Dilemma* means   a. a hard choice.   b. a great danger.   c. a benefit.

4 inclination
(ĭn-klə-nā'shən)
-noun

- My **inclination** is to major in nursing, but I'm going to speak to a few nurses before I make my final decision.
- Our two-year-old has some irritating tendencies, such as her **inclination** to say "no" to everything.

__ *Inclination* means   a. a tendency.   b. a reason.   c. a fate.

5 irate
(ī-rāt')
-adjective

- If Kate got angry only occasionally, I could take her more seriously, but she's always **irate** about something or other.
- I get mad when my wife misplaces the TV's remote control, and she becomes equally **irate** when I write a check and forget to record it in the checkbook.

__ *Irate* means   a. thrilled.   b. selfish.   c. furious.

6 retort
(rĭ-tôrt')
-verb

- When I told my parents I'd wash the supper dishes the next morning, my father **retorted**, "Maybe we should serve you dinner in the mornings, too."
- "What do you want?" the young woman asked Dracula. "Only to drink in your charms," he **retorted**.

__ *Retort* means   a. to approve.   b. to reply.   c. to ask.

7 sabotage
(săb′ə-tŏzh′)
-verb

___ *Sabotage* means

- Terrorist groups train their members to **sabotage** airports and other public places.
- A fired computer operator **sabotaged** the company's computer system by planting a "virus" in it.

  a. to develop.   b. to invest in.   c. to do harm to.

8 subsequent
(sŭb′sĭ-kwənt′)
-adjective

___ *Subsequent* means

- "I was hired as a stock boy," said the company president. "My **subsequent** jobs took me steadily up the company ladder."
- The first time I drove on a highway, I was terrified, but on **subsequent** trips, I felt more relaxed.

  a. first.   b. following.   c. previous.

9 wary
(wâr′ē)
-adjective

___ *Wary* means

- "There's no such thing as a free lunch" means that we should be **wary** about promises of getting something for nothing.
- I'm a little **wary** of people who, when they first meet me, treat me as if I'm their best friend.

  a. careful.   b. tired.   c. welcoming.

10 zeal
(zēl)
-noun

___ *Zeal* means

- Flo attacked her food with such **zeal** that I thought she hadn't eaten for a week!
- My neighbor has so much **zeal** about keeping our neighborhood clean that he sweeps our sidewalk if we don't do it ourselves.

  a. resistance.   b. passion.   c. skill.

Matching Words with Definitions

Following are definitions of the ten words. Clearly write or print each word next to its definition. The sentences above and on the previous page will help you decide on the meaning of each word.

1. _____   A tendency to think, act, or behave in a certain way; a leaning

2. _____   Rudely brief when speaking to someone

3. _____   Cautious; on guard

4. _____   To reply, especially in a quick, sharp, or witty way

5. _____   To lower the spirits of; weaken the confidence or cheerfulness of

6. _____   A situation requiring a difficult choice

7. _____   Following, in time or order; next; later

8. _____   Enthusiastic devotion; intense enthusiasm

9. _____   To deliberately destroy or damage

10. _____   Very angry

CAUTION: Do not go any further until you are sure the above answers are correct. Then you can use the definitions to help you in the following practices. Your goal is eventually to know the words well enough so that you don't need to check the definitions at all.

➤ *Sentence Check 1*

Using the answer line provided, complete each item below with the correct word from the box. Use each word once.

a. curt	b. demoralize	c. dilemma	d. inclination	e. irate
f. retort	g. sabotage	h. subsequent	i. wary	j. zeal

_____ 1. Rob's ___ was whether to go to work feeling sick or to stay home and lose a day's pay.

_____ 2. Be ___ when something sounds too good to be true—it probably is.

_____ 3. I have to watch my budget because I have a(n) ___ to overspend.

_____ 4. The Broadway director cut off most of the auditioning singers with a(n) ___ response: "Thank you. That will be all."

_____ 5. The striking miners planned to ___ one of the mines by blowing up the main entrance.

_____ 6. Breaking up with Phil ___(e)d me so much that I didn't think my spirits could be lower—until I got fired.

_____ 7. The team played miserably in the first game of the season, but they managed to win all ___ games.

_____ 8. My father always became ___ when any of his children came home after curfew. One time he began yelling at me even before my date had left.

_____ 9. If adolescents could apply to their studies just a bit of the ___ they feel for music and partying, their grades would skyrocket.

_____ 10. When the wisecracking waiter said, "That hat looks ridiculous, lady," the woman stated, "I didn't come here to be insulted." "That's what you think!" ___(e)d the waiter.

NOTE: Now check your answers to these questions by turning to page 175. Going over the answers carefully will help you prepare for the next two practices, for which answers are not given.

➤ *Sentence Check 2*

Using the answer lines provided, complete each item below with **two** words from the box. Use each word once.

_____
_____ 1–2. Already angry, the customer became even more ___ when he received only this ___ response: "No returns."

_____
_____ 3–4. When I answer my phone and hear someone demand, "Who is this?" my ___ is to ___, "I'm the person whose phone was ringing. Who is *this*?"

_____ 5–6. Because of terrorist attempts to ___ flights, airline security workers are
_____ ___ of even the most innocent-looking passengers.

_____ 7–8. I began the semester with great ___ for my chemistry class, but the
_____ realization that I didn't have the necessary background quickly ___(e)d
me.

_____ 9–10. Margo intended to accept the job offer to be a salad chef, but a(n) ___
_____ offer for an office position has presented her with a(n) ___: Should she
take the interesting restaurant job, which pays poorly, or the higher-
paying job that may not interest her much?

►*Final Check:* Telephone Salespeople

Here is a final opportunity for you to strengthen your knowledge of the ten words. First read the following selection carefully. Then fill in each blank with a word from the box at the top of the previous page. (Context clues will help you figure out which word goes in which blank.) Use each word once.

If my carpets need cleaning or I want a new freezer, I will do some comparison shopping first. I am not likely to buy anything suddenly just because a complete stranger has phoned—usually during the dinner hour—to sell it. For this and other reasons, I have always been (1)_____ of telephone salespeople. I don't like their cheerful, overly amiable° voices and their nervy suggestions as to how I might easily pay for whatever it is they are selling. My (2)_____ is to get off the phone as soon as possible.

My husband, however, creates a(n) (3)_____ for me when he takes these calls. He doesn't want what is being sold either, but he feels sorry for the salespeople. He doesn't want to (4)_____ them with such a(n) (5)_____ reply as "No." When they begin their sales pitch, he is overcome by their (6)_____ for their product and therefore listens politely. Then he (7)_____s my efforts to discourage (8)_____ calls by suggesting that the salespeople call back later to talk to his wife! I don't know who gets more (9)_____ when that happens—I or the salespeople, disappointed when they realize we never intended to buy a thing. More than once, when I've finally said "No sale" for the last time to an adamant° salesperson who had been refusing to take "no" for an answer, he or she has (10)_____(e)d, "Well, thanks for wasting my time."

Scores Sentence Check 2 _____% ` Final Check _____%

Enter your scores above and in the vocabulary performance chart on the inside back cover of the book.

 SENTENCES

acclaim	exploit
adjacent	methodical
elicit	obsolete
engross	tangible
escalate	terminate

Ten Words in Context

In the space provided, write the letter of the meaning closest to that of each **boldfaced** word. Use the context of the sentences to help you figure out each word's meaning.

1 **acclaim**
(ə-klām′)
-noun

- Any subway system that is clean, quiet, and safe deserves **acclaim**.
- Although Vincent Van Gogh is now considered a genius, the artist received little **acclaim** in his lifetime.

___ *Acclaim* means   a. criticism.   b. praise.   c. change.

2 **adjacent**
(ə-jā′sənt)
-adjective

- Because their desks are **adjacent**, Jeff and Kellie often exchange looks and comments.
- If you keep your dishes in a cupboard that's **adjacent** to the dishwasher, you won't have to walk when putting away the clean dishes.

___ *Adjacent* means   a. close.   b. similar.   c. separated.

3 **elicit**
(ĭ-lĭs′ĭt)
-verb

- Elizabeth Taylor's violet eyes always **elicit** admiration and wonder.
- Wes is such a troublemaker in Mrs. Turner's class that his late arrival one day **elicited** this sharp comment from her: "In your case, Wes, never is better than late."

___ *Elicit* means   a. to stop.   b. to follow.   c. to bring out.

4 **engross**
(ĕn′grōs′)
-verb

- The suspenseful TV movie so **engrossed** Bryan that he didn't even budge when he was called to dinner.
- The fascinating single-file march of black ants along the sidewalk **engrossed** me for several minutes.

___ *Engross* means   a. to hold the interest of.   b. to disgust.   c. to bore.

5 **escalate**
(ĕs′kə-lāt′)
-verb

- The fight between the two hockey players **escalated** into an all-out battle among members of both teams.
- "We need to **escalate** our fund-raising efforts," the theater manager said. "Otherwise, the company won't survive."

___ *Escalate* means   a. to expand.   b. to delay.   c. to weaken.

6 **exploit**
(ĕks-ploit′)
-verb

- At the turn of the century, factory owners **exploited** children by making them work in terrible conditions for as many as eighteen hours a day.
- Ricky **exploited** his parents' absence by having a wild party at their home.

___ *Exploit* means   a. to forget.   b. to take advantage of.   c. to be sad about.

7 methodical
(mə-thŏd′ĭ-kəl)
-adjective

- A **methodical** way to store spices is to shelve them in alphabetical order.
- Joan is so **methodical** about her diet that she classifies the foods in each meal into different nutritional categories.

___ *Methodical* means   a. accidental.   b. out-of-date.   c. orderly.

8 obsolete
(ŏb′sə-lēt′)
-adjective

- Word processors are so common now that they have made typewriters almost **obsolete**.
- In the United States, the automobile quickly made travel by horse and carriage **obsolete**.

___ *Obsolete* means   a. popular.   b. useful.   c. extinct.

9 tangible
(tăn′jə-bəl)
-adjective

- The sculptor loved making her ideas **tangible** by giving them form in metal and stone.
- Corn-chip crumbs, empty soda bottles, and dirty napkins were **tangible** evidence that a party had taken place the night before.

___ *Tangible* means   a. clever.   b. solid.   c. hidden.

10 terminate
(tûr′mə-nāt)
-verb

- The students waited impatiently for the bell to **terminate** Mr. Leeman's boring lecture.
- The referee should have **terminated** the boxing match when he first saw the weaker fighter losing the ability to defend himself.

___ *Terminate* means   a. to end.   b. to revive.   c. to begin.

Matching Words with Definitions

Following are definitions of the ten words. Clearly write or print each word next to its definition. The sentences above and on the previous page will help you decide on the meaning of each word.

1. _____   To draw forth

2. _____   To stop; bring to an end

3. _____   Orderly; systematic

4. _____   Close; near (to something)

5. _____   Able to be touched; having form and matter

6. _____   No longer active or in use; out of date

7. _____   To increase or intensify

8. _____   Great praise or applause; enthusiastic approval

9. _____   To hold the full attention of; absorb

10. _____   To use selfishly or unethically; take unfair advantage of

CAUTION: Do not go any further until you are sure the above answers are correct. Then you can use the definitions to help you in the following practices. Your goal is eventually to know the words well enough so that you don't need to check the definitions at all.

➤ Sentence Check 1

Using the answer line provided, complete each item below with the correct word from the box. Use each word once.

a. **acclaim**	b. **adjacent**	c. **elicit**	d. **engross**	e. **escalate**
f. **exploit**	g. **methodical**	h. **obsolete**	i. **tangible**	j. **terminate**

_____ 1. A wedding ring is a(n) ___ expression of a couple's commitment to each other.

_____ 2. If solar energy becomes as cheap and plentiful as sunshine, nuclear energy, which is expensive, may become ___.

_____ 3. Susan Sarandon's performance in *Dead Man Walking* won the actress an Oscar and the ___ of admiring critics.

_____ 4. Our house is ___ to one with a high wooden fence, so our view on that side is completely blocked.

_____ 5. The shouting match between Rose and her brother ___(e)d until it was so loud that the neighbors complained.

_____ 6. Sometimes an article I'm reading on the bus will ___ me so much that I'll pass my stop.

_____ 7. When workers feel ___(e)d by their employers, they often go on strike for larger salaries and better working conditions.

_____ 8. Diana is very ___ about writing letters. She keeps her writing materials in one spot, makes a list of the people she owes letters to, and writes once a week.

_____ 9. When Luke was caught stealing money on the job, the company ___(e)d his employment and brought him up on criminal charges.

_____ 10. In one disturbing survey, the question "Which do you like better, TV or Daddy?" ___(e)d this response from a number of children: "TV."

NOTE: Now check your answers to these questions by turning to page 175. Going over the answers carefully will help you prepare for the next two practices, for which answers are not given.

➤ Sentence Check 2

Using the answer lines provided, complete each item below with **two** words from the box. Use each word once.

_____
_____ 1–2. The gifted ice skater's routine ___(e)d the audience. It was the epitome° of grace and power combined. At the end, a long, rapid spin ___(e)d a burst of applause.

_____
_____ 3–4. Although hand-crafted furniture is almost ___, mass production hasn't yet ___(e)d all demand for it.

_____ 5–6. Workers want ___ rewards such as money and a pension, but they also
_____   welcome less concrete benefits, such as ___ for a job well done.

_____ 7–8. The more the British ___(e)d the American colonies by taxing them
_____   unfairly, the more the colonists' animosity° toward the British ___(e)d.

_____ 9–10. Patty's ___ baking technique includes arranging all ingredients in a
_____   row, with each one ___ to the one that is used after it.

➤ Final Check: A Cruel Sport

Here is a final opportunity for you to strengthen your knowledge of the ten words. First read the following selection carefully. Then fill in each blank with a word from the box at the top of the previous page. (Context clues will help you figure out which word goes in which blank.) Use each word once.

The nightclub lights dimmed, and a spotlight revealed a short, fat man holding a heavy chain. He tugged the chain, and a muzzled bear appeared. The man, the animal's owner, announced that the bear's name was Sally. He would give a hundred dollars, he said, to anyone who wrestled Sally to the floor. Alex, sitting in the audience, was shocked. He had thought bear wrestling was (1)_____, given up long ago as a cruel sport.

The offer (2)_____(e)d an eager response. "I'll do it!" one man called, winning the (3)_____ of the spectators, who cheered him on. He went up and started to swing at Sally. She tried to back away. The match greatly (4)_____(e)d most of the audience members, who watched every move. A stranger sitting (5)_____ to Alex became so excited that he accidentally knocked over Alex's drink.

"Knock her on her rear!" the owner shouted with zeal°. When Sally finally raised a paw to defend herself, her owner jerked her back with a sharp tug. Sally's opponent could then see that she had no claws. He thus felt more confident, so his attack (6)_____(e)d. But when the man fighting the bear seemed likely to pin Sally, her owner allowed the bear to throw him off. At that, the owner (7)_____(e)d the match, calling out "Next!"

Another man then sprang to his feet. And soon another. There were six subsequent° matches, each with the same result. It was clear to Alex that this show always followed the same (8)_____ routine.

Finally, the owner led Sally away. Her drooping head and labored walk were (9)_____ expressions of the animal's misery. Alex was more certain than ever that bear wrestling (10)_____(e)d the animal for human entertainment. As Sally passed his table, Alex heard her moaning softly. Looking closely, he saw that the bear was old, and completely blind.

Scores Sentence Check 2 _____%	Final Check _____%	

Enter your scores above and in the vocabulary performance chart on the inside back cover of the book.

✱ 5 sentences

deter	innovation
implication	revitalize
inequity	sparse
infirmity	subjective
infringe	succinct

Ten Words in Context

In the space provided, write the letter of the meaning closest to that of each **boldfaced** word. Use the context of the sentences to help you figure out each word's meaning.

1 **deter**
(dĭ-tûr')
-verb

- To **deter** burglars, my father put a sign on our lawn that says, "Beware of German shepherd."
- If the dangers of skydiving don't **deter** Ben, maybe the high cost will.

___ *Deter* means   a. to reward.   b. to stop.   c. to bore.

2 **implication**
(ĭm-plĭ-kā'shən)
-noun

- When the boss said that company profits were down, the **implication** was that nobody would be getting a raise.
- When the salesman winked, the **implication** was that he would give Joaquin a special deal on a car.

___ *Implication* means   a. a minor fault.   b. a demand.   c. something suggested.

3 **inequity**
(ĭn-ĕk'wĭt-ē)
-noun

- In South Africa, Mahatma Gandhi experienced an **inequity** that was all too common at the time—he was thrown off a "whites only" train.
- Most Americans consider it an **inequity** that some millionaires pay less in taxes than ordinary citizens do.

___ *Inequity* means   a. an injustice.   b. a physical weakness.   c. a question.

4 **infirmity**
(ĭn-fûr'mə-tē)
-noun

- Rick uses a wheelchair, but he doesn't let his **infirmity** keep him from traveling.
- Certain **infirmities**, such as arthritis and diabetes, are more likely to affect the elderly.

___ *Infirmity* means   a. a relationship.   b. a disability.   c. a secret.

5 **infringe**
(ĭn-frĭnj')
-verb

- The protesters may picket the nuclear power plant as long as they don't **infringe** on other people's right to enter and exit freely.
- When my mother is doing her homework, no one is allowed to **infringe** on her quiet time.

___ *Infringe* means   a. to interfere with.   b. to protect.   c. to recognize.

6 **innovation**
(ĭn-'ə-vā'shən)
-noun

- When commercial bakers first offered sliced bread, it was considered an exciting **innovation**.
- The high cost of college has led to such financial **innovations** as paying for children's education while they're still infants.

___ *Innovation* means   a. something new.   b. a weakness.   c. an imitation.

7 revitalize
(rē-vīt'əl-īz')
-verb

- When Dwight is tired after work, he finds a brief nap **revitalizes** him for a night on the town with friends.
- The City Council hopes to **revitalize** the currently lifeless shopping district by offering tax breaks for new businesses.

__ *Revitalize* means   a. to refresh.   b. to amuse.   c. to tire out.

8 sparse
(spärs)
-adjective

- There are thick pine forests at the foot of the mountain, but higher up, the trees become **sparse**.
- Unfortunately, the turnout for the team's first pep rally was **sparse**. Organizers hope to have better attendance at the next one.

__ *Sparse* means   a. long.   b. thin.   c. crowded.

9 subjective
(səb-jĕk'tĭv)
-adjective

- Mary, a highly **subjective** judge of her son's abilities, feels he's brilliant in every respect. The boy's father, however, has a less emotional view of him.
- The reporter refused to write about his friend's trial. He knew any story he wrote would be too **subjective** to be published as an unbiased article.

__ *Subjective* means   a. one-sided.   b. boring.   c. impersonal.

10 succinct
(sək-sĭngkt')
-adjective

- Your telegram should be **succinct** so that you get your message across clearly without paying for more words than necessary.
- "What's new?" is a **succinct** way of asking, "Has anything of interest happened to you lately, my friend?"

__ *Succinct* means   a. wordy.   b. prejudiced.   c. brief and clear.

Matching Words with Definitions

Following are definitions of the ten words. Clearly write or print each word next to its definition. The sentences above and on the previous page will help you decide on the meaning of each word.

1. _____   Injustice; unfairness; an instance of injustice

2. _____   A new custom, method, or invention; something newly introduced

3. _____   Based on personal opinions, feelings, and attitudes; not objective

4. _____   To prevent or discourage from doing something

5. _____   Expressed clearly in a few words; to the point; concise

6. _____   To renew the strength and energy of; restore to a vigorous, active condition

7. _____   A physical weakness or defect; ailment

8. _____   Distributed thinly; not thick or crowded

9. _____   To intrude or trespass on; to go beyond the limits considered proper

10. _____   An idea that is communicated indirectly, through a suggestion or hint

CAUTION: Do not go any further until you are sure the above answers are correct. Then you can use the definitions to help you in the following practices. Your goal is eventually to know the words well enough so that you don't need to check the definitions at all.

➤ *Sentence Check 1*

Using the answer line provided, complete each item below with the correct word from the box. Use each word once.

a. **deter**	b. **implication**	c. **inequity**	d. **infirmity**	e. **infringe**
f. **innovation**	g. **revitalize**	h. **sparse**	i. **subjective**	j. **succinct**

_____ 1. Although Marie joked about her broken leg, it was an ___ that kept her from work for a month.

_____ 2. When a restaurant's tables have ashtrays, the ___ is that smoking is permitted.

_____ 3. Our democratic rights do not include the freedom to ___ on other people's rights.

_____ 4. "Now" is a ___ way of saying, "At this particular point in time."

_____ 5. Our grass is ___ along a path at the corner of the lot, where kids take a shortcut through our yard.

_____ 6. An interesting ___ in food packaging is a bottle from which salad dressing is squirted, rather than poured.

_____ 7. The seminar for company employees ___(e)d my interest in my job by giving me new skills and suggesting new goals.

_____ 8. *The Diary of Anne Frank* is a ___ view of events during World War II, from the point of view of a young Jewish girl in hiding.

_____ 9. The company was accused of creating a(n) ___ by paying women less pay than men for doing the same work.

_____ 10. The fact that Beethoven was totally deaf by age 50 did not ___ him from composing at the age of 53 one of his most ambitious and beloved works, the *Ninth Symphony*.

NOTE: Now check your answers to these questions by turning to page 175. Going over the answers carefully will help you prepare for the next two practices, for which answers are not given.

➤ *Sentence Check 2*

Using the answer lines provided, complete each item below with **two** words from the box. Use each word once.

_____
_____ 1–2. When the candidate for mayor saw the ___ turnout for his speech, he knew he had to do something to ___ his campaign.

_____
_____ 3–4. Future ___s in technology may make it easier for a government to ___ on the privacy of citizens' computer records.

_____   5–6. Although arthritis can be a painful ___, Aunt Fern doesn't let it ___ her
_____   from attending her weekly square-dance meetings.

_____   7–8. All editorials are ___—they represent someone's opinions. In an
_____   editorial, for example, writers are free to argue against the ___ of police
                                        brutality, instead of just reporting on it.

_____   9–10. A sign may be brief and still have several ___s. For example, the ___
_____   sign "Dangerous Curve" suggests that drivers should be wary° and
                                        slow down, that the curve ahead is sharp, and that bad accidents have
                                        happened there before.

➤ *Final Check:* **Bald Is Beautiful**

Here is a final opportunity for you to strengthen your knowledge of the ten words. First read the following
selection carefully. Then fill in each blank with a word from the box at the top of the previous page.
(Context clues will help you figure out which word goes in which blank.) Use each word once.

Looking through a hair-care magazine, I noticed many ads for toupees and hair thickeners. The

(1)_____ seemed to be that a man's baldness is a major (2)_____.

Well, I'm not going to let anyone (3)_____ on the right of a man to be bald, or to

demoralize° those who have already lost their hair. Listen, all you baldies. You may feel it's a serious

(4)_____ that some heads have only (5)_____ hair while others

are thickly covered, but I think bald men are terrifically attractive. Sure, that's just my

(6)_____ opinion, but I'm not alone. I know another woman whose boyfriend

went so far as to shave his head in order to (7)_____ their tired romance. My

thick-haired boyfriend hasn't offered to go quite that far, but I wouldn't (8)_____

him from shaving his head if he had an inclination° to do so. I know drug companies manufacture

medications to produce hair on bald heads, but that's one (9)_____ I would

discourage any man from using. I'd even like to see the day when toupees are as obsolete° as hoop

skirts. I hate to see all those beautiful, shiny bald heads covered up. Or, to be more

(10)_____, bald is beautiful.

Scores	Sentence Check 2 _____%	Final Check _____%

Enter your scores above and in the vocabulary performance chart on the inside back cover of the book.

allusion	banal
altruistic	euphemism
appease	mercenary
arbitrary	syndrome
assail	taint

Ten Words in Context

In the space provided, write the letter of the meaning closest to that of each **boldfaced** word. Use the context of the sentences to help you figure out each word's meaning.

1 **allusion**
(ə-lōo′zhən)
-*noun*

- After I suggested that Monty have fruit for dessert instead of chocolate cake, he responded, "Is that an **allusion** to my weight?"
- Ray didn't have the courage to come right out and ask Lucy to marry him. Instead, he made only an **allusion** to marriage by asking, "Wouldn't it be easier if we had to fill out just one tax return?"

___ *Allusion* means   a. a contrast.   b. a reference.   c. an answer.

2 **altruistic**
(ăl′trōo-ĭs′tĭk)
-*adjective*

- When an enemy approaches, ground squirrels show **altruistic** behavior. They risk their own lives to give alarm calls to nearby relatives.
- "I'm not often **altruistic**," Brett admitted. "I usually put my own welfare first."

___ *Altruistic* means   a. unselfish.   b. cheerful.   c. greedy.

3 **appease**
(ə-pēz′)
-*verb*

- My sister was so outraged when I accidentally scratched her favorite old Beatles record that nothing I could say or do would **appease** her.
- Roger was furious when he saw me out with another guy, but I quickly **appeased** him by explaining that the "date" was my cousin.

___ *Appease* means   a. to annoy.   b. to heal.   c. to calm.

4 **arbitrary**
(är′bĭ-trĕr′ē)
-*adjective*

- Professor Miller's students were angry that he graded essays in an **arbitrary** way, rather than using clear-cut standards.
- Parents should not enforce rules according to their moods. Such **arbitrary** discipline only confuses children.

___ *Arbitrary* means   a. steady.   b. slow.   c. impulsive.

5 **assail**
(ə-sāl′)
-*verb*

- The storm **assailed** us with hail and heavy rain.
- The two candidates continuously **assailed** each other with accusations of dishonesty.

___ *Assail* means   a. to attack.   b. to confuse.   c. to support.

6 **banal**
(bə-năl′)
-*adjective*

- The film, with its overused expressions and unimaginative plot, was the most **banal** I had ever seen.
- "Nice to see you" may be a **banal** comment, but what it lacks in originality it makes up for in friendliness.

___ *Banal* means   a. greedy.   b. unoriginal.   c. clever.

7 euphemism
(yōō'fə-mĭz'əm)
-noun

- Common **euphemisms** include "final resting place" (for *grave*), "intoxicated" (for *drunk*), and "powder room" (for *toilet*).
- The Central Intelligence Agency is on record as having referred to assassination with the **euphemism** "change of health."

___ *Euphemism* means   a. a harsh term.   b. a term that doesn't offend.   c. a foreign term.

8 mercenary
(mûr'sə-nĕr'ē)
-adjective

- Ed is totally **mercenary**. His philosophy is, "Pay me enough, and I'll do anything."
- The con man pretended to love the wealthy widow, but he actually married her for **mercenary** reasons.

___ *Mercenary* means   a. jealous.   b. angry.   c. greedy.

9 syndrome
(sĭn'drōm)
-noun

- Headaches are usually harmless, but as part of a **syndrome** including fever and a stiff neck, they may be a sign of a serious illness.
- Jet lag is a **syndrome** resulting from flying long distances; it often includes exhaustion, headache, and loss of appetite.

___ *Syndrome* means   a. a group of symptoms.   b. a cause.   c. something required.

10 taint
(tānt)
-verb

- The involvement of organized crime has **tainted** many sports, including boxing and horse racing.
- The government scandal **tainted** the reputations of everyone involved.

___ *Taint* means   a. to benefit.   b. to damage.   c. to start.

Matching Words with Definitions

Following are definitions of the ten words. Clearly write or print each word next to its definition. The sentences above and on the previous page will help you decide on the meaning of each word.

1. _____   Determined by personal judgment, not rule or reason; based on impulse

2. _____   Motivated only by financial gain; greedy

3. _____   An indirect reference

4. _____   A group of symptoms typical of a particular disease or condition

5. _____   A mild or vague term used as a substitute for one considered offensive or unpleasant

6. _____   To calm, especially by giving in to the demands of

7. _____   Lacking originality; overused; commonplace

8. _____   To stain the honor of someone or something

9. _____   To attack physically or verbally

10. _____   Unselfishly concerned for the welfare of others; unselfish

CAUTION: Do not go any further until you are sure the above answers are correct. Then you can use the definitions to help you in the following practices. Your goal is eventually to know the words well enough so that you don't need to check the definitions at all.

➤ *Sentence Check 1*

Using the answer line provided, complete each item below with the correct word from the box. Use each word once.

a. **allusion**	b. **altruistic**	c. **appease**	d. **arbitrary**	e. **assail**
f. **banal**	g. **euphemism**	h. **mercenary**	i. **syndrome**	j. **taint**

_____ 1. There have been people ___ enough to sell their own children for the right price.

_____ 2. "Someone hasn't shown me his report card," my mother said, making a(n) ___ to my brother.

_____ 3. It takes a(n) ___ person to adopt a disabled child.

_____ 4. The mugger ___ed his victims with a baseball bat.

_____ 5. The local undertaker insists on using a(n) ___ for the chapel of his funeral parlor. He calls it the "slumber room."

_____ 6. The report that the halfback was addicted to drugs ___(e)d the team's image.

_____ 7. The only thing that would ___ the dead boy's parents was imprisonment of the drunk driver who had killed him.

_____ 8. Abraham Lincoln is thought to have had Marfan's ___, a group of symptoms which includes unusually long bones and abnormal blood circulation.

_____ 9. The judge's harsh sentence was ___. Rather than being based on past similar cases or on the seriousness of the crime, it was based on the judge's opinion of the defendant.

_____ 10. "You're special" probably appears on thousands of greeting cards, but when someone says it to you and means it, it never seems ___.

NOTE: Now check your answers to these questions by turning to page 175. Going over the answers carefully will help you prepare for the next two practices, for which answers are not given.

➤ *Sentence Check 2*

Using the answer lines provided, complete each item below with **two** words from the box. Use each word once.

_____
_____ 1–2. ___ people tend to place the public welfare above their own self-interest. In contrast, ___ people will exploit° anyone for a profit—they will even sell harmful products.

_____
_____ 3–4. The angry customer loudly ___(e)d the salesman for having sold her a broken clock. The salesman quickly ___(e)d her by giving her a full refund.

_____   5–6. My boss judges performance in a(n) ___ manner, praising and scolding
_____   according to his moods. And when he says, "Please stay a few minutes
                                 longer today," "a few minutes" is a(n) ___ for "an hour."

_____   7–8. A certain rare ___ includes a very odd symptom—an uncontrollable
_____   urge to use obscene language. This disease can ___ a victim's
                                 reputation, because some people who hear the foul language won't
                                 understand the reason for it.

_____   9–10. The critic hated stale language. Instead of writing a(n) ___ comment
_____   such as "That ballerina is light on her feet," he made an interesting ___
                                 to the dancer's movements: "She was never heavier than moonlight."

➤ _Final Check:_ No Luck with Women

Here is a final opportunity for you to strengthen your knowledge of the ten words. First read the following
selection carefully. Then fill in each blank with a word from the box at the top of the previous page.
(Context clues will help you figure out which word goes in which blank.) Use each word once.

I don't have much luck with women. The other night at a singles dance, I encountered° an
attractive lady and asked her, "Excuse me, do you have the time?" (I admit the question is a bit
(1)_____, but I couldn't think of anything more clever.) She retorted°, "Isn't that
kind of personal?" Another woman got really upset just because I asked, "Haven't we met before, at
Weight Watchers?" Okay, so I was wrong. I didn't mean to make a(n) (2)_____
to her size. Still, after that, nothing I said would (3)_____ her.

Women don't appreciate how nice I am. First of all, I'm not particularly
(4)_____. For instance, I've never considered a woman's wealth the most
important thing about her. It's the second most important thing. And I would never
(5)_____ a woman's reputation by letting her be seen with me in a decent
place. I'm so (6)_____ that I once took care of a guy who was drunk by
sending him home in a cab. Instead of being grateful, his attractive date (who had been in the
ladies' room) became irate° and (7)_____(e)d me with all sorts of accusations.
How was I supposed to know she was his wife?

When I ask women out, they often answer me with (8)_____s such as "I
already have plans" or the curt° "I'm busy." What they really mean is, "I'm busy making plans to
avoid you." You'd think I suffer from some horrible, infectious (9)_____.

Women's behavior is totally (10)_____. At least, I can't see any reason
to it. Last night, for example, a woman I was nice enough to treat to a Coke threw it in my face.
Thank goodness, she didn't get any on my day-glo Mickey Mouse tie.

Scores	Sentence Check 2 _____%	Final Check _____%

Enter your scores above and in the vocabulary performance chart on the inside back cover of the book.

ann, enn	-ly
audi, audio-	non-
cycl, cyclo-	path, -pathy
-hood	pend
hyper-	quart, quadr-

Ten Word Parts in Context

Common word parts—also known as *prefixes, suffixes,* and *roots*—are used in forming many words in English. Figure out the meanings of the following ten word parts by looking *closely* and *carefully* at the context in which they appear. Then, in the space provided, write the letter of the meaning closest to that of each word part.

1 ann, enn

- This year's **annual** family reunion will be held at a campground.
- Our town is having a big **bicentennial** parade exactly two hundred years after the day the town was founded.

__ The word part *ann* or *enn* means   a. four.   b. year.   c. hang.

2 audi, audio-

- The bride's softly spoken wedding vows were not **audible** to those at the back of the church.
- The sound system in the new **auditorium** is so good that music can be heard clearly even in the upper balconies.

__ The word part *audi* or *audio-* means   a. condition.   b. feeling.   c. hearing.

3 cycl, cyclo-

- When Bob asked his parents if he could buy a new "two-wheeler," they didn't realize he meant a **motorcycle**.
- A **cyclone** travels in a circular motion.

__ The word part *cycl* or *cyclo-* means   a. circle.   b. four.   c. condition.

4 -hood

- When children reach **adulthood**, how much help should their parents give them?
- For my great-grandmother, **womanhood** began early—she was married at 15.

__ The word part *-hood* means   a. state of.   b. sound.   c. not.

5 hyper-

- Nancy is **hypersensitive** to conflict. When people disagree with her, she thinks they are rejecting her personally.
- The **hypermarket**, a combination of a department store and a supermarket, is relatively new in the United States.

__ The word part *hyper-* means   a. opposite of.   b. more than normal.   c. fourth.

6 -ly

- One cannot **easily** drown in Utah's Great Salt Lake because the lake's high percentage of salt helps people float.
- During the American Revolution, many brides **proudly** wore red, instead of white, as a symbol of rebellion.

__ The word part *-ly* means   a. fourth.   b. in a certain way.   c. opposite of.

7 **non-**

- The paints used in elementary schools are **nontoxic** so that a child who might swallow some won't be poisoned.
- The story about the aliens was supposed to be **nonfiction**, but it sounded made-up to me.

__ The word part *non-* means   a. condition.   b. not.   c. overly.

8 **path, -pathy**

- When Rich's marriage fell apart, Ben's reaction was very **empathic** because he has also been rejected by a loved one.
- Felicia and her mother claim to have powers of **telepathy**. They say that they know each other's feelings and thoughts without being told.

__ The word part *path* or *-pathy* means   a. feeling.   b. hearing.   c. the opposite.

9 **pend**

- The children's swing is an old tire that's **suspended** from a strong oak branch.
- I can't sit and watch the swinging **pendulum** of a grandfather clock without starting to feel sleepy.

__ The word part *pend* means   a. suffering.   b. to listen.   c. to hang.

10 **quart, quadr-**

- Let's cut the apple into **quarters** so all four of us can have a piece.
- The ad said I would **quadruple** my money in two months. But instead of making four times as much money, I lost what I had invested.

__ The word part *quart* or *quadr-* means   a. overly.   b. two.   c. four.

Matching Word Parts with Definitions

Following are definitions of the ten word parts. Clearly write or print each word part next to its definition. The sentences above and on the previous page will help you decide on the meaning of each word part.

1. _____ Four, fourth

2. _____ Feeling, suffering

3. _____ In a certain manner

4. _____ Hearing, sound

5. _____ To hang

6. _____ State, condition

7. _____ Year

8. _____ More than normal; overly

9. _____ Circle

10. _____ Not; the opposite of

CAUTION: Do not go any further until you are sure the above answers are correct. Then you can use the definitions to help you in the following practices. Your goal is eventually to know the word parts well enough so that you don't need to check the definitions at all.

➤ *Sentence Check 1*

Using the answer line provided, complete each *italicized* word in the sentences below with the correct word part from the box. Use each word part once.

a. **ann**	b. **audi, audio-**	c. **cycl, cyclo-**	d. **-hood**	e. **hyper-**
f. **-ly**	g. **non-**	h. **path, -pathy**	i. **pend**	j. **quart, quadr-**

_____ 1. Chim loves playing the piano, especially when he has a(n) (. . . *ence*) ___ listening to him.

_____ 2. It's hard for me to be (*sym . . . etic*) ___ when my sister complains, because she causes so many of her problems herself.

_____ 3. Because of therapy, Grace is a well-adjusted adult, but her (*child . . .*) ___ years were troubled and unhappy.

_____ 4. When I lost one of my diamond earrings, I had the other one made into a(n) (. . . *ant*) ___ to hang around my neck.

_____ 5. The children's odd (. . . *et*) ___ consisted of a toy-drum player, a building-block clapper, a piano player, and a bell ringer.

_____ 6. We were told to bring only necessary equipment on our camping trip, so I was surprised to see how much (. . . *essential*) ___ gear others brought.

_____ 7. Mrs. Baker said she and her husband had been (*happi . . .*) ___ married for forty-seven years. But Mr. Baker, correcting her, said 1952 wasn't so great.

_____ 8. One of the most difficult vehicles to ride is also one of the simplest: a(n) (*uni . . . e*) ___, a vehicle with only one wheel.

_____ 9. Our boss said we would be evaluated (. . . *ually*) ___ for possible promotions. So if we don't get a promotion one year, we might get one the next.

_____ 10. My grandmother has (. . . *tension*) ___, which is abnormally high blood pressure.

NOTE: Now check your answers to these questions by turning to page 175. Going over the answers carefully will help you prepare for the next two practices, for which answers are not given.

➤ *Sentence Check 2*

Using the answer lines provided, complete each *italicized* word in the sentences below with the correct word part from the box. Use each word part once.

_____ 1–2. Some males act as if their (*man . . .*) really ___ (*de . . . ed*) ___ on how _____ many women they go out with, rather than on maturity and strength of character.

_____ 3–4. The (. . . *ist*) ___ stood there (*helpless . . .*) ___ staring at the tire he _____ had chained to the tree. The rest of the bike had been stolen.

_____ 5–6. Stan, a (. . . *drinker*) ___, is (. . . *critical*) ___ of anyone who touches
_____ alcohol. He is adamant° in his belief that taking even a single drink is
the sign of a self-destructive personality.

_____ 7–8. My nursing class watched an (. . . *visual*) ___ show about the horrible
_____ conditions in a mental institution of the 1950s. The patients looked
(. . . *etic*) ___; clearly, they were suffering.

_____ 9–10. For my research report, I used two magazines—one (. . . *erly*) ___,
_____ published four times a year; and an (. . . *ual*) ___ that appears only
every January.

➤ *Final Check:* **A Taste of Parenthood**

Here is a final opportunity for you to strengthen your knowledge of the ten word parts. First read the following selection carefully. Then complete each *italicized* word in the parentheses below with a word from the box at the top of the previous page. (Context clues will help you figure out which word part goes in which blank.) Use each word part once.

I have a lot of (*sym* . . .) (1)_____ for parents of twins, triplets, and
(. . . *uplets*) (2)_____. I just spent the weekend baby-sitting for my four
nieces and nephews.

First, I altruistically° offered to watch my brother's two children so that he and his wife could
go away for the weekend for their sixth wedding (. . . *iversary*) (3)_____.
Then my sister called and said that her husband, an actor, had a chance to (. . . *tion*)
(4)_____ for a big part in a TV drama. He had to fly to California for the
weekend. She said she'd love to go along if I could watch their children, aged two and three. I
(*willing* . . .) (5)_____ agreed.

What a time I had! I soon learned that the word *baby-sitting* has a false implication°—I did
very little sitting that weekend. The children's activity was (. . . *stop*) (6)_____.
It seemed as if they never sat down, and nothing engrossed° them for more than a few minutes.
They went from pedaling their tiny (*tri* . . . *es*) (7)_____ to building with their
blocks to banging their toy drums. They "washed" the dishes, let the dog loose, and made mud
pies in the tomato garden. By Sunday, I was convinced they were all (. . . *active*)
(8)_____. In addition, all weekend I was assailed° with endless questions:
"Why can't I stay up late?" "Do I have to brush my teeth?" "What do ants eat?"

Besides all the activity and questions, I had to cope with the knowledge that four little ones
were entirely (*de* . . . *ent*) (9)_____ on me for their needs. What if one got hurt?
What if they got sick? Fortunately, we survived without a disaster.

I can't imagine what it must be like for parents with two or more children. I guess I'm not
ready to have kids yet—not even one. At least my responsibilities were terminated° on Sunday
night. But (*parent* . . .) (10)_____ is for keeps. I think I'll wait.

Scores	Sentence Check 2 _____%	Final Check _____%

Enter your scores above and in the vocabulary performance chart on the inside back cover of the book.

UNIT ONE: *Review*

The box at the right lists twenty-five words from Unit One. Using the clues at the bottom of the page, fill in these words to complete the puzzle that follows.

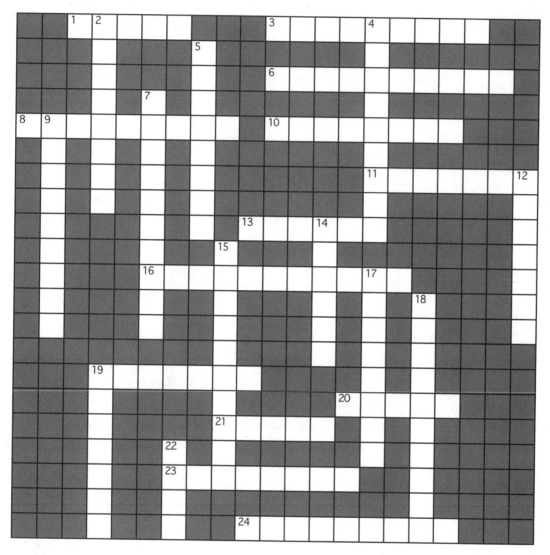

absolve
acclaim
adjacent
altruistic
amiable
animosity
arbitrary
banal
demoralize
deter
eccentric
epitome
escalate
inclination
infringe
innovation
mercenary
obsolete
retort
sparse
subsequent
succinct
taint
terminate
zeal

ACROSS

1. Lacking originality; overused; commonplace
3. Determined by personal judgment; based on impulse
6. To lower the spirits of
8. Motivated only by financial gain; greedy
10. Expressed clearly in a few words; to the point; concise
11. To find innocent or blameless
13. Distributed thinly
16. A tendency to think, act, or behave in a certain way
19. Great praise or applause; enthusiastic approval
20. To prevent or discourage from doing something
21. To stain the honor of someone or something
23. To increase or intensify
24. Bitter hostility

DOWN

2. Close; near (to something)
4. To stop; bring to an end
5. To intrude or trespass on; to go beyond the limits considered proper
7. A new custom, method, or invention; something newly introduced
9. Differing from what is customary; odd
12. A perfect example of a general quality or type
14. To reply, especially in a quick, sharp, or witty way
15. Unselfishly concerned for the welfare of others; unselfish
17. No longer active or in use; out-of-date
18. Following in time or order; next; later; succeeding
19. Good-natured; friendly and pleasant
22. Enthusiastic devotion; intense enthusiasm

UNIT ONE: Test 1

PART A
Choose the word that best completes each item and write it in the space provided.

_____ 1. In the winter, the price of tomatoes ___ while their quality goes down.
a. elicits   b. appeases   c. escalates   d. absolves

_____ 2. A common ___ for *corpse* is "remains."
a. syndrome   b. dilemma   c. euphemism   d. zeal

_____ 3. The taxi driver was so ___ that he charged his own mother for a ride.
a. mercenary   b. amiable   c. curt   d. wary

_____ 4. Do you consider it an ___ that only one percent of Americans own a third of the nation's wealth?
a. allusion   b. inclination   c. inequity   d. acclaim

_____ 5. The plants look ___ now, but within a year or two they'll multiply and fill in the empty spaces.
a. methodical   b. sparse   c. amoral   d. subjective

_____ 6. You probably thought that mail delivery by mule was ___, but it still exists in the Grand Canyon.
a. adamant   b. curt   c. tangible   d. obsolete

_____ 7. You can make your essays ___ by going through them carefully to remove all unnecessary words.
a. succinct   b. adamant   c. tangible   d. eccentric

_____ 8. The ___ of refreshment is drinking an ice-cold lemonade on a sizzling hot day.
a. taint   b. epitome   c. animosity   d. innovation

_____ 9. So ___ that he refused to take money from the public for his discovery of x-rays, Wilhelm Roentgen died poor.
a. wary   b. altruistic   c. amoral   d. curt

_____ 10. To ___ employees from stealing, the Los Angeles Rapid Transit Authority has them wear uniforms without pockets.
a. deter   b. elicit   c. assail   d. engross

_____ 11. Although Marilyn Monroe received great ___ from adoring fans and critics, she never received an Oscar.
a. animosity   b. sabotage   c. innovation   d. acclaim

(Continues on next page)

_____ 12. The model realized that if she wanted to be ___ of the charges, she'd better hire a detective to find the real murderer.

     a. assailed   b. demoralized   c. tainted   d. absolved

_____ 13. You might have a stronger ___ to work for high grades if you were a student in the Cleveland public high schools, where each A earns forty dollars toward college tuition.

     a. animosity   b. infirmity   c. inclination   d. syndrome

PART B
Write **C** if the italicized word is used **correctly**. Write **I** if the word is used **incorrectly**.

_____ 14. Compact disks are already so popular that it's easy to forget how recent an *innovation* they are.

_____ 15. Ants have the *infirmity* of being able to survive under water for up to two weeks.

_____ 16. Students often *exploit* the presence of a substitute teacher by using fake names.

_____ 17. We had to trim the oak tree *adjacent* to our house so that its branches wouldn't reach into the porch.

_____ 18. If you worry about the environment, you're *eccentric*. According to a poll, over three-fourths of Americans are concerned about the environment.

_____ 19. Our *amiable* neighbor scares our children so much that they refuse to knock on his door even on Halloween.

_____ 20. The symptoms of fetal alcohol *syndrome* include deformed limbs and mental retardation.

_____ 21. Teach your young children to be *wary* of strangers.

_____ 22. The passerby showed his *animosity* by entering the burning house and pulling the child to safety.

_____ 23. In 1876, Wild Bill Hickok was in a poker game that was *terminated* by a bullet entering the back of his head.

_____ 24. A wedding ring is a *tangible* expression of a couple's commitment to each other.

_____ 25. Many taxpayers became *irate* when they learned that in a single year, the United States Air Force spent over five million dollars on imported goatskin jackets.

Score (Number correct) _____ x 4 = _____ %

Enter your score above and in the vocabulary performance chart on the inside back cover of the book.

UNIT ONE: *Test 2*

PART A
PART A
Complete each item with a word from the box. Use each word once.

a. **adamant**	b. **allusion**	c. **amoral**	d. **antagonist**	e. **appease**
f. **demoralize**	g. **elicit**	h. **infringe**	i. **retort**	j. **revitalize**
k. **sabotage**	l. **subsequent**	m. **zeal**		

_____ 1. An unhappy employee ___(e)d the company's assembly line by spilling coffee on a gear box.

_____ 2. Do you think that supermarket tabloids ___ on celebrities' privacy?

_____ 3. The ___s in the debate took opposing sides on the question of outlawing cigarettes.

_____ 4. Most Americans show little ___ for the outdoors, spending only about 2 percent of their time there.

_____ 5. Apparently, the chance to be President doesn't ___ much enthusiasm from most Americans—89 percent say they wouldn't want the job.

_____ 6. A permanent involves the contradictory steps of burning hair to a lifeless state and then smearing on conditioners to ___ it.

_____ 7. It's often said that nature is ___. However, humans are part of nature, and most of them *do* have a moral sense.

_____ 8. Our congressional representative, ___ in her opposition to pesticides, often reminds voters that pesticides kill about fourteen thousand people each year.

_____ 9. When a woman told Winston Churchill, "If you were my husband, I'd put poison in your tea," he ___(e)d, "If I were your husband, I'd drink it."

_____ 10. Although failure ___s some people, it encourages others to try harder.

_____ 11. Manny did poorly on his first biology test because he had trouble remembering diagrams. Then he learned a memorization method and did much better on ___ tests.

_____ 12. "Gail isn't the only athlete in the family," Clarence said, making a(n) ___ to Gail's father, a bowling champion.

_____ 13. When Kathleen stood Evan up for the prom, an apology did not ___ him. He's suing her for the cost of his rented tux and the prom tickets.

(Continues on next page)

PART B
Write **C** if the italicized word is used **correctly**. Write **I** if the word is used **incorrectly**.

_____ 14. Cory was so *engrossed* in the film that he fell asleep.

_____ 15. When, during our drive, we *encountered* an unexpected hailstorm, we felt as if we were inside a metal can being pelted with stones.

_____ 16. Movie reviews are never *subjective*—they represent the personal opinions of critics.

_____ 17. My interview with the *curt* personnel officer was the friendliest and most comfortable I've ever experienced.

_____ 18. Phyllis is very *methodical* in her efforts to be the life of any party. She keeps a file box of jokes, indexed by occasion.

_____ 19. The critic *maligned* the folk singer by saying her voice has both richness and sparkle, like velvet trimmed with gold.

_____ 20. Eager to *taint* his opponent's reputation, the candidate spent thousands of dollars on research aimed at uncovering some scandal.

_____ 21. In 1971, three dolphins *assailed* a drowning woman by keeping her afloat and protecting her from sharks across two hundred miles of ocean.

_____ 22. When the evidence in a case is unclear, a jury's decision may be *arbitrary*, based on only the jurors' "gut feeling."

_____ 23. Alice Walker's novel *The Color Purple* won both the Pulitzer Prize and the National Book Award because critics found her writing so *banal*.

_____ 24. Parents of young children often face a *dilemma*: whether both parents should work or one should put a career on hold and stay home for a few years.

_____ 25. When we say something moves "at a snail's pace," the *implication* is that it's moving slowly.

Score (Number correct) _____ x 4 = _____ %

Enter your score above and in the vocabulary performance chart on the inside back cover of the book.

UNIT ONE: Test 3

PART A
Complete each sentence in a way that clearly shows you understand the meaning of the **boldfaced** word. Take a minute to plan your answer before you write.

Example: _____Four feet of snow on the ground_____ would deter me from attending classes.

1. Typewriters are now almost **obsolete** because _____

   _____.

2. I might be **demoralized** if _____

   _____.

3. One **tangible** symbol of affection is _____

   _____.

4. One behavior that makes me **irate** is _____

   _____.

5. I think that _____

   _____ **infringes** on other people's rights.

6. The **eccentric** teacher has a habit of _____

   _____.

7. This year I face a **dilemma**: _____

   _____.

8. The most **altruistic** thing I ever saw anyone do was to _____

   _____.

9. The actor received this **acclaim** for his performance: " _____

   _____."

10. I'm **wary** of driving at night, so I _____

   _____.

(Continues on next page)

PART B

After each **boldfaced** word are a *synonym* (a word that means the same as the boldfaced word), an *antonym* (a word that means the opposite of the boldfaced word), and a word that is neither. On the answer line, write the letter of the word that is the antonym.

Example: __b__ **irate**   a. angry   b. calm   c. well-informed

_____ 11. **terminate**   a. end   b. begin   c. grow

_____ 12. **amoral**   a. ethical   b. costly   c. unprincipled

_____ 13. **amiable**   a. friendly   b. natural   c. unfriendly

_____ 14. **assail**   a. flow   b. attack   c. defend

_____ 15. **subsequent**   a. previous   b. hidden   c. following

PART C

Use five of the following ten words in sentences. Make it clear that you know the meaning of the word you use. Feel free to use the past tense or plural form of a word.

a. **absolve**	b. **adjacent**	c. **animosity**	d. **appease**	e. **curt**
f. **deter**	g. **epitome**	h. **innovation**	i. **methodical**	j. **zeal**

16. _____

_____

17. _____

_____

18. _____

_____

19. _____

_____

20. _____

_____

Score   (Number correct) _____ x 5 = _____ %

Enter your score above and in the vocabulary performance chart on the inside back cover of the book.

UNIT ONE: Test 4 (Word Parts)

PART A
Listed in the left-hand column below are ten common word parts, along with words in which the parts are used. In each blank, write in the letter of the correct definition on the right.

Word Parts	Examples	Definitions
_____ 1. **ann, enn**	annual, bicentennial	a. In a certain manner
_____ 2. **audi, audio-**	audible, auditorium	b. Feeling, suffering
_____ 3. **cycl, cyclo-**	motorcycle, cyclone	c. Circle
_____ 4. **-hood**	adulthood, womanhood	d. To hang
_____ 5. **hyper-**	hypersensitive, hypermarket	e. Year
_____ 6. **-ly**	easily, proudly	f. Four, fourth
_____ 7. **non-**	nontoxic, nonfiction	g. State, condition
_____ 8. **path, -pathy**	empathic, telepathy	h. Not; the opposite of
_____ 9. **pend**	suspend, pendulum	i. Hearing, sound
_____ 10. **quart, quadr-**	quarter, quadruple	j. More than normal; overly

PART B
Using the answer line provided, complete each *italicized* word in the sentences below with the correct word part from the box. Not every word part will be used.

a. **ann**	b. **audi-**	c. **cycl-**	d. **-hood**	e. **hyper-**
f. **-ly**	g. **non-**	h. **-pathy**	i. **pend**	j. **quadr-**

_____ 11. Mickey Mouse had no (*boy . . .*)—he was "born" as an adult.

_____ 12. I enjoy riding an exercise bike because I don't have to (*. . . e*) uphill.

_____ 13. My dog didn't know why I was crying, but I could tell that she felt (*sym . . .*) for me.

_____ 14. The spider, (*sus . . . ed*) from the ceiling on its own silken thread, dangled above a bowl of popcorn.

_____ 15. Children's rhymes include such (*. . . sense*) words as "Hickory, dickory, dock."

(Continues on next page)

PART C

Use your knowledge of word parts to determine the meaning of the **boldfaced** words. On the answer line, write the letter of each meaning.

_____ 16. Ned **secretly** slipped a note under Anna's plate.

      a. in a secret manner   b. at a secret time   c. without being secret

_____ 17. Should I buy a **quart** or a gallon of chocolate milk?

      a. a third of a gallon   b. a fourth of a gallon   c. a half gallon

_____ 18. The public library's **biennial** hobby show will take place next month.

      a. happening every two weeks   b. happening every two months   c. happening every two years

_____ 19. Mrs. Bush was troubled by **hyperthyroidism**.

      a. too little activity   b. too much activity   c. a missing thyroid gland
         of the thyroid gland   of the thyroid gland

_____ 20. There's a problem at the television station. Only the **audio** portion of the show is coming through.

      a. sound   b. picture   c. top

| _Score_ (Number correct) _____ x 5 = _____ % |

Enter your score above and in the vocabulary performance chart on the inside back cover of the book.

Unit Two

calamity	persevere
comprehensive	ponder
conventional	rehabilitate
flagrant	turmoil
fluctuate	venture

Ten Words in Context

In the space provided, write the letter of the meaning closest to that of each **boldfaced** word. Use the context of the sentences to help you figure out each word's meaning.

1 calamity
(kə-lăm′ĭ-tē)
-*noun*

- The survivors of the earthquake slowly rebuilt their homes and lives after the **calamity**.
- Our neighbor's house burned down one night in May. Ever since that **calamity**, our children have been afraid to go to bed at night.

___ *Calamity* means   a. an activity.   b. a tragedy.   c. a risk.

2 comprehensive
(kŏm′prē-hĕn′sĭv)
-*adjective*

- That article on sightseeing in New Orleans was not **comprehensive**. It failed to mention many points of interest in that wonderful city.
- Our company's **comprehensive** insurance plan covers most health services, including hospitals, doctors, and dentists.

___ *Comprehensive* means   a. complete.   b. familiar.   c. continuous.

3 conventional
(kən-vĕn′shə-nəl)
-*adjective*

- The **conventional** Valentine's Day gifts are roses and chocolates.
- Jorge wanted to propose to Elena in the **conventional** manner, so in the middle of a restaurant, he got down on his knees and asked, "Will you marry me?"

___ *Conventional* means   a. out-of-the-way.   b. useful.   c. usual.

4 flagrant
(flā′grənt)
-*adjective*

- The use of campaign funds for the congressman's private business was a **flagrant** violation of the law.
- In **flagrant** disregard of his parents' stated wishes, Art wore a T-shirt and jeans to their dinner party.

___ *Flagrant* means   a. obvious.   b. acceptable.   c. minor.

5 fluctuate
(flŭk′chōō-āt′)
-*verb*

- My weight used to **fluctuate** between 150 and 190 pounds. Now it's steady, at 170 pounds.
- Desert temperatures can **fluctuate** by as much as fifty degrees between daytime and nighttime.

___ *Fluctuate* means   a. to continue.   b. to vary.   c. to follow.

6 persevere
(pûr′sə′vīr)
-*verb*

- "I know you're tired," Jack said, "but we've got to **persevere** and get to the camp before the storm hits."
- It was not easy to attend English classes while working at two jobs, but Nina **persevered** until she could speak English well.

___ *Persevere* means   a. to surrender.   b. to hold back.   c. to keep going.

7 **ponder**
(pŏn′dər)
-*verb*

- Too often we don't take time to **ponder** the possible consequences of our actions.
- Over the years, Mr. Madigan rarely took time to **ponder** the meaning of life. Since his heart attack, however, he's thought a lot about what is important to him.

__ *Ponder* means   a. to wait for.   b. to ignore.   c. to think about.

8 **rehabilitate**
(rē′hə-bĭl′ə-tāt)
-*verb*

- Most prisons make little effort to **rehabilitate** inmates so that they can lead productive, wholesome lives after their release.
- My grandfather learned to walk, write, and speak again in a program that **rehabilitates** stroke victims.

__ *Rehabilitate* means   a. to pay back.   b. to prepare for normal life.   c. to depend upon.

9 **turmoil**
(tûr′moil)
-*noun*

- Without a teacher, the sixth-grade class was in **turmoil**, until the principal entered the room and the students quickly came to order.
- After the **turmoil** of crying babies, active children, and trying to feed 120 people, I'm glad when our family reunions end.

__ *Turmoil* means   a. discussion.   b. disorder.   c. harmony.

10 **venture**
(vĕn′chər)
-*verb*

- "I'll **venture** going on any ride in this amusement park except the Twister," said Nick. "I'll risk getting sick to my stomach, but I won't risk my life."
- At tomorrow's staff meeting, I will **venture** to say what I really think and cross my fingers that I don't get fired.

__ *Venture* means   a. to dare.   b. to remember.   c. to imagine.

Matching Words with Definitions

Following are definitions of the ten words. Clearly write or print each word next to its definition. The sentences above and on the previous page will help you decide on the meaning of each word.

1. _____   a. Shockingly obvious; outrageous

2. _____   b. To take the risk of; dare

3. _____   c. Including all or much

4. _____   d. To restore to a normal life through therapy or education

5. _____   e. To continue with an effort or plan despite difficulties

6. _____   f. Complete confusion; uproar

7. _____   g. An event bringing great loss and misery

8. _____   h. To vary irregularly; to go up and down or back and forth

9. _____   i. To consider carefully; think deeply about

10. _____   j. Customary; ordinary

CAUTION: Do not go any further until you are sure the above answers are correct. Then you can use the definitions to help you in the following practices. Your goal is eventually to know the words well enough so that you don't need to check the definitions at all.

➤ *Sentence Check 1*

Using the answer line provided, complete each item below with the correct word from the box. Use each word once.

a. **calamity**	b. **comprehensive**	c. **conventional**	d. **flagrant**	e. **fluctuate**
f. **persevere**	g. **ponder**	h. **rehabilitate**	i. **turmoil**	j. **venture**

_____ 1. Iris is so vain that she considers it a ___ if a pimple appears anywhere on her face.

_____ 2. Too many people have a child without taking time to ___ parenthood. They give less thought to having a baby than to buying a sofa.

_____ 3. When Charlene lost her job because she spoke up for a fellow employee, it was a ___ violation of her rights.

_____ 4. Our psychology exam will be ___; it will cover everything we've studied since September.

_____ 5. Nobody in Doug's family has a ___ job. His mother is a drummer, his father is a magician, and his uncle is a wine taster.

_____ 6. Learning the computer program was difficult, but when Maria saw how useful it would be in her work, she was glad she had ___(e)d.

_____ 7. It took many months of therapy to ___ my aunt after she lost her sight, but now she can get around her home and neighborhood on her own.

_____ 8. The day we moved, the apartment was in ___. Boxes and people were everywhere, and the baby wouldn't stop crying.

_____ 9. The way my dog's appetite ____(e)d this week worries me. One day she hardly ate anything, and the next she gulped down everything I gave her.

_____ 10. Instead of hiring a lawyer, the defendant will ___ to plead her own case in court.

NOTE: Now check your answers to these questions by turning to page 175. Going over the answers carefully will help you prepare for the next two practices, for which answers are not given.

➤ *Sentence Check 2*

Using the answer lines provided, complete each item below with **two** words from the box. Use each word once.

_____ 1–2. The one time my cousin ___(e)d skydiving, the result was a ___. Her
_____   parachute didn't open, and she was injured so badly in the fall that she almost died.

_____ 3–4. A drug-treatment center can ___ most addicts. Among the failures are
_____   addicts who don't ___ with the treatment and leave the center early.

_____   5–6. When driving alone, Marshall is very ___, obeying all the traffic rules.
_____   But when his friends are with him, he shows off with ___ violations of
the speed limit.

_____   7–8. "We need to ___ all we might do to help families in trouble," said the
_____   social worker to her staff. "We must plan a ___ program, not just a
narrow plan dealing with only one part of their lives."

_____   9–10. Our boss's moods and orders ___ so wildly at times that they throw our
_____   department into ___. As a result, our productivity is at an all-time low,
and it will take a new boss to revitalize° this office.

➤ _Final Check:_ Accident and Recovery

Here is a final opportunity for you to strengthen your knowledge of the ten words. First read the following
selection carefully. Then fill in each blank with a word from the box at the top of the previous page.
(Context clues will help you figure out which word goes in which blank.) Use each word once.

We tried to deter° Anna from jumping, but her (1)_____ disregard of our

warnings led to a (2)_____ that would change her life forever. She dove off a

rock into a river none of us was sure was deep enough. When she hit the bottom, she broke her

back.

I visited Anna at the hospital every day for the next few weeks. I saw her mood

(3)_____ between anger and quiet depression. Her whole life seemed in

(4)_____; she was too confused and demoralized° to think reasonably about

her future.

Within about a month, however, I began to see a change in Anna. She had moved to Henner

House to participate in a very (5)_____ program, designed to meet all the

needs of patients like Anna. The program (6)_____s accident victims so that

they can return to fulfilling lives. Anna gained hope once she saw she could learn to do such

everyday tasks as cooking, cleaning, and bathing. After learning how to get around indoors, she

(7)_____(e)d traveling around the city in her wheelchair. The more she did,

the better she felt. The staff also helped Anna plan for her future. They urged her to

(8)_____ her goals and how she might meet them. At times, it was difficult

for her to (9)_____ with the program, but she didn't quit.

Now, ten months later, Anna is able to live a somewhat (10)_____ life.

Despite her infirmity°, she is able to do many of the ordinary things she used to do—work, drive,

and live in an apartment with a friend. Yes, her life has changed forever. But Anna is once again

glad to be alive.

Scores	Sentence Check 2 _____%	Final Check _____%

Enter your scores above and in the vocabulary performance chart on the inside back cover of the book.

attest	enigma
attribute	exemplify
discern	mobile
dispatch	nocturnal
enhance	orient

Ten Words in Context

In the space provided, write the letter of the meaning closest to that of each **boldfaced** word. Use the context of the sentences to help you figure out each word's meaning.

1 attest
(ə-tĕst')
-verb

- Anyone who has seen the Golden Gate Bridge in the rose-gold light of sunset can **attest** to its beauty.
- Witnesses **attest** to the fact that rainfall makes the ground of Death Valley so slippery that boulders slide across it.

___ *Attest to* means   a. to declare to be true.   b. to wish for.   c. to forget easily.

2 attribute
(ăt'rə-byo͞ot')
-noun

- A three-hundred-page novel written in 1939 has the odd **attribute** of containing no *e*, the most common letter in English.
- In Japan, some cars have such computerized **attributes** as windshield wipers that automatically turn on when it rains.

___ *Attribute* means   a. a tendency.   b. a defect.   c. a characteristic.

3 discern
(dĭ-sûrn')
-verb

- An experienced jeweler can easily **discern** whether a diamond is genuine or fake.
- People who are red-green colorblind can **discern** the colors of traffic lights by recognizing shades of gray.

___ *Discern* means   a. to see clearly.   b. to disregard.   c. to change.

4 dispatch
(dĭ-spăch')
-verb

- I wanted to **dispatch** the letter as quickly as possible, so I took it to the post office instead of dropping it into a mailbox.
- At work Harold is treated like an errand boy. His boss often **dispatches** him to the deli for sandwiches or donuts.

___ *Dispatch* means   a. to represent.   b. to send.   c. to drive.

5 enhance
(ĕn-hăns')
-verb

- Our gym teacher **enhanced** her appearance with a more attractive hairstyle.
- The college catalogue stated that the writing course would "**enhance** all students' writing skills" by improving their grammar and style.

___ *Enhance* means   a. to improve.   b. to recognize.   c. to reduce.

6 enigma
(ĭ-nĭg'mə)
-noun

- How the thief entered our house was an **enigma** until we remembered that the cellar door had been left unlocked.
- The "singing sands" of Scotland remained an **enigma** until scientists learned that footsteps caused the round grains of sand and the surrounding air pockets to make musical vibrations.

___ *Enigma* means   a. a comfort.   b. a puzzle.   c. an error.

7 **exemplify**
(ĭg-zĕm′plə-fī′)
-*verb*

• The many IRS employees who give citizens inaccurate information **exemplify** governmental incompetence.
• Mr. Pell, who emphasizes original thinking and freedom of expression, **exemplifies** the best in teaching.

___ *Exemplify* means   a. to illustrate.   b. to save.   c. to oppose.

8 **mobile**
(mō′bəl)
-*adjective*

• My parents own a **mobile** home, which can be moved from place to place on a long truck.
• Every morning when I was in the hospital, a volunteer wheeled a **mobile** library into my room.

___ *Mobile* means   a. active.   b. expensive.   c. movable.

9 **nocturnal**
(nŏk-tûr′nəl)
-*adjective*

• I know when my brother has enjoyed one of his **nocturnal** feasts because I find a stack of dishes in the sink in the morning.
• Being **nocturnal**, owls are rarely seen during the day.

___ *Nocturnal* means   a. noisy.   b. busy.   c. of the night.

10 **orient**
(ôr′ē-ĕnt)
-*verb*

• When coming up from the subway, I often need to look at a street sign to **orient** myself.
• Drivers of the future may **orient** themselves in unfamiliar places with the help of an electronic map that shows the car's location.

___ *Orient* means   a. to locate.   b. to welcome.   c. to question.

Matching Words with Definitions

Following are definitions of the ten words. Clearly write or print each word next to its definition. The sentences above and on the previous page will help you decide on the meaning of each word.

1. _____   a. A mystery or puzzle

2. _____   b. To send to a specific place or on specific business

3. _____   c. Of, about, or happening in the night; active at night

4. _____   d. To make a statement about something on the basis of personal experience; bear witness; testify

5. _____   e. To determine one's location or direction; to locate in relation to a direction (east, west, etc.)

6. _____   f. To recognize; detect

7. _____   g. To improve

8. _____   h. Moving or able to move from place to place

9. _____   i. A quality or feature of a person or thing

10. _____   j. To be an example of; represent; be typical of

CAUTION: Do not go any further until you are sure the above answers are correct. Then you can use the definitions to help you in the following practices. Your goal is eventually to know the words well enough so that you don't need to check the definitions at all.

➤ *Sentence Check 1*

Using the answer line provided, complete each item below with the correct word from the box. Use each word once.

a. **attest**	b. **attribute**	c. **discern**	d. **dispatch**	e. **enhance**
f. **enigma**	g. **exemplify**	h. **mobile**	i. **nocturnal**	j. **orient**

_____ 1. Fresh garlic may not ___ the breath, but it certainly improves spaghetti sauce.

_____ 2. A witness ___(e)d to the truth of the defendant's claim that she had loved the murdered man.

_____ 3. When I was younger, my mother used to ___ me to the store for milk or some missing cooking ingredient as often as twice a day.

_____ 4. The lives of such reformers as Susan B. Anthony, Gandhi, and Martin Luther King ___ greatness.

_____ 5. Science does not have enough evidence to solve the ___ of whether or not there is other intelligent life in the universe.

_____ 6. The convicts decided on a(n) ___ escape. The darkness would hide them as they fled through the forest.

_____ 7. Sue's hairpiece is so natural looking that it's impossible to ___ where the hairpiece ends and her own hair begins.

_____ 8. The positions of the stars help sailors ___ themselves on the open seas.

_____ 9. My mother is unable to walk, but with her wheelchair she is ___ enough to get around her one-story home, move along a sidewalk, and even shop at a mall.

_____ 10. Giant kelp, a form of seaweed, has some amazing ___s. Not only is it the world's fastest-growing vegetable, but the more it is cut, the faster it grows.

NOTE: Now check your answers to these questions by turning to page 175. Going over the answers carefully will help you prepare for the next two practices, for which answers are not given.

➤ *Sentence Check 2*

Using the answer lines provided, complete each item below with **two** words from the box. Use each word once.

_____
_____ 1–2. Because Helen Keller could not hear or see, the keenness of her other senses was ___(e)d by use. It is said that she could ___ who was in a room simply by using her sense of smell.

_____
_____ 3–4. A ___ robot that collects and delivers mail throughout our office building ___s itself with electric eyes.

_____   5–6. In fables, animals often illustrate human ___s. In the story of the race
_____   between the tortoise and the hare, the tortoise is meant to ___ the human
                                quality of being slow but steady. Despite competing against a much
                                speedier antagonist°, he persevered° and beat the overly confident hare.

_____   7–8. The reason the boss likes to ___ Oliver on lengthy errands is no ___.
_____   Everyone knows that the office functions better with Oliver out of the
                                way.

_____   9–10. Anyone who has ever gone to college can ___ to the fact that, during
_____   finals, many students become ___ animals. They stay up all night before
                                 an exam and then sleep during the daytime after taking the test.

➤ *Final Check:* Animal Senses

Here is a final opportunity for you to strengthen your knowledge of the ten words. First read the following
selection carefully. Then fill in each blank with a word from the box at the top of the previous page.
(Context clues will help you figure out which word goes in which blank.) Use each word once.

Animals possess sensory powers that humans lack. Homing pigeons fly with great speed and

accuracy when (1)_____(e)d with messages to faraway places. How do pigeons

(2)_____ themselves in unfamiliar regions? This remains something of a(n)

(3)_____. The mystery, however, is partly explained by a pigeon's ability to

see ultraviolet light, which reveals the sun's position even through clouds. In addition, pigeons can

hear sound waves that have traveled hundreds of miles. These waves (4)_____

a pigeon's sense of direction by indicating distant mountains and seas. Pigeons even appear to

(5)_____ changes in the earth's magnetic field.

Bats have impressive (6)_____s equally worthy of acclaim°. As

(7)_____ animals, they search for food in complete darkness. They do so by

screeching in tones higher than any human can hear and then locating prey by the returning

echoes.

Scorpions also (8)_____ the night hunter. Tiny leg hairs enable them to

feel vibrations in the sand made by a (9)_____ insect as far as two feet away.

People with knowledge of the pigeon, bat, and scorpion can (10)_____

to the fact that such "innovations"° as the magnetic compass, radar, and the motion detector are

nothing new.

Scores Sentence Check 2 _____%	Final Check _____%

Enter your scores above and in the vocabulary performance chart on the inside back cover of the book.

concurrent	hypothetical
confiscate	nominal
constitute	predominant
decipher	prerequisite
default	recession

Ten Words in Context

In the space provided, write the letter of the meaning closest to that of each **boldfaced** word. Use the context of the sentences to help you figure out each word's meaning.

1 concurrent
(kən-kûr′ənt)
-*adjective*

- Having mistakenly registered for two **concurrent** classes, Joe had to drop one of them and choose a course that met at a different time.
- **Concurrent** with the closing of the steel mill was the opening of a new toy factory in town. As a result, most of the workers laid off from the mill found jobs at the new factory.

___ *Concurrent* means   a. occurring at the same time.   b. resulting.   c. noticeable.

2 confiscate
(kŏn′fĭs-kāt′)
-*verb*

- Not only did the teacher **confiscate** the note I passed to my boyfriend, but she also read it out loud to the entire class.
- Chinese drug agents once **confiscated** $2 million worth of heroin that had been wrapped in plastic and inserted into live goldfish. The agents seized the drugs as they were being sent out of the country.

___ *Confiscate* means   a. to distribute widely.   b. to take possession of.   c. to overlook.

3 constitute
(kŏn′stĭ-tōōt)
-*verb*

- In my opinion, a good movie, a pizza, and animated conversation **constitute** a perfect night out.
- Twelve business and professional people **constitute** the board of directors of the local women's shelter. Among other things, they help raise funds for the shelter.

___ *Constitute* means   a. to repeat.   b. to oppose.   c. to form.

4 decipher
(dĭ-sī′fər)
-*verb*

- Why do contracts have to use language that's so difficult to **decipher**?
- On one of Holly's essays, her English teacher wrote, "Please type your papers. I can't **decipher** your handwriting."

___ *Decipher* means   a. to figure out.   b. to find.   c. to improve.

5 default
(dĭ-fôlt′)
-*verb*

- We won our case against the appliance repairman because he **defaulted** by failing to appear in court.
- Jay's mother said, "I'll co-sign on your car loan, but you have to make every payment. If you **default**, it will hurt my credit rating."

___ *Default* means   a. to act as expected.   b. not to do something required.   c. to begin.

6 hypothetical
(hī′pō-thĕt′ĭ-kəl)
-*adjective*

- Imagine the **hypothetical** situation of going to live alone on an island. Which books and music tapes would you take along?
- Law schools hold pretend court sessions with **hypothetical** cases so that students can practice their skills.

___ *Hypothetical* means   a. sure to happen.   b. dangerous.   c. imaginary.

7 nominal
(nŏm′ə-nəl)
-*adjective*

- Except for a **nominal** registration fee, the camp for needy children is entirely free.
- Professor Banks gave us only **nominal** extra credit for participating in psychology experiments. She wanted our course grade to be based mainly on our test scores.

___ *Nominal* means   a. enormous.   b. very little.   c. helpful.

8 predominant
(prĭ-dŏm′ə-nənt)
-*adjective*

- Rock is the **predominant** music in our dorm, but country music is also popular.
- Alhough the **predominant** type of car in New York City in 1900 used gasoline, a third of the cars ran on electricity.

___ *Predominant* means   a. rare.   b. main.   c. temporary.

9 prerequisite
(prē-rĕk′wĭ-zĭt)
-*noun*

- You can't take Spanish Literature I unless you've taken the **prerequisite**, Spanish III.
- Being allergic to cigarette smoke, Kathy told Joel that his quitting smoking was a **prerequisite** for their marrying.

___ *Prerequisite* means   a. a requirement.   b. a penalty.   c. a method.

10 recession
(rĭ-sēsh′ən)
-*noun*

- While seashore businesses in the North suffer a **recession** in the winter, they do very well from spring to fall.
- The department store laid off twenty workers during the **recession**, but it rehired them when business improved.

___ *Recession* means   a. a rapid growth.   b. a sale.   c. an economic setback.

Matching Words with Definitions

Following are definitions of the ten words. Clearly write or print each word next to its definition. The sentences above and on the previous page will help you decide on the meaning of each word.

1. _____   a. To make up; be the parts of

2. _____   b. To fail to do something required

3. _____   c. Most common or most noticeable

4. _____   d. Something required beforehand

5. _____   e. To seize with authority; legally take possession of

6. _____   f. To interpret or read (something confusing or hard to make out)

7. _____   g. Slight; very small compared with what might be expected

8. _____   h. Happening or existing at the same time; simultaneous

9. _____   i. A temporary decline in business

10. _____   j. Supposed for the sake of argument or examination; imaginary; theoretical

CAUTION: Do not go any further until you are sure the above answers are correct. Then you can use the definitions to help you in the following practices. Your goal is eventually to know the words well enough so that you don't need to check the definitions at all.

➤ *Sentence Check 1*

Using the answer line provided, complete each item below with the correct word from the box. Use each word once.

a. **concurrent**	b. **confiscate**	c. **constitute**	d. **decipher**	e. **default**
f. **hypothetical**	g. **nominal**	h. **predominant**	i. **prerequisite**	j. **recession**

_____ 1. Anger was the ___ emotion among students when they first heard that their tuition would be raised again.

_____ 2. Although the two robberies were ___—both occurred at midnight on Friday—one man had planned them both.

_____ 3. One hundred senators and 435 members of the House of Representatives ___ the United States Congress.

_____ 4. A ___ for taking the driver-education class is passing a written test on the driving laws.

_____ 5. The town library charges only a ___ fine for late books but a higher fine for late videotapes.

_____ 6. Karim has such terrible handwriting that his wife couldn't ___ his message saying she should meet him at the restaurant.

_____ 7. When the shoe factory closed, our little town went into a ___ because the laid-off workers had no money to spend at local businesses.

_____ 8. The phone company refused to install a phone in Glen's new apartment because he had ___(e)d on several of his previous bills.

_____ 9. One of the town's police officers ___s illegal fireworks from teenagers and then sets them off at his own home on the Fourth of July.

_____ 10. To teach young children safety, many parents explain what to do in ___ situations, such as if a stranger asks them to go for a ride.

NOTE: Now check your answers to these questions by turning to page 176. Going over the answers carefully will help you prepare for the next two practices, for which answers are not given.

➤ *Sentence Check 2*

Using the answer lines provided, complete each item below with **two** words from the box. Use each word once.

_____
_____ 1–2. This summer, local children can sign up for art or music lessons for a ___ fee of $3. It's impossible to take both, though, since the classes will be ___.

_____
_____ 3–4. Although cancer and heart disease ___ the leading threats to life in the United States, car accidents are the ___ cause of death for teenagers.

_____ 5–6. "It seems as if a degree in accounting is a ___ for understanding our tax

_____ laws," said Ken. "How else could anyone ___ the tax codes?"

_____ 7–8. The small print on my mortgage stated that if I should ___ on payments,

_____ the bank had the right to ___ my house.

_____ 9–10. When Ms. Howe was interviewed for the job of store manager, the

_____ regional manager asked her a question about a ___ situation. "Imagine that

our business is in a ___," he said. "What would you do to enhance° sales?"

➤ _Final Check:_ Money Problems

Here is a final opportunity for you to strengthen your knowledge of the ten words. First read the following selection carefully. Then fill in each blank with a word from the box at the top of the previous page. (Context clues will help you figure out which word goes in which blank.) Use each word once.

"My car has been stolen!" My neighbor, Martha, ran into my house crying and angry. "I saw them take it."

I called the police for her, and she told an officer the license number and car model. "The (1)_____ color of the car is brown," she added, "but it has a black roof. I had it parked in the lot adjacent° to the beauty shop I own. I saw two men tow it away."

"You saw them tow it?" the officer asked. "Have you (2)_____(e)d on your car loan?"

"What do you mean?" Martha asked.

"If you haven't been making your payments, the bank or dealer has the right to (3)_____ the car."

Martha admitted that she hadn't made any payments for three months. Later she told me she'd ⁻gotten notices in the mail but threw them away because their language was too complicated to (4)_____. She also said she was having money problems. (5)_____ with the car loan was a big home improvement loan. She also had five credit-card bills and regular living expenses to pay. To top it all off, the city was suffering from a (6)_____, so her income was down, something her laid-off employees could certainly attest° to. She was about $12,000 in debt.

At my suggestion, Martha visited a debt counselor who helped her develop a comprehensive° plan to pay her bills. The only (7)_____s for this free service were a regular job and a willingness to pay one's debts in full. The counselor and Martha planned what would (8)_____ a reasonable budget, based on Martha's income and expenses. They then wrote to the companies she owed to arrange to pay a (9)_____ amount each month until the whole debt was paid. They also discussed what she would do in several (10)_____ situations, such as if her refrigerator died or her income changed.

Now, Martha is getting back on her feet again—in more ways than one, since she never got the car back.

Scores Sentence Check 2 _____%	Final Check _____%

Enter your scores above and in the vocabulary performance chart on the inside back cover of the book.

degenerate	sanctuary
implausible	scrutiny
incoherent	sinister
intercede	suffice
intricate	vulnerable

Ten Words in Context

In the space provided, write the letter of the meaning closest to that of each **boldfaced** word. Use the context of the sentences to help you figure out each word's meaning.

1 degenerate
(dĭ-jĕn′ər-āt′)
-*verb*

- Mr. Freedman's family was called to the nursing home when the old man's condition began to **degenerate**. It was feared he didn't have long to live.
- Mel's relationship with his parents **degenerated** when he dropped out of school against their wishes and became a bartender.

__ *Degenerate* means   a. to improve.   b. to remain the same.   c. to worsen.

2 implausible
(ĭm-plô′zə-bəl)
-*adjective*

- As **implausible** as it may sound, Southern Florida sometimes does get snow.
- Insurance companies hear such **implausible** excuses for auto accidents as "I hit the telephone pole when I was blinded by the lights of a flying saucer."

__ *Implausible* means   a. unbelievable.   b. acceptable.   c. valuable.

3 incoherent
(ĭn′kō-hîr′ənt)
-*adjective*

- If Mitch drinks much more, he'll become completely **incoherent**. He's already having trouble expressing his thoughts clearly.
- My sister talks a lot in her sleep, but she's so **incoherent** then that we can never figure out what she's saying.

__ *Incoherent* means   a. calm.   b. unclear.   c. inconvenient.

4 intercede
(ĭn′tər-sēd′)
-*verb*

- When the principal said Harry couldn't play in Friday's football game, the coach **interceded**, hoping to change the principal's mind.
- Inez's parents refused to come to her wedding until her brother **interceded** and persuaded them to come after all.

__ *Intercede* means   a. to give in to someone.   b. to plead for someone.   c. to examine closely.

5 intricate
(ĭn′trĭ-kĭt)
-*adjective*

- *War and Peace* is a long, **intricate** novel that weaves together the detailed life stories of many individuals.
- It's amazing to see the **intricate** gold and silver jewelry that ancient Indians made with only simple tools. It obviously required great patience and skill to create such complex ornaments.

__ *Intricate* means   a. simple.   b. uninteresting.   c. complicated.

6 sanctuary
(săngk′chōō-ĕr′ē)
-*noun*

- Old, unused trains in Grand Central Station serve as a nighttime **sanctuary** for some of New York City's homeless.
- When the houseful of children becomes too noisy, Ned finds the laundry room to be a **sanctuary**, a place where he can read in quiet.

__ *Sanctuary* means   a. a reminder.   b. a shelter.   c. a challenge.

7 scrutiny
(skrōot′ən-ē)
-*noun*

• Store security guards give careful **scrutiny** to people carrying large bags, since the bags may be used for shoplifting.
• Before being published, a book comes under the **scrutiny** of a proofreader, who examines it for grammar and spelling errors.

___ *Scrutiny* means   a. attention.   b. protection.   c. permission.

8 sinister
(sĭn′ĭs-tər)
-*adjective*

• In the movie, a mad scientist thought up the **sinister** scheme of releasing a deadly virus. His evil plot failed when he died from the virus himself.
• Jack the Ripper, one of the more **sinister** criminals in English history, slashed the throats of six women.

___ *Sinister* means   a. illogical.   b. evil.   c. inconsiderate.

9 suffice
(sə-fīs′)
-*verb*

• The amount of research you've done may **suffice** for a high school term paper, but not for a college one.
• I forgot to buy something for lunch tomorrow, but the leftover meatloaf will **suffice**.

___ *Suffice* means   a. to be wasted.   b. to be adequate.   c. to be examined.

10 vulnerable
(vŭl′nər-ə-bəl)
-*adjective*

• Homes in heavily wooded areas are especially **vulnerable** to termites.
• Because they tend to have brittle bones, the elderly are **vulnerable** to fractures.

___ *Vulnerable* means   a. open.   b. safe.   c. attracted.

Matching Words with Definitions

Following are definitions of the ten words. Clearly write or print each word next to its definition. The sentences above and on the previous page will help you decide on the meaning of each word.

1. _____   a. Having many parts arranged in a complicated way; complex

2. _____   b. To be good enough

3. _____   c. To worsen; deteriorate

4. _____   d. A place of safety, protection, or relief

5. _____   e. To make a request or plead on behalf of someone else

6. _____   f. Open to damage or attack; susceptible

7. _____   g. Difficult to believe; unlikely

8. _____   h. Evil; wicked

9. _____   i. Close inspection; careful examination

10. _____   j. Unable to speak in an orderly, logical way

CAUTION: Do not go any further until you are sure the above answers are correct. Then you can use the definitions to help you in the following practices. Your goal is eventually to know the words well enough so that you don't need to check the definitions at all.

➤ *Sentence Check 1*

Using the answer line provided, complete each item below with the correct word from the box. Use each word once.

a. **degenerate**	b. **implausible**	c. **incoherent**	d. **intercede**	e. **intricate**
f. **sanctuary**	g. **scrutiny**	h. **sinister**	i. **suffice**	j. **vulnerable**

_____ 1. Ken's cartoons ___ for the school newspaper, but they wouldn't be good enough for the city papers.

_____ 2. The Joker's name is misleading, for he's a(n) ___ man who takes pleasure in doing evil.

_____ 3. People who live in big cities are more ___ to muggings than are residents of small towns.

_____ 4. The leaves outside the window created a(n) ___ lacy shadow on my bedroom wall.

_____ 5. Although it seems ___, the seemingly dead desert really does blossom after a rainstorm.

_____ 6. People who allow an escaped convict to use their home as a ___ may face criminal charges themselves.

_____ 7. My husband was so upset that he was ___. It wasn't until he calmed down that I understood he had been fired.

_____ 8. Unclaimed bags at airports receive the ___ of security officers watching for drugs or explosives.

_____ 9. When I don't have company, my apartment tends to ___ into a jumble of papers, clothes, and school supplies.

_____ 10. When Dad informed my little sister that she had to be home from her date no later than ten o'clock, Mom ___(e)d and got her a midnight curfew.

NOTE: Now check your answers to these questions by turning to page 176. Going over the answers carefully will help you prepare for the next two practices, for which answers are not given.

➤ *Sentence Check 2*

Using the answer lines provided, complete each item below with **two** words from the box. Use each word once.

_____
_____ 1–2. Birds feel ___ to attack when they are out in the open where shrubbery is sparse°. To attract them to your bird feeder, put it near a ___ of thickly growing trees and large bushes.

_____
_____ 3–4. To get into the party, Mitch made up a flagrant° lie—a(n) ___ story about having lost our invitations in a fire. Surprisingly, the unlikely tale ___(e)d to get us in.

_____ 5–6. When a complicated musical piece is played by a talented orchestra,
_____   audiences can appreciate the ___ structure. But when poor musicians try
                                        the piece, it ___s into nothing more than noise.

_____ 7–8. As he left the bank, the robber shot an elderly man on mere impulse.
_____   Shocked by the ___ act, the bank clerk was at first ___. However, after
                                        calming down, she was able to clearly tell the police about the robbery
                                        and the totally arbitrary° shooting.

_____ 9–10. The children's eager ___ of the carefully arranged candies and cookies
_____   brought a curt° warning from their mother: "Look, but don't touch!"
                                         However, their grandmother ___(e)d and convinced her that it would be
                                         an inequity° to give all the goodies to company and none to the children.

➤ _Final Check:_ The New French Employee

Here is a final opportunity for you to strengthen your knowledge of the ten words. First read the following
selection carefully. Then fill in each blank with a word from the box at the top of the previous page.
(Context clues will help you figure out which word goes in which blank.) Use each word once.

One summer, Nan worked in a factory with an employee who had recently arrived from
France, a soft-spoken young man named Jean-Louis. He spoke little English, but Nan's basic
French (1)_____(e)d for simple conversations and helpful translations.

However, one day when she was called to the foreman's office, she wished she knew no
French at all. FBI agents were there with Jean-Louis. After explaining that Jean-Louis may have
been more (2)_____ than the innocent young man he appeared to be, the
foreman left her there to translate for the agents. The agents said Jean-Louis had been on the run
after committing several jewel thefts in France. Nan struggled to translate their questions, which
were often too (3)_____ for her limited vocabulary. At times, she became so
nervous that she was nearly (4)_____. When Jean-Louis finally deciphered°
what Nan was saying, he said the police were maligning° him. He claimed he was being mistaken
for his no-good twin brother, who was responsible for the robberies. The angry FBI agents found
Jean-Louis's story (5)_____. The conversation soon (6)_____(e)d
into a shouting match, with everyone yelling at poor Nan. When her boss heard the racket, he
(7)_____(e)d, appeased° the agents, and got them to excuse her.

Nan then went to the ladies' room, a (8)_____ from the turmoil° of all
the shouting. After the agents left with Jean-Louis, she was calm enough to go back to work.
But she felt (9)_____ for days as she wondered if she was under the
(10)_____ of jewel thieves who might blame her for Jean-Louis's arrest.

| _Scores_   Sentence Check 2 _____% | Final Check _____% |

Enter your scores above and in the vocabulary performance chart on the inside back cover of the book.

blatant	gloat
blight	immaculate
contrive	plagiarism
garble	qualm
gaunt	retaliate

Ten Words in Context

In the space provided, write the letter of the meaning closest to that of each **boldfaced** word. Use the context of the sentences to help you figure out each word's meaning.

1 blatant
(blā′tənt)
-*adjective*

• Scott's smoking is **blatant**. Not only does he light up everywhere, but his clothes smell of smoke, and his fingers are stained with nicotine.
• The company's disregard of the environment is **blatant**. It makes no effort to stop polluting coastal waters with garbage.

__ *Blatant* means   a. unmistakable.   b. scrambled.   c. not noticeable.

2 blight
(blīt)
-*noun*

• Nothing has hurt our country more than the **blight** of drugs.
• There are two ways of looking at TV: as a **blight** that dulls the mind or as a valuable source of information.

__ *Blight* means   a. something that assists. b. something very obvious. c. something that harms.

3 contrive
(kən′trīv)
-*verb*

• My eight-year-old son could write a book titled *101 Ways I Have **Contrived** to Stay Up Past My Bedtime*.
• Jill has to **contrive** a way to get a day off from work for her friend's wedding. She's already used up her vacation time.

__ *Contrive* means   a. to think up.   b. to mix up.   c. to avoid.

4 garble
(gär′bəl)
-*verb*

• The typesetter accidentally **garbled** the newspaper story, giving the reader only a mixed-up article.
• The company had **garbled** the bike's assembly instructions so badly that we were constantly confused about which step to do next.

__ *Garble* means   a. to read.   b. to lose.   c. to jumble.

5 gaunt
(gônt)
-*adjective*

• Abraham Lincoln's beard made his **gaunt** face look fuller.
• Sharon's eating disorder, called anorexia nervosa, has made her so **gaunt** that she looks like a walking skeleton.

__ *Gaunt* means   a. very thin.   b. wide.   c. confused.

6 gloat
(glōt)
-*verb*

• The coach told his team, "There's only one thing worse than a sore loser, and that's a mean winner. Don't **gloat**."
• Neil's sister always tattles on him and then **gloats** when he's punished, saying, "I told you so."

__ *Gloat* means   a. to apologize fully.   b. to be overly self-satisfied.   c. to pay back.

7 immaculate
(ĭ-măk′yə-lĭt)
-adjective

- It's amazing that while Carolyn always appears **immaculate**, her apartment often seems very dirty.
- Don't expect a child to come home from a birthday party with **immaculate** clothing. Children usually manage to get as much birthday cake on their clothing as in their mouths.

___ *Immaculate* means   a. uncomfortable.   b. spotless.   c. soiled.

8 plagiarism
(plā′jĕ-rĭz′əm)
-noun

- When the author saw a movie with the same plot as one of her novels, she sued for **plagiarism**.
- The teacher warned her students that using an author's exact words as one's own is **plagiarism**.

___ *Plagiarism* means   a. creativity.   b. the stealing of ideas.   c. planning.

9 qualm
(kwŏm)
-noun

- Larry had no **qualms** about stealing from the cafeteria cash register. He didn't even feel guilty when someone else was blamed.
- After hiding Lori's bike as an April Fool's joke, I began to have **qualms**. What if she thought it was stolen and called the police?

___ *Qualm* means   a. a guilty feeling.   b. a proud memory.   c. a clever plan.

10 retaliate
(rĭ-tăl′ē-āt′)
-verb

- When I broke my sister's stereo, she **retaliated** by cutting the cord of my Sony Walkman earphones.
- When Mary told about Flo's secret love affair, Flo **retaliated** by telling their friends about Mary's shoplifting.

___ *Retaliate* means   a. to forgive.   b. to take revenge.   c. to confuse.

Matching Words with Definitions

Following are definitions of the ten words. Clearly write or print each word next to its definition. The sentences above and on the previous page will help you decide on the meaning of each word.

1. _____   a. An uneasy feeling about how right or proper a particular action is
2. _____   b. To mix up or confuse (as a story or message); scramble
3. _____   c. To feel or express delight or self-satisfaction, often spitefully
4. _____   d. Something that weakens, damages, or destroys
5. _____   e. Using someone else's writings or ideas as one's own
6. _____   f. To plan cleverly; think up
7. _____   g. To return an injury for an injury; pay back
8. _____   h. Very obvious, often offensively so
9. _____   i. Perfectly clean
10. _____   j. Thin and bony

CAUTION: Do not go any further until you are sure the above answers are correct. Then you can use the definitions to help you in the following practices. Your goal is eventually to know the words well enough so that you don't need to check the definitions at all.

➤ *Sentence Check 1*

Using the answer line provided, complete each item below with the correct word from the box. Use each word once.

a. **blatant**	b. **blight**	c. **contrive**	d. **garble**	e. **gaunt**
f. **gloat**	g. **immaculate**	h. **plagiarism**	i. **qualm**	j. **retaliate**

_____ 1. A(n) ___ house may be a sign that someone has nothing better to do than clean.

_____ 2. Child abuse is an awful ___ on the physical and mental health of our youth.

_____ 3. My aunt refuses to drive Mr. Elson to bingo because he ___s so much when he wins, which is often.

_____ 4. The F's and D's on my brother's report card are ___ evidence of how little he has studied this term.

_____ 5. Emilio still hopes to ___ a way to get Rita to go out with him, even though she's refused him four times.

_____ 6. I bought an answering machine because my children have ___(e)d several important phone messages.

_____ 7. Every time the Hatfields harmed the McCoys, the McCoys would ___, so the feud went on for years.

_____ 8. Rescued after being lost at sea for nine days, the men were terribly ___, but they put on weight rapidly.

_____ 9. I would feel guilty if I called in sick when I wasn't, but no one else in the office seems to have any ___s about doing that.

_____ 10. Mark Twain joked that charges of ___ were ridiculous because no one can be completely original. He wrote, "We mortals can't create—we can only copy."

NOTE: Now check your answers to these questions by turning to page 176. Going over the answers carefully will help you prepare for the next two practices, for which answers are not given.

➤ *Sentence Check 2*

Using the answer lines provided, complete each item below with **two** words from the box. Use each word once.

_____
_____ 1–2. The living room looked ___ except for a lump under the carpet, a(n) ___ sign that my son had taken a shortcut in cleaning up.

_____
_____ 3–4. After the bully struck him, Jules wanted to ___ by throwing a rock, but he had ___s about doing anything so dangerous.

_____ 5–6. My little girl was so ___ after her illness that I carefully ___(e)d
_____   fattening meals that were sure to arouse her appetite.

_____ 7–8. "At least I know you aren't guilty of ___," said my teacher. "Nobody
_____   else would have ___(e)d the report so badly that it's impossible to
                                  follow."

_____ 9–10. Willie is a ___ on our school. Not only does he start fights with
_____   opposing players on the basketball court, but he also ___s after he's
                                   benched, as if he's proud of causing such turmoil°. In fact, although he's
                                   a great player, the coach is pondering° kicking him off the team.

➤ *Final Check:* A Cruel Teacher

Here is a final opportunity for you to strengthen your knowledge of the ten words. First read the following selection carefully. Then fill in each blank with a word from the box at the top of the previous page. (Context clues will help you figure out which word goes in which blank.) Use each word once.

It has been twenty years since I was in Mr. Brill's tenth-grade biology class, but I still get nervous thinking about it. Mr. Brill was a tall, (1)_____ man who resembled the skeleton at the back of the room. His meanness was (2)_____. For his most difficult questions, he would call on the shyest kids, those most vulnerable° to the pain of embarrassment. And when they nervously (3)_____(e)d their answers, he would (4)_____, as if their poor performance were a personal victory for him. The discomfort of some of his victims was almost tangible°, nearly as solid as the wooden pointer he sometimes slammed across his desk just to shock us. He seemed to (5)_____ situations just to make us miserable. For example, if our fingernails were not (6)_____, we were sent out of class. As if we needed clean hands to dissect a frog! One time I worked extremely hard on a paper for class, but he accused me of (7)_____. He said I must have copied it because I was too dumb to write anything that good. Without a (8)_____, he gave me an F, which ruined my average and demoralized° me for the rest of the year. All of us students would imagine ways to get even with him, but we were too afraid to (9)_____. Why a teacher like that was allowed to continue teaching was an enigma° to us, one I still have not figured out. In all the years since, I've never met a person who was such a (10)_____ on the teaching profession.

Scores	Sentence Check 2 _____%	Final Check _____%

Enter your scores above and in the vocabulary performance chart on the inside back cover of the book.

-ate	forc, fort
bio-	hum
claim, clam	pater, patri-
fin	semi-
flex, flect	-ward

Ten Word Parts in Context

Figure out the meanings of the following ten word parts by looking *closely* and *carefully* at the context in which they appear. Then, in the space provided, write the letter of the meaning closest to that of each word part.

1 -ate

- Teachers often find it difficult to **motivate** students to learn eagerly.
- The TV history series **fascinated** viewers with such details as a seventeenth-century English children's hospital that gave each child two gallons of beer per week.

__ The word part *-ate* means   a. cause to become.   b. call.   c. end.

2 bio-

- Helen Keller wrote a touching **autobiography** titled *The Story of My Life*.
- **Biology** is the science of living things, both plant and animal.

__ The word part *bio-* means   a. bend.   b. life.   c. partly.

3 claim, clam

- In 1965, American movie critics **acclaimed** *The Sound of Music* as the best picture of the year.
- The **exclamation** point emphasizes passionate, sudden, and surprised outcries, such as "Aha!" and "That hurts!"

__ The word part *claim* or *clam* means   a. cry out.   b. father.   c. partly.

4 fin

- The **final** word in many prayers is *amen*, which means "May it be so."
- All the dancers who had appeared in the recital came back on stage for the **finale**, a tap dance performed to "Goodnight, Irene."

__ The word part *fin* means   a. strong.   b. toward.   c. end.

5 flex, flect

- Gymnasts must be extremely **flexible** so that they can bend their bodies into many positions.
- When they enter church, Catholics **genuflect**—that is, they bend one knee, as a sign of reverence.

__ The word part *flex* or *flect* means   a. bend.   b. father.   c. person.

6 forc, fort

- The burglar **forcibly** entered the home by breaking the kitchen window.
- The children made a high wall of pressed snow to **fortify** themselves against a snowball attack by the kids across the street.

__ The word part *forc* or *fort* means   a. person.   b. direction of.   c. strong.

7 hum

- "We have done all that is **humanly** possible to save your grandmother's life," said the doctor.
- A resident of the shelter for the homeless complained, "The treatment here is not **humane**. We want to be treated like people, not objects."

___ The word part *hum* means   a. in the direction of.   b. having to do with people.   c. call.

8 pater, patri-

- Kara filed a **paternity** suit against Mike, to prove he was her baby's father.
- **Patriotism** was so strong that soldiers willingly risked their lives to defend their fatherland.

___ The word part *pater* or *patri-* means   a. partly.   b. toward.   c. father.

9 semi-

- My grandfather is only **semiretired**—he works part-time as a plumber.
- I use **semisweet** chocolate in my frosting to keep it from being too bitter or too sweet.

___ The word part *semi-* means   a. partly.   b. of living things.   c. toward.

10 -ward

- Everyone at the fair looked **skyward** in horror as the colorful hot-air balloon exploded.
- The children tried walking to school **backward** but gave up before even reaching the end of their block.

___ The word part *-ward* means   a. call.   b. in the direction of.   c. of living things.

Matching Word Parts with Definitions

Following are definitions of the ten word parts. Clearly write or print each word part next to its definition. The sentences above and on the previous page will help you decide on the meaning of each word part.

1. _____   a. Bend

2. _____   b. Partly; half

3. _____   c. Life; of living things

4. _____   d. Father

5. _____   e. Cause to become

6. _____   f. In the direction of; toward

7. _____   g. Call; cry out

8. _____   h. Strong

9. _____   i. Person; having to do with people

10. _____   j. End

CAUTION: Do not go any further until you are sure the above answers are correct. Then you can use the definitions to help you in the following practices. Your goal is eventually to know the word parts well enough so that you don't need to check the definitions at all.

➤ *Sentence Check 1*

Using the answer line provided, complete each *italicized* word in the sentences below with the correct word part from the box. Use each word part once.

a. -ate	b. bio-	c. claim, clam	d. fin	e. flex
f. forc, fort	g. hum	h. pater, patri-	i. semi-	j. -ward

_____ 1. Little Jesse loudly (*ex . . . ed*) ___ that his father was the smartest man on the block.

_____ 2. A (*. . . rhythm*) ___ is any cycle of periodic changes in life, such as daily changes in body temperature.

_____ 3. The jury found the disturbed young man guilty of (*. . . cide*) ___, for shooting his father.

_____ 4. After a cold, rainy weekend of camping, the Boy Scouts were relieved to head (*home . . .*) ___.

_____ 5. My mother was so (*in . . . ible*) ___ that she never once bent the rule and let me stay out past curfew.

_____ 6. The candidate's (*. . . eful*) ___ speech in favor of reduced military spending made a powerful impression on me.

_____ 7. Uncle Ken was in a (*. . . private*) ___ room in the hospital. The other man in the room had also suffered a heart attack.

_____ 8. There were only two (*. . . alists*) ___ in the last session of the talent contest, and both were country singers.

_____ 9. Bishop Desmond Tutu of South Africa received the Nobel Peace Prize for his (*. . . anitarian*) ___ efforts to bring justice to his country's people.

_____ 10. In 1961, administrators of New York's Museum of Modern Art were (*humili . . . d*) ___ to learn that for weeks a painting had been displayed upside down.

NOTE: Now check your answers to these questions by turning to page 176. Going over the answers carefully will help you prepare for the next two practices, for which answers are not given.

➤ *Sentence Check 2*

Using the answer lines provided, complete each *italicized* word in the sentences below with the correct word part from the box. Use each word part once.

_____ 1–2. I looked (*down . . .*) ___ and watched the doctor tap my knee to see if its
_____ (*re . . .*) ___ was normal.

_____ 3–4. My boss, Mr. Kane, is (*. . . nal*) ___. He (*en . . . es*) ___ the rules in a
_____ fatherly way—firmly but kindly. In addition, my coworkers are all very amiable°, making for a very friendly atmosphere.

_____ 5–6. After the accident, my brother was (. . . *conscious*) ___ for several
_____ hours. (. . . *ally*)___, around midnight, he became fully alert and
mobile° enough to walk out of the hospital on his own.

_____ 7–8. When the teacher asked students to write a (. . . *graphy*) ___, she meant
_____ the life story of a (. . . *an*) ___. But Harry wrote the life story of Tarzan,
his pet snake.

_____ 9–10. In 1863, Abraham Lincoln issued a (*pro . . . ation*) ___ freeing the
_____ slaves. But it would be almost 100 years after his announcement before
real efforts were made to (*integr . . .*) ___ black people into society's
mainstream.

➤ *Final Check:* **It's Never Too Late**

Here is a final opportunity for you to strengthen your knowledge of the ten word parts. First read the
following selection carefully. Then complete each *italicized* word in the parentheses below with a word
from the box at the top of the previous page. (Context clues will help you figure out which word part goes
in which blank.) Use each word part once.

I almost fell out of my chair last night when my father (*pro . . . ed*) (1)_____,
"I quit my job today. I'm going to college." He realizes that people may think it eccentric° to go to
school at his age, but he's willing to appear odd because he's tired of (. . . *skilled*)
(2)_____ work in a factory. He wants a job that requires more skill and training.
Both of my (. . . *nal*) (3)_____ grandparents died when Dad was a child, so
he and his brothers were forced to quit school early to work. Dad finished high school at night.
Now he will venture° working only part-time in order to (*educ . . .*) (4)_____
himself further. He still isn't sure what his major will be, but he has always liked science. He
definitely wants to take a (. . . *logy*) (5)_____ course because all living
things interest him. He'd like to focus his (*ef . . . s*) (6)_____ in a field that
benefits (. . . *anity*) (7)_____, such as physical therapy, where he could help
rehabilitate° people with certain infirmities°. He's also thinking about nursing. Most men of his
generation think of nursing as women's work, so Dad's interest in this field shows me he is more
(. . . *ible*) (8)_____ in his thinking than I ever realized. Whatever his choice,
he is looking (*for . . .*) (9)_____ to classes with great zeal°. I know that
when he (. . . *ishes*) (10)_____ his schooling, no one will be prouder of him
than I already am.

| *Scores* | Sentence Check 2 _____% | Final Check _____% |

Enter your scores above and in the vocabulary performance chart on the inside back cover of the book.

UNIT TWO: *Review*

The box at the right lists twenty-five words from Unit Two. Using the clues at the bottom of the page, fill in these words to complete the puzzle that follows.

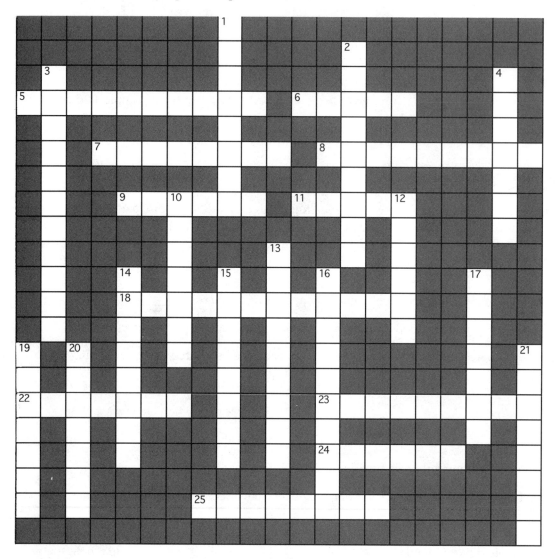

attribute
blatant
calamity
concurrent
contrive
conventional
decipher
default
discern
dispatch
enigma
fluctuate
gaunt
immaculate
implausible
intercede
mobile
nominal
ponder
qualm
recession
scrutiny
sinister
suffice
turmoil

ACROSS

5. Perfectly clean
6. Thin and bony
7. An event bringing great loss and misery
8. A quality or feature of a person or thing
9. To consider carefully
11. An uneasy feeling about how right or proper a particular action is
18. Customary; ordinary
22. To be good enough
23. A temporary decline in business
24. A mystery or puzzle
25. To send to a specific place or a specific business

DOWN

1. To plan cleverly; think up
2. To vary irregularly; to go up and down or back and forth
3. Difficult to believe; unlikely
4. Very obvious, often offensively so
10. Slight; very small compared to what might be expected
12. Moving or able to move from place to place
13. To make a request or plead on behalf of someone else
14. Close inspection; careful examination
15. To interpret or read (something confusing or hard to make out)
16. Happening or existing at the same time; simultaneous
17. Complete confusion; uproar
19. To recognize; detect
20. To fail to do something required
21. Evil; wicked

UNIT TWO: Test 1

PART A
Choose the word that best completes each item and write it in the space provided.

_____ 1. According to legend, vampires are ___ creatures who cannot survive in daylight.

    a. incoherent   b. immaculate   c. nocturnal   d. conventional

_____ 2. The counseling program to ___ addicts includes job training.

    a. rehabilitate   b. contrive   c. ponder   d. exemplify

_____ 3. Unless figure skaters practice regularly, their skills will ___.

    a. retaliate   b. degenerate   c. confiscate   d. decipher

_____ 4. It may sound ___, but a camel can drink twenty-five gallons of water at a time.

    a. implausible   b. gaunt   c. mobile   d. nominal

_____ 5. Movie subtitles should be ___ with the spoken words they are translating.

    a. flagrant   b. hypothetical   c. incoherent   d. concurrent

_____ 6. Even the most ___ people have microscopic creatures clinging to their hair.

    a. sinister   b. immaculate   c. incoherent   d. intricate

_____ 7. Measles remains a serious ___ worldwide, killing over a million people each year.

    a. blight   b. plagiarism   c. qualm   d. prerequisite

_____ 8. The Peace Corps continues to ___ American volunteers to live and work in developing nations.

    a. discern   b. garble   c. dispatch   d. default

_____ 9. The sinking of the ship _Titanic_, which struck an iceberg, was a ___ in which nearly 1,600 people died.

    a. prerequisite   b. sanctuary   c. calamity   d. qualm

_____ 10. The government student loan program is in serious trouble because many students ___ on their payments.

    a. suffice   b. attest   c. intercede   d. default

_____ 11. In a race across New Jersey in 1901, drivers traveling up to thirty miles an hour were arrested for their ___ disregard of the speed limit, which was eight miles an hour.

    a. flagrant   b. hypothetical   c. conventional   d. immaculate

(Continues on next page)

_____ 12. Although our college library charges only a ___ fee to use a computer, I don't think it should charge students any fee at all.

      a. vulnerable   b. nominal   c. mobile   d. comprehensive

_____ 13. The thousands of oak leaves that covered the ground in a Scottish town in 1889 were a(n) ___. The nearest oak trees were eight miles away.

      a. sanctuary   b. attribute   c. enigma   d. recession

PART B

Write **C** if the italicized word is used **correctly**. Write **I** if the word is used **incorrectly**.

_____ 14. Ocean plants *constitute* about 85 percent of all the greenery on Earth.

_____ 15. Jesse Jackson is often praised for his *garbled* speeches.

_____ 16. It's healthier to stay the same weight than to *fluctuate* up and down.

_____ 17. Elise enjoys *intricate* jigsaw puzzles, such as those of detailed flower displays.

_____ 18. Vince *gloated* when he learned that his girlfriend was moving to another state.

_____ 19. Every day, people *enhance* the tropical rainforests by destroying some twenty thousand acres.

_____ 20. Knowing basic math skills is a *prerequisite* for learning the more advanced concepts of algebra.

_____ 21. Adult dolphins often form a protective ring around young ones to keep them *vulnerable* from attack.

_____ 22. Each year, thousands of Americans who think themselves too *gaunt* have some fat surgically removed.

_____ 23. Felix's teacher suspected him of *plagiarism* because his last paper was so much better written than his others.

_____ 24. Before leaving for Antarctica, a team of explorers packed such *conventional* equipment as twenty hula hoops.

_____ 25. In a *blatant* case of injustice, a wealthy and influential North Carolina man received no punishment when he was caught selling cocaine.

Score   (Number correct) _____ x 4 = _____ %

Enter your score above and in the vocabulary performance chart on the inside back cover of the book.

UNIT TWO: *Test 2*

PART A
Complete each item with a word from the box. Use each word once.

a. **attribute**	b. **comprehensive**	c. **confiscate**	d. **decipher**	e. **exemplify**
f. **orient**	g. **persevere**	h. **qualm**	i. **recession**	j. **retaliate**
k. **scrutiny**	l. **sinister**	m. **suffice**		

_____ 1. Marathon runners must ___ beyond the point at which they start to feel pain.

_____ 2. People who can't read must ___ themselves in a city by relating to familiar places, not signs.

_____ 3. A hint to my daughter to take out the garbage won't ___. She needs to be told to do it.

_____ 4. I don't know who sent me the birthday card because I couldn't ___ the signature.

_____ 5. A shortage of a single product, such as sugar, could cause a(n) ___ in several industries.

_____ 6. Don't buy a used car unless you examine it closely and also have a mechanic give it careful ___.

_____ 7. The Russian communists, who opposed private wealth, ___(e)d the property of wealthy landowners.

_____ 8. In some religions, gods and goddesses represent various human ___s, such as strength, beauty, and wisdom.

_____ 9. Through the years, people with ___s about having cheated on their income taxes have sent gifts of money to the IRS.

_____ 10. The Rumanian people ___(e)d against their communist dictátor, who had ordered mass murders, by executing him.

_____ 11. One of the oddest ___ plots of all time was thought up by a wealthy Frenchman. He fed his victims rich foods until they died of overeating.

_____ 12. To get a bachelor's degree from some universities, students must take a ___ exam that tests their overall knowledge of their major field.

_____ 13. Lightning bolts, which travel at millions of miles an hour and produce five times the heat of the sun's surface, ___ nature's tremendous energy.

(Continues on next page)

PART B
Write **C** if the italicized word is used **correctly**. Write **I** if the word is used **incorrectly**.

_____ 14. The Olympic swimmer *pondered* across the pool in record time.

_____ 15. It's hard to *discern* the differences between the Fields twins.

_____ 16. The man *attested* to his crime, pleading not guilty to all charges.

_____ 17. The *turmoil* of a smooth, clear lake always makes me feel at peace.

_____ 18. Our veterinarian has a *mobile* office, a fully equipped van which she drives to patients' homes.

_____ 19. When our English teacher was fired because of his odd teaching practices, our entire class *interceded*, begging the school board to reconsider.

_____ 20. Farm *Sanctuary* offers a safe, comfortable home to farm animals who have been rescued from cruel conditions.

_____ 21. In the *hypothetical* work of Dr. Martin Luther King, Jr., nonviolence was combined with aggressive action.

_____ 22. The Democratic and Republican parties are *predominant* in the United States, but other parties are also represented on our ballots.

_____ 23. A wonderfully *incoherent* speaker, Abraham Lincoln was widely admired for his powerful speeches.

_____ 24. In my dreams, I *venture* to perform feats that I would never dare when awake, such as leaping from roof to roof along a row of houses.

_____ 25. Shortly before his birthday, Bruce *contrived* to get his parents to walk past the toy store so that he could point out the Nintendo game displayed in the window.

Score   (Number correct) _____ x 4 = _____ %

Enter your score above and in the vocabulary performance chart on the inside back cover of the book.

UNIT TWO: Test 3

Complete each sentence in a way that clearly shows you understand the meaning of the **boldfaced** word. Take a minute to plan your answer before you write.

Example: Being **nocturnal** animals, raccoons _____*raid our garbage cans only at night*_____ .

1. The news reported a **calamity** in which _____
   _____.

2. Ray **dispatched** his younger brother to _____
   _____.

3. When I take a bath, I often **ponder** _____
   _____.

4. When Carolyn saw her essay grade, she **gloated**, saying, "_____
   _____."

5. My apartment is so **immaculate** that _____
   _____.

6. Three personal **attributes** that I possess are _____
   _____.

7. The novel's main character is a **sinister** doctor who _____
   _____.

8. When my neighbor cut lilacs off my bush for her home, I **retaliated** by _____
   _____.

9. One advantage of a **mobile** library might be _____
   _____.

10. I plan to **persevere** in _____
   _____.

(Continues on next page)

PART B

After each **boldfaced** word are a *synonym* (a word that means the same as the boldfaced word), an *antonym* (a word that means the opposite of the boldfaced word), and a word that is neither. On the answer line, write the letter of the word that is the antonym.

> *Example:* __b__ **nominal**   a. personal   b. enormous   c. slight

____ 11. **confiscate**   a. give back   b. seize   c. combine

____ 12. **enhance**   a. improve   b. lead   c. weaken

____ 13. **comprehensive**   a. limited   b. broad   c. irregular

____ 14. **intricate**   a. complicated   b. musical   c. simple

____ 15. **persevere**   a. look   b. stop   c. persist

PART C

Use five of the following ten words in sentences. Make it clear that you know the meaning of the word you use. Feel free to use the past tense or plural form of a word.

a. **blight**	b. **decipher**	c. **fluctuate**	d. **implausible**	e. **predominant**
f. **qualm**	g. **rehabilitate**	h. **sanctuary**	i. **turmoil**	j. **vulnerable**

16. _____

_____

17. _____

_____

18. _____

_____

19. _____

_____

20. _____

_____

Score (Number correct) _____ x 5 = _____%

Enter your score above and in the vocabulary performance chart on the inside back cover of the book.

UNIT TWO: Test 4 (Word Parts)

PART A
Listed in the left-hand column below are ten common word parts, along with words in which the parts are used. In each blank, write in the letter of the correct definition on the right.

Word Parts	Examples	Definitions
_____ 1. **-ate**	motivate, fascinate	a. Father
_____ 2. **bio-**	autobiography, biology	b. Call; cry out
_____ 3. **claim, clam**	acclaim, exclamation	c. Partly
_____ 4. **fin**	final, finale	d. End
_____ 5. **flex, flect**	flexible, genuflect	e. Cause to become
_____ 6. **forc, fort**	forcibly, fortify	f. In the direction of; toward
_____ 7. **hum**	humanly, humane	g. Person; having to do with people
_____ 8. **pater, patri-**	paternity, patriotism	h. Strong
_____ 9. **semi-**	semiretired, semisweet	i. Bend
_____ 10. **-ward**	skyward, backward	j. Life; of living things

PART B
Using the answer line provided, complete each *italicized* word in the sentences below with the correct word part from the box. Not every word part will be used.

a. **-ate**	b. **bio-**	c. **clam**	d. **fin**	e. **flex**
f. **fort**	g. **hum**	h. **patri-**	i. **semi-**	j. **-ward**

_____ 11. To (*activ . . .*) ___ yeast, put it in a warm liquid.

_____ 12. When I meditate, I focus (*in . . . ly*) ___ by mentally repeating a nonsense word.

_____ 13. In the seventeenth century, England (*. . . ified*) ___ its weakening wool trade by passing a law that all corpses must be buried in wool.

_____ 14. The French king Louis XIV's (*. . . al*) ___ words before his death were to his servants: "Why do you weep? Did you think I was immortal?"

_____ 15. Why are robots often given a (*. . . anoid*) ___ appearance? Are we more comfortable with "smart" machines that resemble us?

(Continues on next page)

PART C
Use your knowledge of word parts to determine the meaning of the **boldfaced** words. On the answer line, write the letter of each meaning.

_____ 16. The dining club is **semipublic**.

     a. fully public   b. partly public   c. private

_____ 17. A **patriarchy** is a form of social organization in which families are headed by

     a. the strongest.   b. the oldest.   c. the father.

_____ 18. My chemistry instructor also teaches **biochemistry**, which is the chemistry of

     a. life processes.   b. lakes.   c. weather.

_____ 19. Albert Einstein **claimed** that his brain was his laboratory.

     a. realized   b. made known   c. silently wished

_____ 20. The company I work for has decided to experiment with **flextime** for employees.

     a. longer work hours   b. shorter work hours   c. adjustable work hours

Score   (Number correct) _____ x 5 = _____%

Enter your score above and in the vocabulary performance chart on the inside back cover of the book.

Unit Three

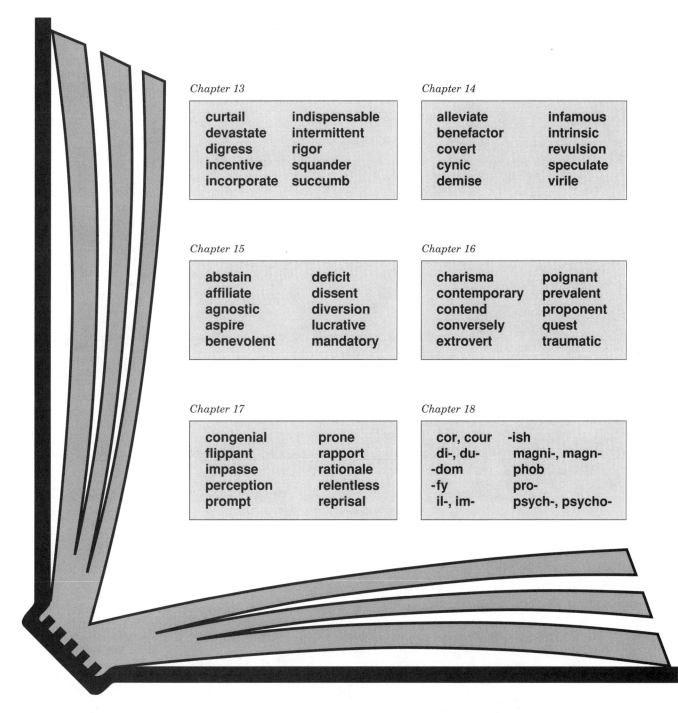

curtail	indispensable
devastate	intermittent
digress	rigor
incentive	squander
incorporate	succumb

Ten Words in Context

In the space provided, write the letter of the meaning closest to that of each **boldfaced** word. Use the context of the sentences to help you figure out each word's meaning.

1 curtail
(kər-tāl′)
-*verb*

- Upon hearing reports of a tornado, our boss **curtailed** the meeting so we all could go home early.
- I need to **curtail** my volunteer activities so that I can spend more time earning money to pay back a loan.

___ *Curtail* means   a. to combine.   b. to shorten.   c. to extend.

2 devastate
(dĕv′əs-tāt′)
-*verb*

- Learning that their son had been arrested for armed robbery **devastated** the Huttons. They couldn't believe he'd do such a terrible thing.
- Vera is so fond of Andy. She'll be **devastated** to hear he has cancer.

___ *Devastate* means   a. to thrill.   b. to annoy.   c. to upset greatly.

3 digress
(dī-grĕs′)
-*verb*

- Professor Rubin never **digresses** during a lecture. Even his jokes relate to the day's topic.
- I tried teaching my three-year-old his phone number, but we **digressed** to a discussion of whether Winnie the Pooh has a telephone.

___ *Digress* means   a. to listen carefully.   b. to go off the subject.   c. to get up.

4 incentive
(ĭn′sĕn′tĭv)
-*noun*

- The insurance company offers an **incentive**—a free vacation—to encourage its representatives to make more sales.
- The thought of myself in a bathing suit next summer provides me with an adequate **incentive** to exercise.

___ *Incentive* means   a. encouragement.   b. liberty.   c. change.

5 incorporate
(ĭn-kôr′pər-āt′)
-*verb*

- Jerry **incorporated** all of his favorite desserts into one: a chocolate-covered banana-cream pecan pie.
- Since the number of young children has gone down in my neighborhood, the two elementary schools have been **incorporated** into one.

___ *Incorporate* means   a. to give up.   b. to join together.   c. to raise.

6 indispensable
(ĭn-dĭ-spĕn′sə-bəl)
-*adjective*

- Because there's no bus or train service nearby, a car is **indispensable** in my neighborhood.
- When you're broke, you find that many things you thought were **indispensable** aren't actually necessary after all.

___ *Indispensable* means   a. free.   b. needed.   c. expensive.

7 intermittent
(ĭn′tər-mĭt′ənt)
-*adjective*

- You have to work steadily with your dog to train him well. **Intermittent** practice won't work.
- Dora realized that weight loss would be **intermittent** when she dieted, so she didn't give up when the losses stopped and started.

__ *Intermittent* means   a. irregular.   b. too much.   c. steady.

8 rigor
(rĭg′ər)
-*noun*

- New Marines must go through the **rigors** of boot camp, such as completing an obstacle course and running several miles a day.
- The **rigor** of working at two part-time jobs while going to school proved too much for Joseph. Exhausted, he dropped both jobs.

__ *Rigor* means   a. a gamble.   b. an expense.   c. a hardship.

9 squander
(skwŏn′dər)
-*verb*

- It's sad to see such a wonderful artist **squander** her talent designing labels for baked-bean cans.
- The company lunchroom now closes promptly at one o'clock so that workers can't **squander** time on long lunch breaks.

__ *Squander* means   a. to share.   b. to misuse.   c. to upset.

10 succumb
(sə-kŭm′)
-*verb*

- Leah **succumbed** to her daughter's begging and bought her a pet lizard for her birthday.
- Once the suspect was arrested, he quickly **succumbed** and confessed to stealing the car stereo.

__ *Succumb* means   a. to yield.   b. to delay.   c. to anger.

Matching Words with Definitions

Following are definitions of the ten words. Clearly write or print each word next to its definition. The sentences above and on the previous page will help you decide on the meaning of each word.

1. _____   a. To waste; spend or use foolishly

2. _____   b. To cut short or reduce

3. _____   c. Something that moves one to take action or work harder; a motivation

4. _____   d. To turn aside, or stray, especially from the main topic in speaking or writing

5. _____   e. Great hardship or difficulty; harshness; severity

6. _____   f. To upset deeply; overwhelm

7. _____   g. To give in; stop resisting

8. _____   h. Necessary

9. _____   i. To unite into a single whole; combine

10. _____   j. Starting and stopping from time to time; off-and-on

CAUTION: Do not go any further until you are sure the above answers are correct. Then you can use the definitions to help you in the following practices. Your goal is eventually to know the words well enough so that you don't need to check the definitions at all.

➤ *Sentence Check 1*

Using the answer line provided, complete each item below with the correct word from the box. Use each word once.

a. **curtail**	b. **devastate**	c. **digress**	d. **incentive**	e. **incorporate**
f. **indispensable**	g. **intermittent**	h. **rigor**	i. **squander**	j. **succumb**

_____ 1. ___ rain kept interrupting the ballgame.

_____ 2. The sight of her bandaged husband in an oxygen tent ___(e)d Claire.

_____ 3. Someone has managed to ___ a tomato and a potato into one plant.

_____ 4. A home computer and a telephone are ___ tools for many self-employed people.

_____ 5. Airlines offer "frequent flyer credits" toward free trips as an ___ to get people to fly often.

_____ 6. Many teenagers don't foresee the ___s of parenthood, such as staying up all night with a sick child.

_____ 7. By examining her last two months of spending, Coretta discovered that she had ___(e)d money on too many expensive meals.

_____ 8. The man on the corner offered to sell me a watch, but he quickly ___(e)d his sales pitch when he saw a police officer approaching.

_____ 9. Because our history teacher loved to gab, we often could get him to ___ from the lesson to talk about school athletics or school politics.

_____ 10. Carl resisted Lola's charms for months, thinking she was too young for him, but he finally ___(e)d and asked her out to dinner.

NOTE: Now check your answers to these questions by turning to page 176. Going over the answers carefully will help you prepare for the next two practices, for which answers are not given.

➤ *Sentence Check 2*

Using the answer lines provided, complete each item below with **two** words from the box. Use each word once.

_____ 1–2. Duane feels he ___(e)d too many years in inactivity, so now he
_____ welcomes the ___s of an exercise program.

_____ 3–4. The company decided to ___ the construction of its new plant until the
_____ architects could decide on how to ___ an employee gym into the new building.

_____ 5–6. My aunt has only ___ success in quitting smoking. Every few months
_____ she ___s to temptation, and then she has to quit all over again.

_____ 7–8. As Leo explained a failed business deal that had once ___(e)d him, he
_____   ___(e)d into the even more interesting tale of his romance with Molly,
                                 his business partner.

_____ 9–10. The vitamin saleswoman offered me free samples, ninety-day trials, and
_____   every other ___ she could think of to get me to buy. However, I found
                                  her sales pitch highly implausible°. I simply could not believe that her
                                  products, and her products alone, were ___ to my well-being.

➤ *Final Check:* Learning to Study

Here is a final opportunity for you to strengthen your knowledge of the ten words. First read the following
selection carefully. Then fill in each blank with a word from the box at the top of the previous page.
(Context clues will help you figure out which word goes in which blank.) Use each word once.

Linda never had to work very hard to make good grades in high school. But in college, where
the (1)_____s of course work were greater, her casual high-school study
habits would no longer suffice°. It was also much easier in college for Linda to
(2)_____ time on dates and parties. She didn't realize how badly she was
doing until she saw her midterm grades, which (3)_____(e)d her. She knew
she had to make some changes right away and began to ponder° what they should be. As a(n)
(4)_____ to work harder, she tried studying with her friend Denise. But that
didn't work; their conversation would (5)_____ from European history to
personal topics, such as dates or favorite singers.

Linda decided she'd have to go it alone. She began to skip weekday parties and also to
(6)_____ the time she spent talking with friends. She discovered that a
good place to study was (7)_____ to her new study habits. She found the
library's silent third floor a sanctuary°, a place with no temptations to which she could
(8)_____. She also became more methodical° in her study habits, keeping
an assignment book, writing due dates on a calendar, and setting up a study schedule. At first,
Linda's performance fluctuated°, and so the improvement in her grades was
(9)_____—A's and B's alternated with C's and D's. But little by little, she
learned to (10)_____ a social life with serious study and get grades she
was proud of.

Scores   Sentence Check 2 _____%   Final Check _____%

Enter your scores above and in the vocabulary performance chart on the inside back cover of the book.

alleviate	infamous
benefactor	intrinsic
covert	revulsion
cynic	speculate
demise	virile

Ten Words in Context

In the space provided, write the letter of the meaning closest to that of each **boldfaced** word. Use the context of the sentences to help you figure out each word's meaning.

1 alleviate
(ə-lē′vē-āt′)
-verb

- To **alleviate** his loneliness, the widower moved closer to his daughter and her family.
- After a long game in the August heat, the young baseball players **alleviated** their thirst with ice-cold lemonade.

___ *Alleviate* means   a. to consider.   b. to hide.   c. to ease.

2 benefactor
(běn′ə-făk′tər)
-noun

- The Second Street Bank is a long-time **benefactor** of the arts. This year it will sponsor a series of free jazz concerts in the parks.
- The wealthy **benefactor** who paid for the child's operation prefers to remain anonymous.

___ *Benefactor* means   a. a financial supporter.   b. a social critic.   c. a cooperative person.

3 covert
(kŭv′ərt)
-adjective

- Miriam and David's relationship is so **covert** that they never eat out. Even Miriam's parents don't know she is seeing him.
- If you enjoy **covert** activities, become a secret agent.

___ *Covert* means   a. obvious.   b. concealed.   c. easy to bear.

4 cynic
(sĭn′ĭk)
-noun

- Her parents' nasty divorce has made Libby a **cynic** about marriage.
- Mr. Bryant was a **cynic** about people until he fell down on a street corner and several strangers rushed to his aid.

___ *Cynic* means   a. someone who believes the worst.   b. someone who gives help.   c. someone with a bad reputation.

5 demise
(dĭ-mīz′)
-noun

- Drugs have led to the **demise** of numerous athletes, such as the great basketball player Len Bias.
- In 1567, a beard caused a man's **demise**. Hans Steininger's beard was so long that he stepped on it while climbing a staircase, lost his balance, fell down the steps, and died.

___ *Demise* means   a. popularity.   b. secret.   c. dying.

6 infamous
(ĭn′fə-məs)
-adjective

- King Henry VIII of England was **infamous** throughout Europe for executing two of his six wives.
- Visitors to the dungeons of ancient castles always want to see the instruments of torture, including the **infamous** Iron Maiden—a body-shaped box with spikes inside.

___ *Infamous* means   a. known unfavorably.   b. thought to be annoying.   c. giving hope.

7 intrinsic
(ĭn-trĭn′sĭk)
-adjective

- Trust is **intrinsic** to any good friendship.
- Because Lian has an **intrinsic** desire to learn, she doesn't need the reward of good grades to motivate her studies.

__ *Intrinsic* means
a. secret.
b. fundamental.
c. unnecessary.

8 revulsion
(rĭ-vŭl′shən)
-noun

- Whenever I read about child abuse in the newspaper, I am filled with such **revulsion** that I often cannot finish the article.
- When Sharon met the man who had cheated her father, she was overcome with **revulsion**.

__ *Revulsion* means
a. interest.
b. hatred.
c. understanding.

9 speculate
(spĕk′yə-lāt′)
-verb

- It's interesting to **speculate** how history might have been different if Abraham Lincoln had lived a few years longer.
- The therapist asked Cassy to **speculate** about what might happen if she told Ralph her true feelings.

__ *Speculate* means
a. to remember.
b. to announce.
c. to guess.

10 virile
(vîr′əl)
-adjective

- Men who are unsure about their masculinity sometimes try to "prove" they are **virile** by being overly aggressive.
- When a male heron stamps his feet and sticks his neck out, and then drops his head and says "plop-buzz," the female finds him very **virile**. In fact, that behavior is how the male attracts a mate.

__ *Virile* means
a. having attractive male qualities.
b. lacking in confidence.
c. unselfish.

Matching Words with Definitions

Following are definitions of the ten words. Clearly write or print each word next to its definition. The sentences above and on the previous page will help you decide on the meaning of each word.

1. _____
a. Secret; hidden

2. _____
b. A person who believes the worst of people's behavior and motives; someone who believes people are motivated only by selfishness

3. _____
c. Belonging to a person or thing by its very nature (and thus not dependent on circumstances)

4. _____
d. Having a very bad reputation; widely known for being vicious, criminal, or deserving of contempt

5. _____
e. A person or organization that gives help, especially financial aid

6. _____
f. Manly; masculine

7. _____
g. Death

8. _____
h. To come up with ideas or theories about a subject; theorize

9. _____
i. To relieve; make easier to endure

10. _____
j. Great disgust or distaste

CAUTION: Do not go any further until you are sure the above answers are correct. Then you can use the definitions to help you in the following practices. Your goal is eventually to know the words well enough so that you don't need to check the definitions at all.

➤ *Sentence Check 1*

Using the answer line provided, complete each item below with the correct word from the box. Use each word once.

a. **alleviate**	b. **benefactor**	c. **covert**	d. **cynic**	e. **demise**
f. **infamous**	g. **intrinsic**	h. **revulsion**	i. **speculate**	j. **virile**

_____ 1. Problems are ___ to life; they're unavoidable.

_____ 2. My hunger isn't fully satisfied, but the apple ___(e)d it somewhat.

_____ 3. Teenage guys usually welcome a deepening voice and a thickening beard as signs that they are becoming more___.

_____ 4. The selfless work of the nuns in the slums of India is enough to touch the hearts of most hardened ___s.

_____ 5. Though she was tried and found not guilty, Lizzie Borden is still ___ for killing her parents with a hatchet.

_____ 6. The children loved the ___ activities involved in preparing their mother's surprise party.

_____ 7. The mass murderer's neighbors were overcome with ___ when they learned what their "friend" had been doing in his basement.

_____ 8. "As no group has claimed responsibility, we can only ___ on the motives for the bombing," said the newscaster.

_____ 9. Roger Novak had been a well-known ___ of AIDS research, so it was no surprise that he left a lot of money for the research in his will.

_____ 10. It's a good idea for married couples to discuss their funeral plans in case of each other's ___. For example, do they wish to be buried or cremated?

NOTE: Now check your answers to these questions by turning to page 176. Going over the answers carefully will help you prepare for the next two practices, for which answers are not given.

➤ *Sentence Check 2*

Using the answer lines provided, complete each item below with **two** words from the box. Use each word once.

_____
_____ 1–2. Nursing is a good career for Dee because it's a(n) ___ part of her personality to try to ___ people's pain. In addition, since she is physically and mentally strong, she will be able to handle the rigors° of nursing, such as intense stress and long hours.

_____
_____ 3–4. Although everything about the Nazis filled the Dutch spy with ___, his ___ assignment was to make friends with top Nazi scientists. He had few qualms° about faking such friendships—he would have felt more guilty if he hadn't done everything in his power to fight the Nazis.

_____   5–6. The ___s in town said that Joyce Lester's sorrow over her husband's
_____   ___ was much less than her joy in getting the money from his insurance
                              policy.

_____   7–8. Young men who are bullies usually think of themselves ___, but a ___
_____   of the weak is far more manly than someone who takes advantage of
                              weakness.

_____   9–10. With all the stories told about Jesse James, the Dalton Gang, and other
_____   ___ figures of the Wild West, we can only ___ as to how much is fact
                              and how much is fiction.

►_Final Check:_ The Mad Monk

Here is a final opportunity for you to strengthen your knowledge of the ten words. First read the following
selection carefully. Then fill in each blank with a word from the box at the top of the previous page.
(Context clues will help you figure out which word goes in which blank.) Use each word once.

Shortly before the Russian Revolution, an eccentric° man named Rasputin became
(1)_____ as the "mad monk." Because he dressed like a peasant, drank
heavily, and rarely bathed, the nobility often felt (2)_____ when they
encountered° him at the palace.

Yet despite his outward appearance, Rasputin possessed a(n) (3)_____
charm that drew many to him, including the Russian empress. She thought him a great man of God
and a special (4)_____ of her seriously ill son, whose condition she felt
Rasputin (5)_____(e)d.

Many (6)_____s believed otherwise. To them, Rasputin was no healer
but a man who exploited° his relationship with the empress for his own benefit. Rather than praise
Rasputin, his enemies preferred to malign° him. In a pamphlet titled _The Holy Devil,_ one of his
critics described him as a sinister° man. This author even dared to (7)_____
that the monk and the empress were romantically involved. This theory was strengthened by the
fact that the empress's "holy man" pursued many women and boasted about how
(8)_____ he was.

Finally, a group of Russian noblemen made (9)_____ plans to kill
Rasputin. Somehow, the secret must have gotten out, for a Russian official warned Rasputin of a
plot against him. He nevertheless accepted the noblemen's invitation to a dinner party, where they
served him poisoned wine and cake. When Rasputin did not appear to succumb° to the poison, his
enemies hastened his (10)_____ by shooting and stabbing him and then
dumping him into an icy river. An autopsy revealed that he had died by drowning.

| _Scores_   Sentence Check 2 _____% | Final Check _____% |

Enter your scores above and in the vocabulary performance chart on the inside back cover of the book.

abstain	deficit
affiliate	dissent
agnostic	diversion
aspire	lucrative
benevolent	mandatory

Ten Words in Context

In the space provided, write the letter of the meaning closest to that of each **boldfaced** word. Use the context of the sentences to help you figure out each word's meaning.

1 abstain
(ăb-stān′)
-verb

- Although Lou has given up cigarettes, he doesn't **abstain** from tobacco. Now he chews it.
- My sister called off her engagement to Clayton because he wouldn't **abstain** from dating other women.

___ *Abstain from* means   a. to desire.   b. to believe in.   c. to deny oneself.

2 affiliate
(ə-fĭl′ē-āt′)
-verb

- Diane is neither a Democrat nor a Republican. She isn't **affiliated** with any political party.
- The young singer could have earned more if she had been **affiliated** with the musicians' union, but she couldn't afford the membership dues.

___ *Affiliate with* means   a. to join.   b. to study.   c. to hold back from.

3 agnostic
(ăg-nŏs′tĭk)
-noun

- Iris believes there is a God, and Marcia feels sure there isn't. Jean, an **agnostic**, feels that we can't be certain one way or the other.
- My uncle, who was an **agnostic**, used to say, "Humans cannot understand a flower, let alone whether or not there's a God."

___ *Agnostic* means   a. one who denies God's existence.   b. one who feels we can't know if God exists.   c. one who is sure there is a God.

4 aspire
(ə-spīr′)
-verb

- Twelve-year-old Derek, who loves drawing buildings, **aspires** to be a great architect.
- Millions of young people **aspire** to be professional athletes, but only a few will succeed.

___ *Aspire* means   a. to fear.   b. to wish.   c. to volunteer.

5 benevolent
(bə-nĕv′ə-lənt)
-adjective

- People are more **benevolent** when they get tax deductions for their donations.
- In 1878, William Booth founded a **benevolent** association to help the poor of London. He called it the Salvation Army.

___ *Benevolent* means   a. recreational.   b. profitable.   c. charitable.

6 deficit
(dĕf′ə-sĭt)
-noun

- The United States has spent so much more than it has taken in that it now has a huge budget **deficit**.
- Residents are asked not to water their lawns because a **deficit** of rain has dangerously lowered the water supply.

___ *Deficit* means   a. a lack.   b. an overflow.   c. a collection.

7 dissent
(dĭ-sĕnt′)
-noun

- The committee was so torn by **dissent** that its members could not agree even on whether or not to schedule another meeting.
- The dictator permitted people to agree with his policies or keep silent about them, but not to express **dissent**.

___ *Dissent* means   a. plans.   b. opposition.   c. relief.

8 diversion
(də-vûr′zhən)
-noun

- My history teacher says that one of her favorite **diversions** during summer vacation is reading mystery novels.
- Skip likes his job, but he also enjoys such **diversions** as playing video games, watching baseball, and reading humorous stories.

___ *Diversion* means   a. a recreation.   b. something easy.   c. an assignment.

9 lucrative
(lōō′krə-tĭv)
-adjective

- Investments in the stock market can be **lucrative**. However, they can also result in great financial loss.
- "Teaching at a small college isn't **lucrative**," Professor Baum admitted, "but I've never felt the need to make lots of money."

___ *Lucrative* means   a. required.   b. financially rewarding.   c. risky.

10 mandatory
(măn′də-tôr′ē)
-adjective

- Members of the basketball team have to follow strict rules. For example, it's **mandatory** that each player attend at least 80 percent of the practices.
- "A research paper isn't **mandatory**," the instructor said, "but if you write one, you'll get extra credit."

___ *Mandatory* means   a. unimportant.   b. helpful.   c. essential.

Matching Words with Definitions

Following are definitions of the ten words. Clearly write or print each word next to its definition. The sentences above and on the previous page will help you decide on the meaning of each word.

1. _____   a. To strongly desire; to be ambitious (to do something or to get something)

2. _____   b. Profitable; well-paying

3. _____   c. A shortage; a lack (in amount)

4. _____   d. To hold oneself back from something; refrain

5. _____   e. Charitable

6. _____   f. A person who believes we cannot know whether or not there is a God

7. _____   g. Required

8. _____   h. An amusement or pastime; anything that relaxes or amuses

9. _____   i. To associate; join

10. _____   j. Disagreement

CAUTION: Do not go any further until you are sure the above answers are correct. Then you can use the definitions to help you in the following practices. Your goal is eventually to know the words well enough so that you don't need to check the definitions at all.

➤ *Sentence Check 1*

Using the answer line provided, complete each item below with the correct word from the box. Use each word once.

a. **abstain**	b. **affiliate**	c. **agnostic**	d. **aspire**	e. **benevolent**
f. **deficit**	g. **dissent**	h. **diversion**	i. **lucrative**	j. **mandatory**

_____ 1. My kid brother ___s to become the video-game champion of the world.

_____ 2. The ___ fund at my church collects money to help poor families in our parish.

_____ 3. My parents enjoy card games, but my sister and I like such ___s as computer games and music videos.

_____ 4. An entrance fee wasn't ___, but a sign at the museum entrance suggested that visitors make a donation.

_____ 5. Because Hank needs to lose weight, his doctor recommended that he ___ from all sweets and fatty foods.

_____ 6. We could overcome a(n) ___ of organs for transplants if more people would agree to have their organs donated after they die.

_____ 7. There was no ___ in the family on whether or not to start a vegetable garden this year. We all agreed it was a great idea.

_____ 8. Yong could have joined the all-male club, but he prefers to ___ with organizations that welcome both men and women.

_____ 9. "When someone who believes in God marries someone who does not," the comic asked, "do they give birth to a(n) ___?"

_____ 10. Acting is ___ for only a small percentage of performers. The rest need additional sources of income, such as waiting on tables or driving a cab.

NOTE: Now check your answers to these questions by turning to page 176. Going over the answers carefully will help you prepare for the next two practices, for which answers are not given.

➤ *Sentence Check 2*

Using the answer lines provided, complete each item below with **two** words from the box. Use each word once.

_____
_____ 1–2. My uncle decided to splurge and ___ with a country club because golf is his main ___.

_____
_____ 3–4. Gale didn't ___ from smoking cigarettes at the office until her employer made not smoking ___. Keeping her job was a very good incentive° to get her to quit.

_____ 5–6. Some people think that since Stan is a(n) ___, he must be amoral°. It's
_____ true he's not sure if God exists, but that doesn't mean he lacks a moral
sense. In fact, he recently founded a ___ society at work to raise money
for disabled children in the area.

_____ 7–8. The ___ in the township treasury is causing a lot of ___ over whether or
_____ not taxes should be raised.

_____ 9–10. Because my father ___s to make enough money to send his children to
_____ college, he's working hard to make his auto repair business as ___ as
possible.

➤ _Final Check:_ Conflict Over Holidays

Here is a final opportunity for you to strengthen your knowledge of the ten words. First read the following
selection carefully. Then fill in each blank with a word from the box at the top of the previous page.
(Context clues will help you figure out which word goes in which blank.) Use each word once.

While Jeanne and Paul are generally a happily married couple, they do struggle over one point of

(1)_____. They disagree as to how their family should observe religious holidays.

"The emphasis on presents," says Jeanne, "has made the season (2)_____ for

all those mercenary° retailers who overcharge at holiday time. Also, people who should be watching

their expenses create unnecessary (3)_____s in their budgets by squandering°

money on unimportant gifts." She complains that exchanging presents at Christmas is practically

(4)_____, whether or not one believes in the holiday's religious significance.

Jeanne (5)_____s to keep her home free of all such nonreligious customs

and thus wants her children to (6)_____ from traditions such as gift-giving

and dyeing Easter eggs. She feels the family's money would be better spent if it were donated to a

(7)_____ organization for helping the poor. Some of Jeanne's neighbors assume

that she is a(n) (8)_____ because of her lack of holiday spirit. They are wrong,

however. Jeanne believes deeply in God and is (9)_____(e)d with a church.

While Paul understands Jeanne's concerns, he prefers the conventional° way of celebrating

holidays. "Children enjoy the customary (10)_____s that are connected with the

holidays," he says. "What would Christmas be without a visit to Santa and gifts under the tree? What

would Easter be without colorful eggs and an Easter egg hunt? These are pleasant practices that

enhance° the joy of the season."

Scores Sentence Check 2 _____% Final Check _____%

Enter your scores above and in the vocabulary performance chart on the inside back cover of the book.

charisma	poignant
contemporary	prevalent
contend	proponent
conversely	quest
extrovert	traumatic

Ten Words in Context

In the space provided, write the letter of the meaning closest to that of each **boldfaced** word. Use the context of the sentences to help you figure out each word's meaning.

1 **charisma**
(kə-rĭz′mə)
-noun

- Kamal has such **charisma** that when he ran for class president, almost every person in the tenth grade voted for him. Such magnetism will benefit him throughout his life.
- Great Britain's Princess Diana obviously has great **charisma**. Despite her family problems, she still has numerous loyal fans worldwide.

___ *Charisma* means   a. feelings.   b. personal appeal.   c. luck.

2 **contemporary**
(kən-tĕm′pə-rĕr′ē)
-adjective

- Beth likes **contemporary** furniture, but her husband prefers antiques.
- My grandfather says that compared to kids in his day, **contemporary** youngsters are soft and lazy.

___ *Contemporary* means   a. common.   b. old-fashioned.   c. current.

3 **contend**
(kən-tĕnd′)
-verb

- The defense attorney **contended** that his client was insane and therefore could not be held responsible for the murder.
- Scientists **contend** that no two snowflakes are identical, but how could they possibly prove it?

___ *Contend* means   a. to wish.   b. to deny.   c. to declare.

4 **conversely**
(kən-vûrs′lē)
-adverb

- Ron, who is basically bored by food, eats in order to live. **Conversely**, Nate loves food so much that he seems to live in order to eat.
- Mary drives her children to school whenever it rains. **Conversely**, I make my kids walk because I think a little rain never hurt anyone.

___ *Conversely* means   a. in contrast.   b. in a modern way.   c. similarly.

5 **extrovert**
(ĕk′strə-vûrt′)
-noun

- Surprisingly, not all performers are **extroverts**. Offstage, many are quiet and shy.
- Ms. Stein hired Robert to greet and chat with her clients because he's such an **extrovert**.

___ *Extrovert* means   a. a supporter of causes.   b. a timid person.   c. a sociable person.

6 **poignant**
(poin′yənt)
-adjective

- The service honoring American soldiers missing in action was touching. A speech by a friend of one of the soldiers was particularly **poignant**.
- I cried when I read a **poignant** story about a dying girl who gave away all of her dolls to "poor children."

___ *Poignant* means   a. affecting the emotions.   b. correct.   c. lively.

7 prevalent
(prĕv′ə-lənt)
-*adjective*

- Unemployment was **prevalent** during America's Great Depression. By 1932, over twelve million people were out of work.

- Television sets are more **prevalent** in the United States than bathtubs. Over half of American homes have two or more TVs. Far fewer homes have more than one bathtub.

__ *Prevalent* means   a. favorable.   b. found frequently.   c. unlikely.

8 proponent
(prō-pō′nənt)
-*noun*

- I voted for Senator Williams, a **proponent** of improved services for the elderly, because I feel that many older people need greater assistance.

- Although Elaine quit work to take care of her children, she is a **proponent** of employer-supported day care.

__ *Proponent* means   a. a recipient.   b. an opponent.   c. a supporter.

9 quest
(kwĕst)
-*noun*

- During Carlo's **quest** for the perfect pizza, he sampled the cheese pizza at twenty-seven different restaurants.

- Ponce de Leon's **quest** was for the Fountain of Youth; what he found instead was Florida.

__ *Quest* means   a. a hunt.   b. a question.   c. design.

10 traumatic
(trô-măt′ĭk)
-*adjective*

- Divorce can be less **traumatic** for children if their fears and feelings are taken into account as the divorce takes place.

- My cousin has had nightmares ever since his **traumatic** experience of being trapped in a coal mine.

__ *Traumatic* means   a. familiar.   b. reasonable.   c. upsetting.

Matching Words with Definitions

Following are definitions of the ten words. Clearly write or print each word next to its definition. The sentences above and on the previous page will help you decide on the meaning of each word.

1. _____   a. In an opposite manner; in an altogether different way

2. _____   b. The quality of a leader which captures great popular devotion; personal magnetism; charm

3. _____   c. A search; pursuit

4. _____   d. Widespread; common

5. _____   e. To state to be so; claim; affirm

6. _____   f. Modern; up-to-date

7. _____   g. Someone who supports a cause

8. _____   h. Emotionally moving; touching

9. _____   i. Causing painful emotions, with possible long-lasting psychological effects

10. _____   j. An outgoing, sociable person

CAUTION: Do not go any further until you are sure the above answers are correct. Then you can use the definitions to help you in the following practices. Your goal is eventually to know the words well enough so that you don't need to check the definitions at all.

➤ *Sentence Check 1*

Using the answer line provided, complete each item below with the correct word from the box. Use each word once.

a. **charisma**	b. **contemporary**	c. **contend**	d. **conversely**	e. **extrovert**
f. **poignant**	g. **prevalent**	h. **proponent**	i. **quest**	j. **traumatic**

_____   1. I study best in the morning. ___, my sister concentrates better at night.

_____   2. Nancy is a(n) ___ by nature, but since she's become depressed, she has avoided other people.

_____   3. At the airport, I was very moved by the ___ reunion of family members who had been separated for years.

_____   4. Underage drinking was so ___ in the fraternity house that college officials ordered the house closed for a year.

_____   5. "This woman ___s that she was here before you," said the supermarket checkout clerk. "Is it her turn now?"

_____   6. Felipe is a(n) ___ of exercising for good health. He even encourages his young children to swim or cycle every day.

_____   7. Certain movie stars may not be great actors, but they have a(n) ___ that makes people want to see their films.

_____   8. Abby didn't like the apartment with the old-fashioned tub and radiators. She preferred a more ___ place.

_____   9. Repeating third grade was ___ for my brother. It still pains him to think about it, even though he's a successful businessman now.

_____   10. Over the past three hundred years, several people have gone on a(n) ___ for Noah's ark. Some have looked for it in northeastern Turkey, on Mount Ararat, sixteen thousand feet above sea level.

NOTE: Now check your answers to these questions by turning to page 176. Going over the answers carefully will help you prepare for the next two practices, for which answers are not given.

➤ *Sentence Check 2*

Using the answer lines provided, complete each item below with **two** words from the box. Use each word once.

_____   1–2. Many people are surprised to learn how ___ poverty is in ___ America.
_____   Today, millions live below the poverty line, and the number seems to escalate° daily.

_____   3–4. Judy and Martin Reed exemplify° the old saying "Opposites attract." A(n)
_____   ___, Judy chooses work that brings her into constant contact with others. ___, Marty prefers jobs in which he mainly works alone.

_____   5–6. Ever since the ___ experience of finding her twelve-year-old son dead
_____   from a drug overdose, Sophie has been a strong ___ of mandatory° drug
education in the public schools. If drug education isn't required, she
says, schools may cut corners and omit it.

_____   7–8. My mother ___s that _Romeo and Juliet_ is the most ___ story ever
_____   written, but my sister claims _Love Story_ is more moving.

_____   9–10. Mahatma Gandhi's ___ and vision inspired millions of fellow Indians to
_____   join him enthusiastically in the ___ for peaceful solutions to national
problems. Gandhi incorporated° nonviolence and political activism into
a highly effective method for social change: passive resistance.

➤ _Final Check:_ Dr. Martin Luther King, Jr.

Here is a final opportunity for you to strengthen your knowledge of the ten words. First read the following
selection carefully. Then fill in each blank with a word from the box at the top of the previous page.
(Context clues will help you figure out which word goes in which blank.) Use each word once.

(1)_____ young people may be able to list the many accomplishments

of the Reverend Dr. Martin Luther King, Jr. They may know that he was a civil rights leader who

aspired° to achieve racial harmony and was a(n) (2)_____ of peaceful

but direct action. They may know that he fought the discrimination against blacks that was so

(3)_____ in our country in the 1950s and 1960s. They may also know that

he received a great deal of acclaim° for his work. For example, in 1964 he won the Nobel Peace

Prize. They may even (4)_____ that he is the most important social

reformer in the history of our nation.

But can the young really know the (5)_____, the powerful personal

magnetism of this man? He was a perfect blend of quiet, considerate thinker and bold, outspoken

(6)_____. When Dr. King spoke, people listened. He had such a forceful

yet (7)_____ way of speaking that those who heard him felt his message

deep within. For most, this meant a stronger belief in and respect for the man and his ideals.

(8)_____, for bigots, it meant hatred and fear of what he stood for.

Dr. King's (9)_____ for equal rights for all was clear when he said, "I

have a dream that this nation will rise up and live out the true meaning of its creed: 'We hold these

truths to be self-evident; that all men are created equal.'" He gave his time, his leadership, and, in

the end, his life. His murder was a(n) (10)_____ event in the lives of

many Americans, who will never fully recover from that awful day. But because of Martin Luther

King, Americans live with greater dignity. And many have taken up his fight against the

inequities° of racism.

| _Scores_   Sentence Check 2 _____%   Final Check _____% |

Enter your scores above and in the vocabulary performance chart on the inside back cover of the book.

congenial	**prone**
flippant	**rapport**
impasse	**rationale**
perception	**relentless**
prompt	**reprisal**

Ten Words in Context

In the space provided, write the letter of the meaning closest to that of each **boldfaced** word. Use the context of the sentences to help you figure out each word's meaning.

1 **congenial**
(kən-jēn′yəl)
-*adjective*

- Our coworkers are very **congenial** except for Walter, who has remained distant and unfriendly toward everyone.
- I was nervous being at a party where I didn't know anyone, but the other guests were so **congenial** that I soon felt at ease.

___ *Congenial* means   a. persistent.   b. intelligent.   c. sociable.

2 **flippant**
(flĭp′ənt)
-*adjective*

- "Don't give me a **flippant** answer," George's father told him. "Your financial situation is a serious matter."
- When I told my son for the third time to clean his room, he gave this **flippant** response: "Why should I? I just cleaned it last month."

___ *Flippant* means   a. rude.   b. serious.   c. incorrect.

3 **impasse**
(ĭm′păs)
-*noun*

- The jurors had reached an **impasse**. They couldn't agree on a verdict— some thought the defendant was the murderer and others were sure he was innocent.
- If you think you've reached an **impasse** when trying to solve a problem, take a break. The solution may come to mind while you're doing something else.

___ *Impasse* means   a. a deadlock.   b. a relationship.   c. an opportunity.

4 **perception**
(pər-sĕp′shən)
-*noun*

- Brenda's **perceptions** of others are usually accurate. She is a good judge of character.
- Our **perceptions** of our problem differ. Rob thinks money is the main issue, but I believe it's a question of who controls the purse strings.

___ *Perception* means   a. a memory.   b. a view.   c. a desire.

5 **prompt**
(prŏmpt)
-*verb*

- To **prompt** Byron to get a job, I pinned the want ads to his pillow.
- Fast-food clerks **prompt** customers to buy more by asking such questions as "Would you like cookies or apple pie with that?"

___ *Prompt* means   a. to allow.   b. to agree with.   c. to motivate.

6 **prone**
(prōn)
-*adjective*

- Mr. Walker is **prone** to sleep problems, so he limits his intake of caffeine.
- **Prone** to fits of laughter during class, Chris sometimes controls the sound by biting into his pen.

___ *Prone* means   a. tending.   b. immune.   c. attracted.

7 **rapport**
(ră-pŏr′)
-*noun*

- In high school, I had such good **rapport** with my gym teacher that our close relationship continues to this day.
- If no **rapport** develops between you and your therapist after a month or two, start looking for a counselor who makes you feel comfortable.

__ *Rapport* means   a. report.   b. personal connection.   c. financial situation.

8 **rationale**
(răsh′ə-năl′)
-*noun*

- Danielle's **rationale** for majoring in business was simple. She said, "I want to make a lot of money."
- The **rationale** for not lowering the drinking age to 18 is that self-control and good judgment are not usually well developed at that age.

__ *Rationale* means   a. a situation.   b. a explanation.   c. a question.

9 **relentless**
(rĭ-lĕnt′lĭs)
-*adjective*

- The dog's **relentless** barking got on my nerves. He barked the entire two hours his owners were out.
- In a large city, the noise of crowds and heavy traffic is so **relentless** that it can be difficult to find peace and quiet.

__ *Relentless* means   a. occasional.   b. exciting.   c. nonstop.

10 **reprisal**
(rĭ-prī′zəl)
-*noun*

- In **reprisal** for being fired, a troubled man shot several people at the factory where he used to work.
- Fear of **reprisal** may keep a woman from pressing charges against a man who has abused her.

__ *Reprisal* means   a. disrespect.   b. revenge.   c. delay.

Matching Words with Definitions

Following are definitions of the ten words. Clearly write or print each word next to its definition. The sentences above and on the previous page will help you decide on the meaning of each word.

1. _____   a. Insight or understanding gained through observation; impression

2. _____   b. Having a tendency; inclined

3. _____   c. Persistent; continuous

4. _____   d. The underlying reasons for something; logical basis

5. _____   e. Disrespectful and not serious enough

6. _____   f. Agreeable or pleasant in character; friendly

7. _____   g. To urge into action

8. _____   h. The paying back of one injury or bad deed with another

9. _____   i. A situation with no way out; dead end

10. _____   j. Relationship, especially one that is close, trusting, or sympathetic

CAUTION: Do not go any further until you are sure the above answers are correct. Then you can use the definitions to help you in the following practices. Your goal is eventually to know the words well enough so that you don't need to check the definitions at all.

➤ *Sentence Check 1*

Using the answer line provided, complete each item below with the correct word from the box. Use each word once.

a. **congenial**	b. **flippant**	c. **impasse**	d. **perception**	e. **prompt**
f. **prone**	g. **rapport**	h. **rationale**	i. **relentless**	j. **reprisal**

_____ 1. Raquel is ___ to accidents, so her car insurance rates are quite high.

_____ 2. You will get along better in life if you are ___ to other people, rather than unpleasant.

_____ 3. My brother hides his lack of confidence by being ___. He rarely treats anything seriously.

_____ 4. It took his best friend's heart attack to ___ my dad to start exercising and eating right.

_____ 5. There was instant ___ between Duke and Otis. They talked as if they'd known each other for years.

_____ 6. At the movie's turning point, the bad guys reached a(n) ___. On one side of them was the police; on the other was a steep cliff.

_____ 7. During April and May, the rain was so ___ that we thought we might have to start building an ark.

_____ 8. Floyd's ___ of human nature is strongly colored by some bad experiences. He thinks everyone is basically selfish.

_____ 9. When Lacey and John divorced, she tried to get over half his income. In ___, he tried not to give her any of his income at all.

_____ 10. The ___ behind encouraging pregnant women to gain about twenty-five pounds is that low weight gain can lead to dangerously low birth weights.

NOTE: Now check your answers to these questions by turning to page 176. Going over the answers carefully will help you prepare for the next two practices, for which answers are not given.

➤ *Sentence Check 2*

Using the answer lines provided, complete each item below with **two** words from the box. Use each word once.

_____
_____ 1–2. Because Wade is so ___ and easy to talk to, we established a warm ___ the first day we met.

_____
_____ 3–4. Although the company president explained the ___ behind the pay cuts, his announcement ___(e)d an employee protest. However, once it was learned that the president was also taking a big pay cut, the employees' dissent° died down.

_____   5–6. My mother was ___ to anger and quick to punish me if I spoke to her in
_____   what she thought was a ___ way. I avoided being with her any more
                                          than necessary, so as not to risk eliciting° her rage.

_____   7–8. My ___ of the situation is that talks between the factory management
_____   and union officials reached a(n) ___ because neither side would
                                          compromise on salaries. In such situations, flexibility is a prerequisite°
                                          to progress.

_____   9–10. Abby could put up with occasional kidding, but her brother's teasing
_____   was often ___, going on for weeks at a time. Sick of it all, she finally
                                          planned a(n) ___ that would embarrass him in front of his friends.

➤ *Final Check:* **Relating to Parents**

Here is a final opportunity for you to strengthen your knowledge of the ten words. First read the following
selection carefully. Then fill in each blank with a word from the box at the top of the previous page.
(Context clues will help you figure out which word goes in which blank.) Use each word once.

How do you respond when your parents deny you permission to do something? For example,

if you want to travel and work around the country for the summer but your parents say you're too

young, do you yell and demand that they stop curtailing° your rights? Do you plan a(n)

(1)_____, vowing to sabotage° their summer plans because they've ruined

yours? Or do you explain the (2)_____ behind your request, so that your

parents will understand your reasoning?

The way you behave when you and your parents reach a(n) (3)_____ on

an issue can have a big effect on how they view you. Sure, you could retort°, "Fine. Just fine. I'll

go buy a leash so you can really run my life." But if you are consistently

(4)_____ like that, you'll just strengthen their (5)_____

of you as being too immature to be on your own. Also, if you are (6)_____ in

your begging, asking three hundred times a day, "But *why* won't you let me go?" they may tell you

where to go, and it won't be on a cross-country trip.

Instead, approach your parents in a (7)_____ way and try to develop a

strong, friendly (8)_____ with them. An amiable°, respectful relationship

will make them more (9)_____ to see things your way. Even if you can't

(10)_____ them to change their minds about this summer's plans, your

chances of getting their support will be better the next time you want to try something new.

Scores Sentence Check 2 _____%	Final Check _____%

Enter your scores above and in the vocabulary performance chart on the inside back cover of the book.

cor, cour	-ish
di-, du-	magni-, magn-
-dom	phob
-fy	pro-
il-, im-	psych-, psycho-

Ten Word Parts in Context

Figure out the meanings of the following ten word parts by looking *closely* and *carefully* at the context in which they appear. Then, in the space provided, write the letter of the meaning closest to that of each word part.

1 cor, cour

- I felt truly welcomed by my **cordial** hosts. Their kindness and generosity were heartfelt.
- Emmy was **courageous** enough to face the bully without backing down. I'm too chicken-hearted to do the same.

__ The word part *cor* or *cour* means   a. resembling.   b. double.   c. heart.

2 di-, du-

- When we got **divorced**, we had to spend a difficult day dividing our household possessions into two groups.
- One of the three band members didn't show up, so only a **duo** played at the dance.

__ The word part *di-* or *du-* means   a. make.   b. two.   c. great.

3 -dom

- A few actors achieve overnight success, but for most, the road to **stardom** is long and difficult.
- One sure way to put my husband into a deep state of **boredom** is to take him with me when I shop for shoes.

__ The word part *-dom* means   a. like.   b. state of being.   c. fear.

4 -fy

- Would it **simplify** matters if I held your baby while you go into the dressing room to try on the slacks?
- First **liquefy** the ice cream over heat. Then mix in the strawberry jam.

__ The word part *-fy* means   a. cause to become.   b. again.   c. dislike.

5 il-, im-

- Nita doesn't seem to care that it's **illegal** to park in front of a fire hydrant.
- My brother-in-law is so **immature** that he often acts as if he is 16 instead of a married man of 26.

__ The word part *il-* or *im-* means   a. not.   b. double.   c. like.

6 -ish

- My **devilish** brother once videotaped me huffing and puffing my way through aerobics, and now he shows the tape to every new friend I bring home.
- Of all the girls at school, Jessy was the most **stylish**, wearing only the latest clothing featured in the fashion magazines.

__ The word part *-ish* means   a. forth.   b. characteristic of.   c. mind.

7 magni-, magn-

- My grandmother uses a **magnifying** glass to make the small print in the newspaper appear larger.
- Eight years after starting Standard Oil in 1870, oil **magnate** John D. Rockefeller controlled about 85 percent of the country's oil industry.

__ The word part *magni-* or *magn-* means

a. forward.   b. fear.   c. large.

8 phob

- One of the most unusual **phobias** is the fear of peanut butter sticking to the roof of one's mouth.
- Marilyn's mother has developed **agoraphobia** to the point that she is afraid even of going to the mailbox at the end of the driveway.

__ The word part *phob* means

a. forth.   b. quality.   c. fear.

9 pro-

- **Proceed** down to the end of this hallway, make a left, and you will see the x-ray department.
- One scientist **propels** his car with a fuel he gets by burning garbage.

__ The word part *pro-* means

a. forward.   b. resembling.   c. dislike.

10 psych-, psycho

- A **psychiatrist** is a medical doctor who specializes in treating disorders of the mind.
- A **psychoactive** drug is one that affects mental processes.

__ The word part *psych-* or *psycho-* means

a. mind.   b. make.   c. again.

Matching Word Parts with Definitions

Following are definitions of the ten word parts. Clearly write or print each word part next to its definition. The sentences above and on the previous page will help you decide on the meaning of each word part.

1. _____   a. Great; large

2. _____   b. Cause to be or become; make

3. _____   c. Forward; forth

4. _____   d. Fear

5. _____   e. Two; double

6. _____   f. Resembling; like; characteristic of

7. _____   g. Heart

8. _____   h. Mental processes; mind

9. _____   i. State of being; condition

10. _____   j. Not

CAUTION: Do not go any further until you are sure the above answers are correct. Then you can use the definitions to help you in the following practices. Your goal is eventually to know the word parts well enough so that you don't need to check the definitions at all.

➤ *Sentence Check 1*

Using the answer line provided, complete each *italicized* word in the sentences below with the correct word part from the box. Use each word part once.

a. **cour**	b. **di-, du-**	c. **-dom**	d. **-fy**	e. **il-, im-**
f. **-ish**	g. **magni-**	h. **phob**	i. **pro-**	j. **psycho-**

_____ 1. Despite her (*boy . . .*) ___ hairdo, Paula looks very feminine.

_____ 2. (*Wis . . .*) ___ is what we gain when we learn from our mistakes.

_____ 3. The parents were greatly (*dis . . . aged*) ___ when every attempt to find their son failed.

_____ 4. To keep the accident victim (. . . *mobile*) ___, the paramedics tied her to a stretcher.

_____ 5. The reason these life-size dolls are so expensive is that only one hundred are (. . . *duced*) ___ each year.

_____ 6. The funhouse mirror (. . . *fied*) ___ my reflection so that I looked fifty pounds heavier.

_____ 7. I always (. . . *plicate*) ___ important papers and letters so that if the original gets lost, I still have the copy.

_____ 8. Barb's (. . . *analyst*) ___ asked her to write down her dreams, as they might be helpful in understanding her problems.

_____ 9. If you want to find a job before all the graduates start looking for employment next month, you'd better (*intensi . . .*) ___ your search.

_____ 10. It's lucky Santa Claus doesn't have (*claustro . . . ia*) ___. Otherwise, he would be too frightened of confined spaces to come down the chimney.

NOTE: Now check your answers to these questions by turning to page 176. Going over the answers carefully will help you prepare for the next two practices, for which answers are not given.

➤ *Sentence Check 2*

Using the answer lines provided, complete each *italicized* word in the sentences below with the correct word part from the box. Use each word part once.

_____ 1–2. The apartment the realtor showed us was (. . . *ficent*) ___, but it was
_____ (. . . *practical*) ___ for us. Not only was it too large, but it would also make an uncomfortable dent in our budget.

_____ 3–4. Everyone has fears, but (. . . *ic*) ___ people need to gain (*free . . .*) ___
_____ from the extreme fears that devastate° them and their families.

_____ 5–6. The purpose of (. . . *therapy*) ___ is to (. . . *mote*) ___ mental health.
_____

_____   7–8. Florence and I felt (*fool . . .*) ___ when we sang a (*. . . et*) ___ of "The

_____   Star-Spangled Banner" and forgot the words halfway through.

_____   9–10. The mayor didn't allow racial tensions to (*dis . . . age*) ___ him. He just

_____   made more of an effort to (*uni . . .*) ___ the city.

➤ *Final Check:* **Held Back by Fears**

Here is a final opportunity for you to strengthen your knowledge of the ten word parts. First read the following selection carefully. Then complete each *italicized* word in the parentheses below with a word from the box at the top of the previous page. (Context clues will help you figure out which word part goes in which blank.) Use each word part once.

At age 24, Gina is facing a major (*. . . lemma*) (1)_____. She desperately

wants to live and work beyond her hometown, but she is prevented from traveling by her (*. . . ias*)

(2)_____. She suffers from (*. . . logical*) (3)_____ but

intense fears of bridges and airplanes that are so traumatic° that they cause nightmares and

breathing problems. Gina is convinced that if she doesn't fall off a bridge or crash in an airplane,

the mere possibility of such a calamity° will so (*terri . . .*) (4)_____ her

that she'll succumb° to a heart attack.

For some time now, Gina's friends have tried to persuade her to start seeing a (*. . . logist*)

(5)_____. They believe her problem will only increase in (*. . . tude*)

(6)_____ if she doesn't get help. But her relatives often make flippant°

remarks about Gina's condition, saying that she is just too cheap to travel. Accusing her of being

(*child . . .*) (7)_____, her brothers call her "baby" and "chicken." They say

if she only had a little more (*. . . age*) (8)_____, she would be able to go

places. They don't realize that if she could have controlled her fears by now, she would have.

Gina is seriously considering her friends' advice because she feels she has squandered° too

much of her time and energy on her fears. She hopes she will make rapid (*. . . gress*)

(9)_____ in gaining (*free . . .*) (10)_____ from her fears

so that she can start to live a full life.

UNIT THREE: Review

The box at the right lists twenty-five words from Unit Three. Using the clues at the bottom of the page, fill in these words to complete the puzzle that follows.

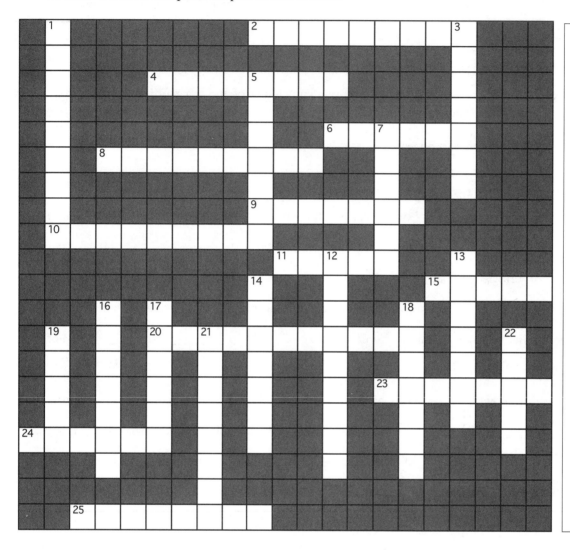

abstain
alleviate
aspire
charisma
congenial
contend
curtail
cynic
deficit
demise
digress
dissent
extrovert
impasse
incorporate
intrinsic
lucrative
poignant
prompt
prone
quest
reprisal
rigor
succumb
virile

ACROSS

2. Belonging to a person or thing by its very nature (and thus not dependent on circumstances)
4. The paying back of one injury or bad deed with another
6. To strongly desire; to be ambitious (to do something or to get something)
8. To relieve; make easier to endure
9. To give in; stop resisting
10. Profitable; well paying
11. A search; pursuit

15. Great hardship or difficulty
20. To unite into a single whole; combine
23. Disagreement
24. Death
25. Emotionally moving; touching

DOWN

1. Agreeable or pleasant in character; friendly
3. To state to be so; claim
5. A situation with no way out; dead end
7. To urge into action

12. An outgoing, sociable person
13. To turn aside, or stray, especially from the main topic in speaking or writing
14. To cut short or reduce
16. To hold oneself back from something; refrain
17. Manly; masculine
18. A shortage; a lack (in amount)
19. Having a tendency; inclined
21. The quality of a leader which captures great popular devotion; personal magnetism
22. A person who believes the worst of people's behavior

UNIT THREE: Test 1

PART A
Choose the word that best completes each item and write it in the space provided.

_____ 1. The muscle ointment ___ the pain of my sprained neck.

    a. alleviated   b. speculated   c. squandered   d. contended

_____ 2. It was ___ to see the bear immediately adopt the orphaned cub.

    a. benevolent   b. poignant   c. relentless   d. infamous

_____ 3. In irregular bursts of energy, dying stars give off ___ radio signals.

    a. virile   b. intermittent   c. congenial   d. flippant

_____ 4. Scientists ___ that the average life span of a dinosaur was probably 100 to 120 years.

    a. speculate   b. digress   c. detract   d. squander

_____ 5. Freud, being a(n) ___, believed that all people are driven primarily by selfish desires.

    a. agnostic   b. benefactor   c. extrovert   d. cynic

_____ 6. The ___ of a Connecticut man was strange indeed. He died when his five-hundred-pound wife sat on him.

    a. diversion   b. charisma   c. perception   d. demise

_____ 7. A power failure ___ our viewing of the TV mystery, so we never found out who had committed the murder.

    a. prompted   b. curtailed   c. contended   d. dissented

_____ 8. The CIA's ___ activities often include "bugging" people's telephone lines with tiny, hidden microphones.

    a. covert   b. traumatic   c. virile   d. congenial

_____ 9. ___ of gun control point out that gun accidents in American homes result in over a thousand deaths each year.

    a. Quests   b. Incentives   c. Proponents   d. Rigors

_____ 10. Alcohol is involved in nearly half of all traffic deaths in the United States, so people should ___ from drinking when they need to drive.

    a. affiliate   b. abstain   c. contend   d. aspire

_____ 11. The talks between the two countries reached a(n) ___ when each side claimed the oil-rich border area as its own.

    a. benefactor   b. rapport   c. diversion   d. impasse

(Continues on next page)

_____ 12. ___ to oversleeping, Sherman keeps his alarm clock across the room so he has to get out of bed to turn it off.

     a. Intrinsic   b. Lucrative   c. Prone   d. Covert

_____ 13. When I realized that I didn't have enough money for holiday gifts, I decided to overcome the ___ by taking an extra part-time job in December.

     a. charisma   b. perception   c. dissent   d. deficit

PART B
Write **C** if the italicized word is used **correctly**. Write **I** if the word is used **incorrectly**.

____ 14. The *benevolent* boss laid workers off without even giving them a week's pay.

____ 15. A typewriter or word processor is *indispensable* for preparing a college term paper.

____ 16. The beautiful sunset, with dramatic red swirls in a pink sky, filled us with *revulsion*.

____ 17. Since baldness is a masculine trait, why don't more men view it as attractively *virile?*

____ 18. Fran often *squanders* her money by walking through rain or snow instead of paying for a cab.

____ 19. Eric has often had cats, but never dogs. *Conversely,* Joan has often had dogs, but never cats.

____ 20. A course in American history isn't *mandatory* at most colleges, but our school does require first-year students to take one.

____ 21. I don't consider retirement benefits a sufficient *incentive* to stick with a job I dislike.

____ 22. Priests, rabbis, and other *agnostics* signed the petition asking for aid to the homeless.

____ 23. Since my brother and I live next door to each other, we've *incorporated* our back yards into one big playground for our children.

____ 24. At the restaurant, Kevin *prompted* me to save room for dessert by saying, "They make the world's best chocolate layer cake here."

____ 25. Halloween has *contemporary* roots. Each year, the ancient Irish would dress as demons and witches to frighten away ghosts who might otherwise claim their bodies.

Score   (Number correct) _____ x 4 = _____%

Enter your score above and in the vocabulary performance chart on the inside back cover of the book.

UNIT THREE: Test 2

PART A
Complete each item with a word from the box. Use each word once.

a. **benefactor**	b. **contend**	c. **devastate**	d. **extrovert**	e. **flippant**
f. **lucrative**	g. **prevalent**	h. **quest**	i. **rapport**	j. **rationale**
k. **reprisal**	l. **rigor**	m. **succumb**		

_____ 1. Jill was ____(e)d when she lost her job and, with it, her hopes of affording a house.

_____ 2. I have excellent ___ with my brother, but I haven't spoken to my sister for years.

_____ 3. Rudy is such a(n) ___ that he makes friends with most of the customers at his beauty salon.

_____ 4. Before the turn of the century, the ___s of prizefighting included boxing without gloves.

_____ 5. The owner of the restaurant ___(e)d to public pressure and established a nonsmoking section.

_____ 6. My ___ for using cloth napkins is that they result in fewer trees being cut down to make paper napkins.

_____ 7. With violent crime so ___, some newspaper reporters now wear bulletproof vests when they cover a story.

_____ 8. Halloween is ___ for candy manufacturers. The holiday earns them about a billion dollars a year.

_____ 9. In some fairy tales, the hero searches far and wide, on a(n) ___ for some precious object or missing person.

_____ 10. The high school's chief ___ has offered to pay all college costs for any low-income student who graduates from the school.

_____ 11. When her brother kept taking her bike without asking, Meg's ___ was simply not to warn him that one of the tires was going flat.

_____ 12. The street's residents ___ that they complained for months about the huge pothole before the city government did anything about it.

_____ 13. When the principal asked Randy why he had spilled milk on some girls in the lunchroom, his ___ response was "Because they were thirsty."

(Continues on next page)

PART B
Write **C** if the italicized word is used **correctly**. Write **I** if the word is used **incorrectly**.

____ 14. Our English teacher said, "Be sure to *digress*. A short essay needs a tight focus."

____ 15. For two weeks, the newspapers reported on the crimes of the *infamous* serial killer.

____ 16. The *relentless* beat of my neighbor's stereo gave me an equally persistent headache.

____ 17. Kira *aspired* to go to the dentist, but her tooth hurt so badly that she had no choice.

____ 18. Whenever it snowed, the *congenial* boy next door would throw tightly packed snowballs at me.

____ 19. Groucho Marx once joked that he wouldn't want to *affiliate* himself with any club that would accept him as a member.

____ 20. Bob's near-fatal auto accident was so *traumatic* for him that, a year later, he still refuses to get inside a car.

____ 21. The candidate lost the TV debate partly because of his *charisma*, which included sweating and stammering.

____ 22. The student meeting went extremely smoothly. There was quite a bit of *dissent* to giving the retiring art teacher a set of fine oil paints.

____ 23. The desire to aid others seems *intrinsic* to many animals. Baboons, for example, will try to free other baboons who are caged.

____ 24. Vanessa's current *diversion* is as a night-shift clerk in a supermarket. She took the part-time job temporarily to pay off some bills.

____ 25. Fashion designers influence our *perceptions* of what is attractive. For example, who would have thought a few years ago that jeans filled with holes would be considered good-looking?

Score   (Number correct) _____ x 4 = _____%

Enter your score above and in the vocabulary performance chart on the inside back cover of the book.

UNIT THREE: Test 3

PART A
Complete each sentence in a way that clearly shows you understand the meaning of the **boldfaced** word. Take a minute to plan your answer before you write.

Example: As an **incentive** to work better, the company *gives bonuses to workers who show special effort*.

1. One sight that makes me feel **revulsion** is _____

_____.

2. A good way to **squander** your money is to _____

_____.

3. Jon, who is a **proponent** of daily exercise, advised me, " _____

_____."

4. At our school, it is **mandatory** to _____

_____.

5. I **aspire** to _____

_____.

6. During the math class, the teacher **digressed** by _____

_____.

7. Our father told us how **traumatic** it was for him to _____

_____.

8. My **rationale** for going to college is _____

_____.

9. The reason the plan was **covert** was that _____

_____.

10. When asked by the restaurant owner to pay his bill, the young man's **flippant** reply was " _____

_____."

(Continues on next page)

PART B

After each **boldfaced** word are a *synonym* (a word that means the same as the boldfaced word), an *antonym* (a word that means the opposite of the boldfaced word), and a word that is neither. On the answer line, write the letter of the word that is the antonym.

Example: __c__ **contemporary** a. modern   b. rapid   c. ancient

_____ 11. **benevolent**   a. cruel   b. gifted   c. kind

_____ 12. **alleviate**   a. relieve   b. worsen   c. raise

_____ 13. **indispensable**   a. essential   b. expensive   c. unnecessary

_____ 14. **prevalent**   a. heavy   b. rare   c. common

_____ 15. **congenial**   a. disagreeable b. clever   c. pleasant

PART C

Use five of the following ten words in sentences. Make it clear that you know the meaning of the word you use. Feel free to use the past tense or plural form of a word.

a. **affiliate**	b. **contend**	c. **curtail**	d. **cynic**	e. **diversion**
f. **perception**	g. **rapport**	h. **relentless**	i. **squander**	j. **virile**

16. _____

_____

17. _____

_____

18. _____

_____

19. _____

_____

20. _____

_____

Score   (Number correct) _____ x 5 = _____ %

Enter your score above and in the vocabulary performance chart on the inside back cover of the book.

UNIT THREE: Test 4 (Word Parts)

PART A
Listed in the left-hand column below are ten common word parts, along with words in which the parts are used. In each blank, write in the letter of the correct definition on the right.

Word Parts	Examples	Definitions
_____ 1. **cor, cour**	cordial, courageous	a. Two; double
_____ 2. **di-, du-**	divorced, duo	b. Mental processes; mind
_____ 3. **-dom**	stardom, boredom	c. Not
_____ 4. **-fy**	simplify, liquefy	d. Fear
_____ 5. **il-, im-**	illegal, immature	e. Heart
_____ 6. **-ish**	devilish, stylish	f. Forward; forth
_____ 7. **magni-, magn-**	magnifying, magnate	g. Great; large
_____ 8. **phob**	phobia, agoraphobia	h. State of being; condition
_____ 9. **pro-**	proceed, propel	i. Cause to be or become; make
_____ 10. **psych-, psycho-**	psychiatrist, psychologist	j. Resembling; like; characteristic of

PART B
Using the answer line provided, complete each *italicized* word in the sentences below with the correct word part from the box. Not every word part will be used.

a. **cour**	b. **-dom**	c. **du-**	d. **-fy**	e. **il-**
f. **-ish**	g. **magni-**	h. **phob**	i. **pro-**	j. **psycho-**

_____ 11. Considering all the books, movies, and TV programs in everyday life, there's no reason for (*bore . . .*) ___.

_____ 12. The car that is used for driving instruction has (*. . . al*) ___ controls, one set for the student and one for the teacher.

_____ 13. Bacteria (*puri . . .*) ___ soil in which bodies are buried by destroying germs.

_____ 14. The (*nightmar . . .*) ___ experience of constantly hiccuping can be stopped with drugs.

_____ 15. A victim of (*acro . . . ia*), a fear of heights, Diane refused any job that required working higher than the second floor.

(Continues on next page)

PART C
Use your knowledge of word parts to determine the meaning of the **boldfaced** words. On the answer line, write the letter of each meaning.

_____ 16. "Go through the red double doors," said the secretary, "and then **proceed** down the hallway."

    a. go quickly   b. go fearfully   c. go forward

_____ 17. A blue moon is **improbable**.

    a. shocking   b. unlikely   c. beautiful

_____ 18. We bought a **magnum** of champagne.

    a. a large bottle   b. a medium-sized bottle   c. a little bottle

_____ 19. Ken's report emphasized the **core** of the plan.

    a. the details   b. the background   c. the central part

_____ 20. Belle suffered from a **psychosis**.

    a. a physical disease   b. a mental disorder   c. a heart problem

Score (Number correct) _____ x 5 = _____%

Enter your score above and in the vocabulary performance chart on the inside back cover of the book.

Unit Four

benign	glib
blasé	haughty
comprise	libel
condescend	pseudonym
facade	redundant

Ten Words in Context

In the space provided, write the letter of the meaning closest to that of each **boldfaced** word. Use the context of the sentences to help you figure out each word's meaning.

1 benign
(bĭ-nīn′)
-adjective

- Finding a stranger on our doorstep startled me, but the **benign** expression on his face told me not to worry.
- Gorilla mothers, usually loving and **benign**, become abusive toward their babies when caged with them.

__ *Benign* means a. realistic.   b. kindhearted.   c. bored.

2 blasé
(blă-zā′)
-adjective

- The new staff members were enthusiastic at the weekly meetings, but the old-timers were pretty **blasé**.
- No matter how many games I see, I will never become **blasé** about baseball. Each game is new and exciting to me.

__ *Blasé* means a. unexcited.   b. obvious.   c. repetitive.

3 comprise
(kŏm-prīz′)
-verb

- The United Kingdom **comprises** England, Scotland, Wales, and Northern Ireland.
- Saliva **comprises** about sixty ingredients, including minerals that help repair tooth enamel.

__ *Comprise* means a. to cause.   b. to reveal.   c. to be made up of.

4 condescend
(kŏn-dĭ-sĕnd′)
-verb

- The snobby millionaire wouldn't **condescend** to associate with anyone who wasn't also rich.
- Although everyone else in the office took turns making coffee, Bill would not **condescend** to perform "such a lowly task."

__ *Condescend* means a. to lower oneself. b. to dare something frightening. c. to remember.

5 facade
(fə-sŏd′)
-noun

- The **facade** of the old department store was cleaned this summer. Now the store's brick front is an inviting bright orange-red.
- The **facade** of the hotel—facing Main Street—was marble, but the sides and back were made of plain brick.

__ *Facade* means a. an inside.   b. a top.   c. a front.

6 glib
(glĭb)
-adjective

- Always ready with a slick promise, the **glib** politician smoothly talked his way into being re-elected.
- The man thought his conversation would impress Sandra, but she found it **glib** and insincere.

__ *Glib* means a. bored.   b. strict.   c. smooth.

7 haughty
(hô′tē)
-adjective

- The Smiths acted as though they were better than anybody else. Not surprisingly, their **haughty** manner made them unpopular with their neighbors.
- After being promoted to manager, Gil was **haughty** with his old office buddies, saying he now had more important things to do than gab with them.

___ *Haughty* means   a. snobbish.   b. angry.   c. wordy.

8 libel
(lī′bəl)
-noun

- When Nick saw his name listed in the article as a gang member, he was furious. "That's **libel**," he yelled. "How dare they print such a lie about me?"
- Many magazine editors double-check the facts they publish about a person. Then, if they are accused of **libel**, they can prove that they stated the truth.

___ *Libel* means   a. a false name.   b. a printed falsehood.   c. a repeated expression.

9 pseudonym
(sōō′də-nĭm′)
-noun

- When writing a personal story for a family magazine, Bev used a **pseudonym**. She didn't want everyone in town to know about her problems.
- The author Stephen King uses a **pseudonym** on some of his books so readers won't be aware that so many of the horror novels on the market are his.

___ *Pseudonym* means   a. a weak vocabulary.   b. a personal experience.   c. a false name.

10 redundant
(rĭ-dŭn′dənt)
-adjective

- The TV ad for a headache medicine was so **redundant** that it gave me a headache! The name of the product was repeated at least a dozen times.
- The teacher wrote "**redundant**" in several spots in the essay where Eric had repeated a point or used extra, unneeded words.

___ *Redundant* means   a. grammatical.   b. proud.   c. repetitious.

Matching Words with Definitions

Following are definitions of the ten words. Clearly write or print each word next to its definition. The sentences above and on the previous page will help you decide on the meaning of each word.

1. _____   a. A false name used by an author; a pen name
2. _____   b. To do something one feels is beneath oneself
3. _____   c. Unexcited or bored about something already experienced repeatedly
4. _____   d. The front of a building
5. _____   e. Wordy or needlessly repetitive
6. _____   f. Kindly; gentle
7. _____   g. The publishing of false information that harms a person's reputation
8. _____   h. Proud of one's appearance or accomplishments to the point of looking down on others; arrogant
9. _____   i. To consist of
10. _____   j. Characterized by a smooth, easy manner of speaking that often suggests insincerity or thoughtlessness

CAUTION: Do not go any further until you are sure the above answers are correct. Then you can use the definitions to help you in the following practices. Your goal is eventually to know the words well enough so that you don't need to check the definitions at all.

➤ *Sentence Check 1*

Using the answer line provided, complete each item below with the correct word from the box. Use each word once.

a. **benign**	b. **blasé**	c. **comprise**	d. **condescend**	e. **facade**
f. **glib**	g. **haughty**	h. **libel**	i. **pseudonym**	j. **redundant**

_____ 1. My job as a receptionist ___s answering the phone, greeting customers, opening the mail, dealing with messengers, and smiling.

_____ 2. My aunt's letters are annoyingly ___, repeating "news" she has already given us by telephone.

_____ 3. Since becoming a fashion model, Nora has been very ___, even snubbing some of her old, unglamorous friends.

_____ 4. One actress sued a magazine for ___ because it printed a false and damaging story about her being drunk in public.

_____ 5. Harry, always ready with some made-up excuse, is ___ enough to talk himself out of any difficulty at the snap of a finger.

_____ 6. In his usual ___ manner, my neighbor carefully picked up the ant in his kitchen, brought it outside, and gently put it down on the sidewalk.

_____ 7. When my sister first got her job at the recording studio, she was thrilled to go to work each day. Now, after ten years, she's ___ about her work and wants to change jobs.

_____ 8. Lidia's grandfather made her a dollhouse with a ___ just like the front of her family's house: black shutters, a red front door, and even the same address.

_____ 9. The conceited young baseball player wouldn't ___ to talk to his fans until an old-timer reminded him that the fans are the ones who made him a star.

_____ 10. Samuel Langhorne Clemens wasn't the first author to use the ___ Mark Twain. A newspaper writer of the time used the same pen name.

NOTE: Now check your answers to these questions by turning to page 176. Going over the answers carefully will help you prepare for the next two practices, for which answers are not given.

➤ *Sentence Check 2*

Using the answer lines provided, complete each item below with **two** words from the box. Use each word once.

_____
_____ 1–2. Believing he was better than everyone else at the supermarket, Dan was so ___ that he would rarely ___ to speak to the other cashiers.

_____
_____ 3–4. One author was accused of ___ when he wrote a damaging article about the governor's wife. After that, he used a ___ so people wouldn't know he was the author whose facts were in doubt.

_____   5–6. At first Joanne thought Barry was too ___, that his smooth talk was all
_____   show. As she got to know him better, however, her perception° of him
                                  changed. She found that his easy manner reflected a friendly and ___
                                  nature.

_____   7–8. The scenery crew for the summer theatre ___(e)d three artists and a set
_____   designer. They built an intricate° model of a palace ___ , complete with
                                  curving staircases, a carved door, and a moat.

_____   9–10. The writing teacher had become ___ from repeatedly seeing the same
_____   problems: careless organization, lack of focus, and writing so ___ that
                                   paragraphs held only a sentence of meaning. In addition, students often
                                   turned to plagiarism° rather than use their own words.

➤ _Final Check:_ Interview with a Rude Star

Here is a final opportunity for you to strengthen your knowledge of the ten words. First read the following
selection carefully. Then fill in each blank with a word from the box at the top of the previous page.
(Context clues will help you figure out which word goes in which blank.) Use each word once.

When a famous actress arrived in town to work on a movie, an editor asked me to interview
her. Because this was my first interview assignment, I felt far from (1)_____
about it. Instead, I was both excited and scared. Would a star (2)_____ to
see me, an unknown, inexperienced reporter?

When I arrived at the movie set, I saw the actress standing in front of the painted
(3)_____ of a mansion. During a break in the filming, I approached her and
introduced myself. Trying to be as congenial° as possible, I smiled and told her I was pleased to
meet her. "Well, let's get this over with," she said, clearly annoyed.

The interview went terribly. My dream of establishing a comfortable rapport° with the star
soon vanished as the interview degenerated° into an awkward, demoralizing° situation that I just
wanted to end. Although it (4)_____(e)d carefully thought-out questions,
she sighed or rolled her eyes at every one of them. And no matter how
(5)_____ my manner, she seemed to view me as some sort of threat. At
one point, she became irate° and yelled, "That's (6)_____! I don't have
time to answer the same question twice." When I asked her about serious issues, her answers were
totally (7)_____—insincere and shallow.

Now that the interview is over, I have to write about her. Should I say that she's a
(8)_____, rude woman who thinks only of herself and expects others to do the
same? If I do, she might accuse me of maligning° her and sue me for (9)_____.
I wonder if the editor would let me use a (10)_____, so my real name won't
appear on an article about this miserable woman.

Scores	Sentence Check 2 _____%	Final Check _____%

Enter your scores above and in the vocabulary performance chart on the inside back cover of the book.

averse	endow
detract	expulsion
disdain	mortify
divulge	nullify
elation	ominous

Ten Words in Context

In the space provided, write the letter of the meaning closest to that of each **boldfaced** word. Use the context of the sentences to help you figure out each word's meaning.

1 averse
(ə-vûrs')
-*adjective*

- My son was once so **averse** to tomatoes that the very sight of them made him gag.
- Being **averse** to screaming crowds, I'd rather stay home and listen to my CD's than go to a rock concert.

__ *Averse* means   a. opposed.   b. accustomed.   c. open.

2 detract
(dĭ-trăkt')
-*verb*

- Julius thinks the scar on his cheek **detracts** from his good looks, but it's barely noticeable.
- All of the litter in the park certainly **detracts** from the beauty of the trees and flowers.

__ *Detract* means   a. to result.   b. to benefit.   c. to take away.

3 disdain
(dĭs-dān')
-*noun*

- The snobby waiter in the French restaurant viewed Tanya with **disdain** because she couldn't pronounce anything on the menu.
- I was afraid my request to see the state senator would be treated with **disdain**. Instead, the senator's secretary politely made an appointment for me.

__ *Disdain* means   a. pride.   b. disrespect.   c. sorrow.

4 divulge
(dĭ-vŭlj')
-*verb*

- My father wouldn't **divulge** the type of car he had bought, saying only, "It's a surprise."
- It's against the law to ask people to **divulge** their age at a job interview.

__ *Divulge* means   a. to hide.   b. to recall.   c. to tell.

5 elation
(ĭ-lā'shən)
-*noun*

- The principal shouted with **elation** when the school team scored the winning touchdown.
- Roy had expected to feel **elation** at his graduation. Instead, he felt sadness at the thought of parting with some of his high school friends.

__ *Elation* means   a. anger.   b. confusion.   c. happiness.

6 endow
(ĕn-dou')
-*verb*

- Nature has **endowed** hummingbirds with the ability to fly backward.
- Oscar Wilde was **endowed** with the ability to find humor in any situation. While dying, he said of the ugly wallpaper in his hotel room, "One of us had to go."

__ *Endow* means   a. to equip.   b. to curse.   c. to threaten.

7 expulsion
(ĕks-pŭl′shən)
-noun

- The manager told us we risked **expulsion** from the theater if we continued to talk during the movie.
- **Expulsion** from school is intended as a punishment, but some students may consider not being allowed to attend classes to be a reward.

__ *Expulsion* means   a. being canceled.   b. being forced out.   c. being embarrassed.

8 mortify
(môr′tə-fī′)
-verb

- It would **mortify** me if my voice were to crack during my choir solo.
- I doubt anything will ever **mortify** me more than the streamer of toilet paper that clung to my shoe as I returned from the ladies' room to rejoin my date in a fancy restaurant.

__ *Mortify* means   a. to shame.   b. to insult.   c. to delay.

9 nullify
(nŭl′ə-fī′)
-verb

- The college will **nullify** my student ID at the end of the term unless I update it with a new sticker.
- A soft drink company decided to **nullify** its contract with a well-known athlete because he was convicted of drunken driving.

__ *Nullify* means   a. to renew.   b. to reveal.   c. to cancel.

10 ominous
(ŏm′ə-nəs)
-adjective

- To many, cemeteries have an **ominous** quality, particularly at night or on Halloween, when the threat of ghosts can seem very real.
- The sore's failure to heal was **ominous**, a possible sign of cancer.

__ *Ominous* means   a. embarrassing.   b. threatening.   c. unworthy.

Matching Words with Definitions

Following are definitions of the ten words. Clearly write or print each word next to its definition. The sentences above and on the previous page will help you decide on the meaning of each word.

1. _____   To provide with a talent or quality

2. _____   An attitude or feeling of contempt; scorn

3. _____   The act or condition of being forced to leave

4. _____   Threatening harm or evil; menacing

5. _____   To reveal; make known

6. _____   Having a feeling of dislike or distaste for something

7. _____   To humiliate or embarrass

8. _____   To lessen what is admirable or worthwhile about something

9. _____   A feeling of great joy or pride

10. _____   To make legally ineffective; cancel

CAUTION: Do not go any further until you are sure the above answers are correct. Then you can use the definitions to help you in the following practices. Your goal is eventually to know the words well enough so that you don't need to check the definitions at all.

➤ *Sentence Check 1*

Using the answer line provided, complete each item below with the correct word from the box. Use each word once.

a. **averse**	b. **detract**	c. **disdain**	d. **divulge**	e. **elation**
f. **endow**	g. **expulsion**	h. **mortified**	i. **nullified**	j. **ominous**

_____ 1. People talking in a movie theater greatly ___ from the enjoyment of watching a film.

_____ 2. Because of the dark, ___ storm clouds, we canceled the softball game.

_____ 3. I'm ___ to speaking in public because I don't enjoy making a fool of myself.

_____ 4. When he received the college scholarship, my brother felt such ___ that he wept with joy.

_____ 5. The results of the mayoral election were ___ after the townspeople found evidence of voting fraud.

_____ 6. The American water shrew is ___(e)d with feet that have air pockets, enabling the small animal to walk on water.

_____ 7. Some want a law calling for the ___ of illegal immigrants. Others want all immigrants to be allowed to stay in the United States.

_____ 8. Vinnie's repeated boasts about his muscle-building backfired. They caused his date to look at him with ___, not admiration.

_____ 9. Never trust Esta with a secret. She'll ___ it the minute you turn your back.

_____ 10. The reporter was ___ when he learned that he had delivered much of his news story facing away from the operating TV camera.

NOTE: Now check your answers to these questions by turning to page 176. Going over the answers carefully will help you prepare for the next two practices, for which answers are not given.

➤ *Sentence Check 2*

Using the answer lines provided, complete each item below with **two** words from the box. Use each word once.

_____
_____ 1–2. Some people are so ___ to living near a nuclear plant that they want the the plant's license to be ___. They say the plant infringes° on every homeowner's right to safety.

_____
_____ 3–4. Shannon is ___(e)d with beautiful curly red hair, but her self-image is so low that she feels her hair ___s from her looks. However, others find her hair to be one of her many attractive physical attributes°.

_____
_____ 5–6. When someone ___(e)d to college officials that a certain student was selling drugs, an investigation began that led to that student's ___ from school.

_____   7–8. Amy was ___ by the low grade she received for her class speech, a
_____   grade she considered a sign of the teacher's ___ for her. However, the
                          teacher's rationale° for the grade was that the speech was incoherent°.
                          In addition to the lack of logic, it contained little solid information.

_____   9–10. Marty had believed his headaches and blurred vision were ___ signs of
_____   some terrible syndrome°, so he felt ___ when he learned that he simply
                          needed glasses.

➤ _Final Check:_ The Nightmare of Gym

Here is a final opportunity for you to strengthen your knowledge of the ten words. First read the following
selection carefully. Then fill in each blank with a word from the box at the top of the previous page.
(Context clues will help you figure out which word goes in which blank.) Use each word once.

I was not (1)_____(e)d with athletic ability. In a frequent nightmare,
I'm still trying to pass my mandatory° gym class so that I can graduate from high school. The
situation always looks grim. For one thing, the teacher has threatened me with
(2)_____ from school for refusing to take a group shower. Also appearing
in my dream is the terrifying vault horse, the very sight of which (3)_____s
from my mental health. I run toward the horse, leap, and nose-dive into the mat. Ignoring my
despair, the rest of the gym class laughs. Once again, I am (4)_____ by my
athletic performance.

Next, a single (5)_____ rope threatens overhead, where it hangs from the
ceiling. I try to contrive° some excuse to get out of climbing it. However, my excuses are so
incoherent° that my teacher says, "I don't understand anything you're saying. Get started."
Wondering if anyone has ever died from rope burn, I struggle to climb it. Almost to the top, I
sweat so much that I slide back to the floor, landing at the gym teacher's feet. "What a loser," the
teacher mutters with an expression of total (6)_____.

Because I've always been (7)_____ to square-dancing, that too appears
in the nightmare. Having forgotten my sneakers, I'm forced to dance in my socks. I slip, rather
than dance, around the polished floor. During one high-speed turn, I go sliding—right into the
men's locker room, where the smell causes me to pass out.

The only pleasant part of the dream comes near the end. With amazement and
(8)_____, I learn that I will graduate after all. I smile, thinking I'll never
have to face the rigors° of gym class again.

But then, the principal (9)_____s the terrible truth. I haven't managed
to pass gym. My graduation depends on my agreeing to take four more years of gym when I get to
college. If I don't, my high school diploma will be (10)_____.

Scores	Sentence Check 2 _____%	Final Check _____%

Enter your scores above and in the vocabulary performance chart on the inside back cover of the book.

CHAPTER 21

credible	interim
cursory	latent
designate	secular
deviate	shun
improvise	simulate

Ten Words in Context

In the space provided, write the letter of the meaning closest to that of each **boldfaced** word. Use the context of the sentences to help you figure out each word's meaning.

1 credible
(krĕd'-ə-bəl)
-adjective

- Some jurors doubted the witness's testimony, but most of them found it **credible**.
- As **credible** as Mr. Bower's résumé may seem, I don't think you should hire him without checking that it really is truthful.

___ *Credible* means   a. long.   b. boring.   c. believable.

2 cursory
(kûr'sə-rē)
-adjective

- Most people do only a **cursory** job of brushing their teeth. To avoid cavities, however, you must take the time to brush carefully.
- Because I had to work late, I had only enough time to give my apartment a **cursory** cleaning before my parents arrived.

___ *Cursory* means   a. careful.   b. consistent.   c. quick.

3 designate
(dĕz'ĭg-nāt')
-verb

- At the party, Betty drank soda rather than beer, so her friends **designated** her as the driver for the trip home.
- A coworker was **designated** to present Vonnie with the "Employee of the Year" award at the company banquet.

___ *Designate* means   a. to forbid.   b. to assign.   c. to hire.

4 deviate
(dē'vē-āt')
-verb

- Having taken the wrong exit off the highway, I had to **deviate** somewhat from the route marked on the map.
- If you **deviate** even a little from the test's directions, you might hurt your grade.

___ *Deviate* means   a. to follow.   b. to depart.   c. to gain.

5 improvise
(ĭm'prə-vīz')
-verb

- Nadia can **improvise** accompaniments on the piano to songs that she's never heard before. I don't know how she plays so well without any preparation or sheet music.
- When I rang the doorbell, I wasn't expecting Ellen's father to come to the door, so I had to quickly **improvise** a false explanation for my visit.

___ *Improvise* means   a. to remember.   b. to keep away from.   c. to invent.

6 interim
(ĭn'tər-ĭm)
-noun

- Cassie hadn't seen her nephews for years. In the **interim**, they had grown from troubled boys into serious young men.
- After our secretary left, it took two weeks for her replacement to arrive. In the **interim**, we had to do our own typing.

___ *Interim* means   a. the time between.   b. the future.   c. the place.

7 latent
(lāt′ənt)
-adjective

- Certain viruses, such as the one for AIDS, can be **latent** in the body for years before symptoms appear.
- After he retired, my father discovered his **latent** artistic talent. He took up oil painting and now sells much of his work.

___ *Latent* means   a. partial.   b. inactive.   c. absent.

8 secular
(sĕk′yə-lər)
-adjective

- While our government is **secular**, some governments are directly tied to a religion.
- Devoting himself to a deeply religious life, the Hindu holy man denied himself most **secular** pleasures.

___ *Secular* means   a. spiritual.   b. reliable.   c. nonreligious.

9 shun
(shŭn)
-verb

- I used to see a lot of Tracy, but since our argument, she **shuns** me whenever possible.
- The Amish live without many modern conveniences. For example, they **shun** automobiles and electric lights.

___ *Shun* means   a. to keep away from.   b. to recognize.   c. to observe.

10 simulate
(sĭm′yoo-lāt′)
-verb

- The tan plastic of our kitchen table, with its wood-grain design, **simulates** oak.
- Equipment that **simulates** a human heart can keep someone alive only temporarily, until an actual heart can be substituted.

___ *Simulate* means   a. to contrast with.   b. to imitate.   c. to be made of.

Matching Words with Definitions

Following are definitions of the ten words. Clearly write or print each word next to its definition. The sentences above and on the previous page will help you decide on the meaning of each word.

1. _____   To compose, perform, or provide without preparation

2. _____   Believable

3. _____   The period of time in between; meantime

4. _____   To name to an office or duty; appoint

5. _____   To act or look like; imitate

6. _____   Not directly related to religion; not spiritual; worldly

7. _____   Done quickly and without attention to detail

8. _____   To keep away from; avoid consistently

9. _____   Present but hidden or inactive

10. _____   To turn aside or stray, as from a path, direction, or standard

CAUTION: Do not go any further until you are sure the above answers are correct. Then you can use the definitions to help you in the following practices. Your goal is eventually to know the words well enough so that you don't need to check the definitions at all.

➤ *Sentence Check 1*

Using the answer line provided, complete each item below with the correct word from the box. Use each word once.

a. **credible**	b. **cursory**	c. **designate**	d. **deviate**	e. **improvise**
f. **interim**	g. **latent**	h. **secular**	i. **shun**	j. **simulate**

_____ 1. My daughter's ___ talent for sarcasm became apparent when she turned 12. Her answers had once been respectful, but now they were witty and biting.

_____ 2. Presidents ___ as Supreme Court justices people who share their political views.

_____ 3. I hear Andy dropped out of college. What caused him to ___ from his plan to get his degree?

_____ 4. Because his story about a flat tire sounded ___, my parents allowed the stranger to use our telephone.

_____ 5. In the ___ between applying to college and getting the letter of acceptance, I spent a lot of time worrying.

_____ 6. Margo couldn't identify the driver of the car that had hit her. She'd given him only a(n) ___ glance at the time of the accident.

_____ 7. The chorus is known for its gospel music, but it also performs ___ compositions, including show tunes.

_____ 8. When the actor forgot his lines, he was forced to ___ some dialog until the stage manager whispered to him from offstage.

_____ 9. Tony found the hardest part of overcoming his addiction was learning to ___ people and places that would tempt him to use drugs again.

_____ 10. The zoo's exhibits ___ the natural environments of its animals. The orangutans, for example, live in a space that looks much like an Asian rain forest.

NOTE: Now check your answers to these questions by turning to page 177. Going over the answers carefully will help you prepare for the next two practices, for which answers are not given.

➤ *Sentence Check 2*

Using the answer lines provided, complete each item below with **two** words from the box. Use each word once.

_____
_____ 1–2. In seventh grade, I looked upon girls with great disdain°. Then, in the ___ between seventh and eighth grades, my ___ interest in them suddenly surfaced.

_____
_____ 3–4. In looking for a college, Luke gave only ___ attention to ___ schools. He was quite sure he wanted to attend a Catholic school.

_____   5–6. Matt told his mother he was late because he had fallen while running
_____   home. To make his lie more ___, he had scratched his knee with a rock
                               to ___ an injury from a fall.

_____   7–8. Della wanted to be a cheerleader, but she willingly ___(e)d from that
_____   goal when she was ___(e)d class mascot and got to wear a polar bear
                               costume to all the games.

_____   9–10. Proud of his ability to create new dishes, Franco tended to ___ cook-
_____   books. He preferred to ___ meals, using whatever ingredients happened
                               to be on hand. In fact, cooking was one of his favorite diversions°.

➤ *Final Check:* Skipping Church

Here is a final opportunity for you to strengthen your knowledge of the ten words. First read the following
selection carefully. Then fill in each blank with a word from the box at the top of the previous page.
(Context clues will help you figure out which word goes in which blank.) Use each word once.

I remember so well the time my mother's back injury prevented her from going to church with
my brother and me. For five weeks we were to go by ourselves. Zack and I then preferred
(1)_____ activities to religious ones, so we decided to (2)_____
church while Mom was recovering. We (3)_____(e)d the churchgoers
she wanted us to be by getting dressed in our good clothes and leaving home and returning at the
right times. We spent the (4)_____ at a restaurant or at the movies. Of
course, we knew Mom would question us about the service. Each week one of us was
(5)_____(e)d to invent a sermon. I thought Zack's sermons sounded not
only (6)_____, but also inspiring. I, in contrast, tended to
(7)_____ on the spot and didn't sound so believable. But Mom never seemed
to notice how weak my sermons were or how (8)_____ our answers were
when she asked whom we'd seen and what news we'd heard.

Finally, she was ready to attend church again. Over dinner Saturday evening, she began what
seemed to be an innocent conversation. Gently, but showing a previously (9)_____
talent for cross-examination that could have made her a star attorney, she questioned us in a quiet
but relentless° manner about our "church-going." The more she persisted, the more Zack and I
stumbled and (10)_____(e)d from our official story. We eventually
concluded we were caught, and the realization mortified° us. Looking downward in shame, we
divulged° all the details of our "secret" scheme. We felt pretty foolish when we learned she'd
known all along that we had never set foot in church.

Scores Sentence Check 2 _____%	Final Check _____%

Enter your scores above and in the vocabulary performance chart on the inside back cover of the book.

commemorate	empathy
complacent	menial
consensus	niche
deplete	transcend
diligent	waive

Ten Words in Context

In the space provided, write the letter of the meaning closest to that of each **boldfaced** word. Use the context of the sentences to help you figure out each word's meaning.

1 **commemorate**
(kə-mĕm′ə-rāt′)
-*verb*

• Thomas devoted himself to feeding the hungry. So on the anniversary of his death, it seems wrong to **commemorate** his life with a fancy dinner party that only the rich can attend.

• Each year, my parents **commemorate** their first date by having dinner at McDonalds, the place where they first met.

__ *Commemorate* means   a. to share.   b. to celebrate.   c. to believe.

2 **complacent**
(kəm-plā′sənt)
-*adjective*

• Elected officials cannot afford to be **complacent** about winning an election. Before long, they'll have to campaign again for the voters' support.

• Getting all A's hasn't made Ivy **complacent**. She continues to work hard at school.

__ *Complacent* means   a. very eager.   b. reasonable.   c. too much at ease.

3 **consensus**
(kən-sen′səs)
-*noun*

• A vote revealed strong agreement among the teachers. The **consensus** was that they would strike if the school board did not act quickly to raise their pay.

• The family **consensus** was that we should go camping again this summer. Ray was the only one who wanted to do something else for a change.

__ *Consensus* means   a. a majority view.   b. an unusual idea.   c. a question.

4 **deplete**
(dĭ-plēt′)
-*verb*

• I'd like to help you out with a loan, but unexpected car repairs have managed to **deplete** my bank account.

• In order not to **deplete** their small quantity of canned food, the shipwreck survivors searched the island for plants they could eat.

__ *Deplete* means   a. to use up.   b. to forget.   c. to find.

5 **diligent**
(dĭl′ə-jənt)
-*adjective*

• I wish I had been nore **diligent** about practicing piano when I was younger. It would be nice to be able to play well now.

• Diane was lazy when she first joined the family business, but she became so **diligent** that she inspired others to work harder.

__ *Diligent* means   a. self-satisfied.   b. lucky.   c. hard-working.

6 **empathy**
(ĕm′pə-thē)
-*noun*

• Families who lost loved ones in the crash of TWA Flight 800 have **empathy** for one another because of their shared grief.

• Ms. Allan is an excellent career counselor partly because of her great **empathy**. She understands each student's feelings and point of view.

__ *Empathy* means   a. a common opinion.   b. a sympathetic understanding.   c. an efficiency.

7 **menial**
(mē′nē-əl)
-*adjective*

- Victor seems to think my summer job delivering pizza is **menial** work, but I've found that it requires some skills.
- Every job can be done with pride. Even **menial** jobs such as washing windows or scrubbing floors can be performed with care.

__ *Menial* means   a. unskilled.   b. steady.   c. satisfying.

8 **niche**
(nĭch)
-*noun*

- Although her degree was in accounting, Laura decided her **niche** was really in business management, so she went back to school for more training.
- Dom spent the years after college moving restlessly from job to job, never finding a comfortable **niche** for himself.

__ *Niche* means   a. a shared opinion.   b. a suitable place.   c. an education.

9 **transcend**
(trăn-sĕnd′)
-*verb*

- The psychic convinced her clients that she could **transcend** time and space and talk directly with the dead.
- Yoga can help one **transcend** the cares of the world and reach a state of relaxation.

__ *Transcend* means   a. to participate in.   b. to go past.   c. to use up.

10 **waive**
(wāv)
-*verb*

- The defendant decided to **waive** his right to an attorney and, instead, speak for himself in court.
- Since Lin had studied so much math on her own, the school **waived** the requirement that she take high school algebra.

__ *Waive* means   a. to lose.   b. to honor.   c. to give up.

Matching Words with Definitions

Following are definitions of the ten words. Clearly write or print each word next to its definition. The sentences above and on the previous page will help you decide on the meaning of each word.

1. _____   Not requiring special skills or higher intellectual abilities

2. _____   The ability to share in someone else's feelings or thoughts

3. _____   To rise above or go beyond the limits of; exceed

4. _____   To honor the memory of someone or something, as with a ceremony; celebrate; observe

5. _____   To willingly give up (as a claim, privilege, or right); do without

6. _____   An opinion held by everyone (or almost everyone) involved

7. _____   Self-satisfied; feeling too much satisfaction with oneself or one's accomplishments

8. _____   Steady, determined, and careful in work

9. _____   An activity or situation especially suited to a person

10. _____   To use up

CAUTION: Do not go any further until you are sure the above answers are correct. Then you can use the definitions to help you in the following practices. Your goal is eventually to know the words well enough so that you don't need to check the definitions at all.

➤ *Sentence Check 1*

Using the answer line provided, complete each item below with the correct word from the box. Use each word once.

a. **commemorate**	b. **complacent**	c. **consensus**	d. **deplete**	e. **diligent**
f. **empathy**	g. **menial**	h. **niche**	i. **transcend**	j. **waive**

_____ 1. The old man decided to ___ any claim he had to the family fortune, preferring to see the money go to the younger generation.

_____ 2. The American Inventors' Association gathered at a banquet to ___ Thomas Edison.

_____ 3. My grandfather, who's recovering from heart surgery, is weak, so it doesn't take much effort for him to ___ the little energy he has.

_____ 4. Many people believe that Shakespeare's works ___ those of all other authors.

_____ 5. The restaurant got off to a good start, but then the owners became ___ about their success and stopped trying to attract new customers.

_____ 6. Several sessions with a career counselor helped Suzanne consider what her ___ in the working world might be.

_____ 7. The children help out at the family restaurant, but they are able to perform only ___ tasks such as mopping floors and cleaning tables.

_____ 8. Arnie has been ___ in his study of German because he hopes to speak the language with his relatives from Germany when they visit next summer.

_____ 9. I had hoped the restaurant would be good, but our group's ___ was that the food was only so-so and the service was even worse.

_____ 10. Dr. Grange is a brilliant mathematician, but she lacks ___ for her students. She doesn't understand how they can find some problems so difficult.

NOTE: Now check your answers to these questions by turning to page 177. Going over the answers carefully will help you prepare for the next two practices, for which answers are not given.

➤ *Sentence Check 2*

Using the answer lines provided, complete each item below with **two** words from the box. Use each word once.

_____
_____ 1–2. Lynn begged the bank to ___ the overdraft charge of thirty dollars, telling them that it would entirely ___ her savings.

_____
_____ 3–4. In high school, Victor was voted "Most Likely to Become a Psychologist." It was the ___ of his classmates that he was the student endowed° with the most ___ for other people.

_____
_____ 5–6. My mother could have stayed in her comfortable ___ as part of the secretarial pool, but she wanted to ___ the limits of that job and become an executive herself.

_____

_____ 7–8. "On this, our hundredth anniversary celebration," said the company president, "I'd like to ___ our founder with a toast. He ran the company from top to bottom, doing even such ___ jobs as emptying garbage cans. He truly exemplified° the values of dedication and hard work."

_____

_____ 9–10. Dr. Roberts and Dr. Krill practice medicine very differently. Dr. Roberts is ___ about reading journals and learning new techniques. Conversely°, Dr. Krill is more ___ and never tries anything new.

➤ *Final Check:* **A Model Teacher**

Here is a final opportunity for you to strengthen your knowledge of the ten words. First read the following selection carefully. Then fill in each blank with a word from the box at the top of the previous page. (Context clues will help you figure out which word goes in which blank.) Use each word once.

At Eastman High School reunions, the conversation usually gets around to the question "Who was the best teacher in school?" And year after year, the (1)_____ of the graduates has been that Mr. MacDonald was the best. Many remember Joe MacDonald as the epitome° of teaching—the teacher against whom they measured all others.

He had started his professional life as a highly paid attorney. However, never at home with the law, he left his lucrative° practice and found his (2) _____ as an English teacher in the shabby classrooms at Eastman. Mr. MacDonald somehow helped his students (3)_____ their broken-down surroundings and experience the magic in the words of Shakespeare, Dickinson, or Frost. Even those who tended to shun° reading began to think there might be something to this literature stuff after all.

Mr. MacDonald's enthusiasm for his work was never (4)_____(e)d. In fact, instead of being used up, his enthusiasm actually increased through the years. Other teachers became (5)_____ about their work and did only cursory° lesson preparation. But Mr. MacDonald was as (6)_____ as an eager first-year teacher. He could often be found talking with students after school, as his great (7)_____ had given him the reputation of being someone who understood students' problems. He was fun, too. On the first really beautiful spring day of each year, he'd (8)_____ his lesson plan and take the class out into the sunshine to sit under the blue sky and talk about literature. And no task was too (9)_____ for him. He was often seen picking up trash from the grounds—something other teachers would never condescend° to do.

After Mr. MacDonald's retirement, his former students wanted to honor him in some way. They thought about a statue, but decided to (10)_____ his teaching in the way that he'd like best, with a college scholarship for an Eastman student, which was established in his name.

Scores	Sentence Check 2 _____%		Final Check _____%	

Enter your scores above and in the vocabulary performance chart on the inside back cover of the book.

bizarre	gist
conducive	hamper
falter	paradox
flaunt	repertoire
frenzy	viable

Ten Words in Context

In the space provided, write the letter of the meaning closest to that of each **boldfaced** word. Use the context of the sentences to help you figure out each word's meaning.

1 **bizarre**
(bĭ-zär′)
-adjective

- Some mentally ill people have **bizarre** ideas. For example, they may think that the TV is talking to them or that others can steal their thoughts.
- Wally's outfits may seem **bizarre**, but if you see him with his even stranger-looking friends, his clothing looks quite ordinary.

__ *Bizarre* means   a. limited.   b. ordinary.   c. odd.

2 **conducive**
(kən-dōō′sĭv)
-adjective

- A deliciously warm and sunny April day is **conducive** to a bad case of spring fever.
- Learning to budget an allowance at a young age is **conducive** to good spending habits later in life.

__ *Conducive* means   a. favorable.   b. similar.   c. damaging.

3 **falter**
(fôl′tər)
-verb

- Vince **faltered** on the first few notes of his piano piece but then played the rest without pausing.
- Even public speakers who now sound smooth and confident must have **faltered** when giving their first speeches.

__ *Falter* means   a. to show off.   b. to hesitate.   c. to succeed.

4 **flaunt**
(flônt)
-verb

- Instead of enjoying their wealth quietly, the Stewarts **flaunt** every new thing they buy in front of their poor relatives.
- Cindy never **flaunted** her high grades. In fact, I didn't know that she was first in her class until she received the highest awards at graduation.

__ *Flaunt* means   a. to interfere with.   b. to approve of.   c. to exhibit.

5 **frenzy**
(frĕn′zē)
-noun

- When I couldn't find my little son in the department store, I went into a **frenzy** and didn't calm down until I knew he was safe.
- The holiday season always includes a **frenzy** of last-minute shopping.

__ *Frenzy* means   a. a calm condition.   b. an angry condition.   c. an excited condition.

6 **gist**
(jĭst)
-noun

- We asked Alex to skip the details and get right to the **gist** of the argument.
- The **gist** of the novel is that a family got stranded on an island and had to struggle to survive.

__ *Gist* means   a. the small parts.   b. the main idea.   c. the benefit.

7 hamper
(hăm′pər)
-verb

- "We never meant to **hamper** your struggle for independence," Tom's parents said. "From now on, we'll let you handle your own life, including your laundry and meals."
- The breakdown of telephone lines **hampered** business all along the West Coast today.

___ *Hamper* means   a. to restrict.   b. to show off.   c. to promote.

8 paradox
(păr′ə-dŏx′)
-noun

- My mother used to recite this **paradox** to my father: "When a husband brings his wife flowers for no reason, there's a reason."
- When Della kept postponing her decision about whether or not to go back to school, I reminded her of the **paradox** "No decision is also a decision."

___ *Paradox* means   a. an outburst.   b. a simple statement.   c. a seeming contradiction.

9 repertoire
(rĕp′ər-twŏr′)
-noun

- The actor's **repertoire** includes drama, storytelling, song, and dance.
- In order to be successful in college, it's important to have a **repertoire** of study strategies from which to choose.

___ *Repertoire* means   a. a variety of skills.   b. a reason to do something.   c. a statement of intent.

10 viable
(vī′ə-bəl)
-adjective

- The parties in the labor dispute can reach a **viable** agreement only if both sides benefit equally.
- My young son quickly learned that using plastic tape is not a **viable** solution to mending a broken vase.

___ *Viable* means   a. practical.   b. attractive.   c. expensive.

Matching Words with Definitions

Following are definitions of the ten words. Clearly write or print each word next to its definition. The sentences above and on the previous page will help you decide on the meaning of each word.

1. _____   The main point or essential part of a matter; central idea

2. _____   To act or speak with uncertainty; hesitate

3. _____   To limit, interfere with, or restrict

4. _____   A wild outburst of excited feelings or actions

5. _____   Workable; capable of being successful or effective

6. _____   A statement that seems contradictory yet may be true

7. _____   A range or collection of skills or accomplishments

8. _____   Dramatically unusual, as in manner or appearance; strange

9. _____   Tending to promote or bring about

10. _____   To show off (something)

CAUTION: Do not go any further until you are sure the above answers are correct. Then you can use the definitions to help you in the following practices. Your goal is eventually to know the words well enough so that you don't need to check the definitions at all.

➤ *Sentence Check 1*

Using the answer line provided, complete each item below with the correct word from the box. Use each word once.

| a. **bizarre** | b. **conducive** | c. **falter** | d. **flaunt** | e. **frenzy** |
| f. **gist** | g. **hamper** | h. **paradox** | i. **repertoire** | j. **viable** |

_____ 1. Halloween offers everyone the chance to look as ___ as possible.

_____ 2. Dustin Hoffman's ___ includes both modern dramas and Shakespearean plays.

_____ 3. When a reporter asked Senator Drake a difficult question, the senator ___(e)d for a moment.

_____ 4. For snails, heat is ___ to sleep. In fact, desert snails may sleep three or four years.

_____ 5. The ___ of Kelly's essay was that school should be open only four days a week, from 8 a.m. to 6 p.m.

_____ 6. Since ordinary clothes may ___ movement, sweat suits and leotards are recommended for the exercise class.

_____ 7. This morning, the staff could not come up with a ___ plan to improve business. Every suggestion had a drawback.

_____ 8. When Chun's parents said they worried when he didn't call home, he said, "Remember that well-known ___—no news is good news."

_____ 9. I was in a ___ because I had locked my keys in the car and I was already twenty minutes late for work.

_____ 10. Lucas believed the only way he could get a date was to ___ his wealth by wearing thick gold chains and driving expensive sports cars.

NOTE: Now check your answers to these questions by turning to page 177. Going over the answers carefully will help you prepare for the next two practices, for which answers are not given.

➤ *Sentence Check 2*

Using the answer lines provided, complete each item below with **two** words from the box. Use each word once.

_____
_____ 1–2. Although Jenny chose the songs from her ___ that she knew best, she wasn't complacent° about being prepared. Afraid she would ___ the night of the concert, she practiced the songs over and over.

_____
_____ 3–4. The ___ of the lecture was that although the United States encourages free trade, some other countries ___ it.

_____ 5–6. The joking at today's staff meeting wasn't ___ to finding a way to alleviate° the town's parking problem. No one could think of a ___ plan to increase the number of parking spaces.

_____

_____ 7–8. Bob is so prone° to changing his mind that his rapid shifts of opinion sometimes make me furious. Once, in a ___ of anger, I shouted this ___: "You're always the same—always changing your mind!"

_____

_____ 9–10. My mother took me aside at the party and said, "That looks more like a strange costume than a dress. It's bad enough your clothing looks so ___, but do you have to mortify° me and ___ it in front of all my friends?"

_____

➤ Final Check: My Talented Roommate

Here is a final opportunity for you to strengthen your knowledge of the ten words. First read the following selection carefully. Then fill in each blank with a word from the box at the top of the previous page. (Context clues will help you figure out which word goes in which blank.) Use each word once.

"If you've got it, (1)_____ it!" That's the (2)_____ of Georgia's philosophy. Georgia is my dorm roommate. A dance and theater major, she is a true extrovert°—always showing off, always "on-stage." It seems she is in constant motion, going from graceful leaps down the hall to such (3)_____ acrobatics as swinging by her knees from the clothes rod in her closet. Some days Georgia performs her entire (4)_____ right in our room. The (5)_____ "less is more" doesn't apply to her on those occasions, when she delights by acting, singing, and dancing everything she's ever learned. Attracted by her talent and charisma°, an audience always gathers to watch. The lack of space in our room never seems to (6)_____ her movements. Since Georgia's shows are not very (7)_____ to good studying on my part, I join the crowd drawn by her magnetism. She is so smooth and confident that I have never seen her (8)_____. She moves easily from ballet to tap to jazz. She'll tell jokes, sing part of an opera, and perform a scene from _Romeo and Juliet_. Not knowing all the words never stops her—she simply improvises° lines as she goes along. When she finishes, her audience breaks into a (9)_____ of applause. Many drama students will probably end up in other careers, but I contend° Georgia is talented enough to build a (10)_____ career in show business.

Scores   Sentence Check 2 _____%   Final Check _____%

Enter your scores above and in the vocabulary performance chart on the inside back cover of the book.

aster-, astro-	mis-
contra-	omni-
-er, -or	pop
-gamy	rect
geo-	the, theo-

Ten Word Parts in Context

Figure out the meanings of the following ten word parts by looking *closely* and *carefully* at the context in which they appear. Then, in the space provided, write the letter of the meaning closest to that of each word part.

1 aster-, astro-

- The **aster** is a lovely flower named for its starlike shape: its petals point outward from a yellow disk.
- **Astrologers** claim to interpret the influence of the stars and planets on our lives.

__ The word part *aster-* or *astro-* means

   a. someone who does something.   b. star.   c. marriage.

2 contra-

- **Contrary** to his campaign promise, the mayor is going to raise taxes.
- **Contraceptive** pills were a revolutionary way of guarding against pregnancy when they first went on sale in the United States in 1960.

__ The word part *contra-* means

   a. all.   b. straight.   c. against.

3 -er, -or

- When the opera **singer** Enrico Caruso had his first professional pictures taken, his only shirt was in the laundry, so he draped a bedspread around his shoulders.
- American **visitors** to Canadian cities are often struck by how clean the streets are.

__ The word part *-er* or *-or* means

   a. god.   b. wrong.   c. someone who does something.

4 -gamy

- Jackson's wife was charged with **bigamy** after he learned that she hadn't divorced her first husband.
- King Mongut of Siam, whose story was told in the musical *The King and I*, practiced **polygamy**. He was reported to have had 9,000 wives.

__ The word part *-gamy* means

   a. marriage.   b. opposite.   c. god.

5 geo-

- Pierce County, North Dakota, has the distinction of being the **geographic** center of North America.
- **Geophysics** is the science of the matter and forces of the Earth, including oceans, volcanos, and earthquakes.

__ The word part *geo-* means

   a. earth.   b. people.   c. outer space.

6 mis-

- I think there must be something wrong with a child who never **misbehaves**.
- The telephone caller **misrepresented** herself. She said she was doing a survey, but she really wanted to sell me life insurance.

__ The word part *mis-* means

   a. for.   b. straight.   c. badly.

7 omni-

- For many years, the mobs seemed **omnipotent**. However, once the government began convicting gangsters, the mobs lost their all-powerful image.
- Some dinosaurs ate only plants, and others ate only meat. Still others, **omnivorous** dinosaurs, ate all kinds of food.

__ The word part *omni-* means   a. right.   b. all.   c. wrong.

8 pop

- In 1770, the United States was not very **populous**. Only about two million people lived here then.
- In order to **populate** the West, the government gave free land to people who would build on it.

__ The word part *pop* means   a. people.   b. everywhere.   c. opposite.

9 rect

- Whenever I play Monopoly, I manage to pick the card that reads, "Go **directly** to jail. Do not pass Go. Do not collect $200."
- "Suck in those stomachs!" yelled the coach. "Pull back those shoulders, and stand **erect**!"

__ The word part *rect* means   a. opposite.   b. straight.   c. wrong.

10 the, theo-

- **Monotheism** is the belief there there is only one God.
- **Theology** is the study of the nature of God and religious truth.

__ The word part *the* or *theo-* means   a. god.   b. everywhere.   c. for.

Matching Word Parts with Definitions

Following are definitions of the ten word parts. Clearly write or print each word part next to its definition. The sentences above and on the previous page will help you decide on the meaning of each word part.

1. _____   Wrong; badly

2. _____   Straight

3. _____   Star, outer space

4. _____   People

5. _____   Someone who (does something)

6. _____   Earth; geography

7. _____   A god or God

8. _____   All; everywhere

9. _____   Marriage

10. _____   Against; contrasting; opposite

CAUTION: Do not go any further until you are sure the above answers are correct. Then you can use the definitions to help you in the following practices. Your goal is eventually to know the word parts well enough so that you don't need to check the definitions at all.

➤ *Sentence Check 1*

Using the answer line provided, complete each *italicized* word in the sentences below with the correct word part from the box. Use each word part once.

a. **aster-, astro-**	b. **contra-**	c. **-er, -or**	d. **-gamy**	e. **geo-**
f. **mis-**	g. **omni-**	h. **pop**	i. **rect**	j. **the, theo-**

_____ 1. Wade, a professional (*act . . .*) ___, seems to be playing a part even when he's off-stage.

_____ 2. The study of the chemical makeup of the Earth's crust is called (*. . . chemistry*) ___.

_____ 3. Poverty is (*. . . present*) ___ in large cities in India, where people beg on every street.

_____ 4. A small starlike figure called an (*. . . isk*) ___ (*) is often used in books and magazines to indicate a footnote.

_____ 5. On a movie set, the (*di . . . or*) ___ is the person who keeps everyone and everything running on course.

_____ 6. John Wesley was the eighteenth-century British (*. . . logian*) ___ who founded Methodism.

_____ 7. If I don't hang my car keys on a special hook in the kitchen as soon I walk into the house, I'll (*. . . place*) ___ them.

_____ 8. My daughter is going through a stage in which she (*. . . dicts*) ___ everything I say. If I say yes, she will certainly say no.

_____ 9. (*Mono . . .*) ___ doesn't stop people from having as many husbands or wives as they like. It only requires them to marry one at a time.

_____ 10. The few places on Earth that have not yet been (*. . . ulated*) ___ by humans probably would not appeal to many. Who wants to live on the snowcapped peak of a mountain?

NOTE: Now check your answers to these questions by turning to page 177. Going over the answers carefully will help you prepare for the next two practices, for which answers are not given.

➤ *Sentence Check 2*

Using the answer lines provided, complete each *italicized* word in the sentences below with the correct word part from the box. Use each word part once.

_____ 1–2. The kindergartners were asked to draw a (*. . . angle*) ___, but several
_____ made a (*. . . take*) ___ and drew a circle instead.

_____ 3–4. (*Pan . . . ists*) ___ believe that God is not a personality but an
_____ (*. . . present*) ___ force of nature, present throughout the universe.

_____   5–6. (*Doct . . .*) ___ Fisher was very (*. . . ular*) ___ with the townspeople
_____   because she always took the time to answer their questions and had
                            great empathy° for her patients' suffering.

_____   7–8. The two Mayfield brothers made (*. . . ry*) career decisions. One is an
_____   archaeologist who speculates° about what our past might have been
                            like. The other is an (*. . . naut*) who thinks about our future in space.

_____   9–10. In (*. . . graphy*) ___ class, we learned not only about the location and
_____   climate of various countries but also about customs. For example, in
                            some African nations, (*exo . . .*) ___, or marrying outside the tribe, is
                            not allowed and can result in expulsion° from one's native community.

➤ *Final Check:* **Fascinating Courses**

Here is a final opportunity for you to strengthen your knowledge of the ten word parts. First read the
following selection carefully. Then complete each *italicized* word in the parentheses below with a word
from the box at the top of the previous page. (Context clues will help you figure out which word part goes
in which blank.) Use each word part once.

Each semester, I like to choose one fascinating course unrelated to my major. Last fall, for

example, I took a(n) (*. . . logy*) (1)_____ course that focused on the

remarkable changes in the Earth's surface over time. Then in the spring, I took (*. . . nomy*)

(2)_____. When I looked at the stars through a telescope, I felt tiny and

insignificant in (*. . . st*) (3)_____ to the enormous sizes and distances of

outer space. This experience made me ponder° the nature of God and prompted° me to look for a

class on religion.

So this semester I'm taking a course in (*. . . logy*) (4)_____. One day we

spent three hours discussing this question: If God is (*. . . potent*) (5)_____,

then why hasn't He or She alleviated° all of humanity's suffering? We've also talked about how

much (*. . . understanding*) (6)_____ arises when people do not knowing

about each other's beliefs. This confusion hampers° the pursuit of unity in the world. For example,

I've long heard my (*minist . . .*) (7)_____ preach that we should be true

to one spouse, but I never knew that in some other religions, (*poly . . .*)

(8)_____ is quite acceptable.

If we were to take a survey of the world's (*. . . ulation*) (9)_____, many

people would probably say they look to their church for (*di . . . ion*) (10)_____

in their lives. I've learned that there's a rationale° for understanding other religions as well.

| *Scores* | Sentence Check 2 _____% | Final Check _____% |

Enter your scores above and in the vocabulary performance chart on the inside back cover of the book.

UNIT FOUR: *Review*

The box at the right lists twenty-five words from Unit Four. Using the clues at the bottom of the page, fill in these words to complete the puzzle that follows.

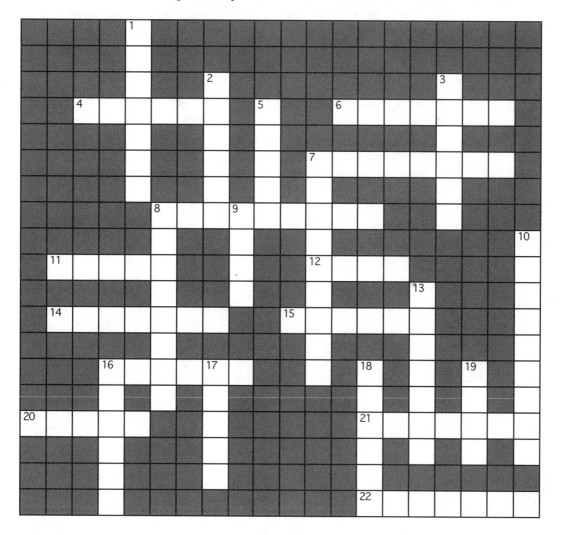

averse
benign
consensus
credible
designate
diligent
disdain
elation
empathy
endow
facade
falter
frenzy
gist
glib
latent
libel
mortify
niche
paradox
redundant
secular
shun
viable
waive

ACROSS

4. Workable; capable of being successful or effective
6. An attitude of contempt; scorn
7. Steady, determined, and careful in work
8. An opinion held by most or all involved
11. An activity or situation especially suited to a person
12. The main point or essential part of a matter; central idea
14. To humiliate or embarrass
15. The front of a building
16. To act or speak with uncertainty; hesitate
20. The publishing of false information that harms a person's reputation
21. A feeling of great joy or pride
22. The ability to share in another's feelings or thoughts

DOWN

1. A statement that seems contradictory yet may be true
2. Kindly; gentle
3. Present but hidden or inactive
5. To willingly give up; do without
7. To name to an office or duty; appoint
8. Believable
9. To keep away from; avoid consistently
10. Wordy or needlessly repetitive
13. Not directly related to religion; not spiritual; worldly
16. A wild outburst of excited feelings or actions
17. To provide with a talent or quality
18. Having a feeling of dislike or distaste for something
19. Characterized by a smooth, easy manner of speaking that often suggests insincerity

UNIT FOUR: Test 1

PART A
Choose the word that best completes each item and write it in the space provided.

_____ 1. Admiring his build in the mirror, Lee gave himself a(n) ___ smile.

    a. ominous   b. complacent   c. latent   d. menial

_____ 2. The rain ___ the work of the road construction crew.

    a. hampered   b. improvised   c. flaunted   d. designated

_____ 3. Suddenly dizzy from the heat, the speaker ___ and covered his eyes.

    a. transcended   b. simulated   c. faltered   d. waived

_____ 4. It's hard to become ___ about great music. No matter how often you hear it, you never tire of it.

    a. viable   b. haughty   c. blasé   d. secular

_____ 5. In becoming a priest, Brian certainly ___ from his plan to become a stockbroker.

    a. improvised   b. deviated   c. simulated   d. divulged

_____ 6. My boss asked me into his office in such a(n) ___ tone that I was sure he was about to fire me.

    a. benign   b. secular   c. ominous   d. menial

_____ 7. When Scott won the gymnastics competition, his parents' ___ was as great as his own joy and pride.

    a. elation   b. facade   c. niche   d. libel

_____ 8. My nephew's ___ of tricks for getting his own way includes pouting, crying, and throwing tantrums.

    a. interim   b. empathy   c. consensus   d. repertoire

_____ 9. I'm not quick with home repairs, but I'm ___. I work steadily and carefully until I get the job done.

    a. diligent   b. glib   c. haughty   d. cursory

_____ 10. Because the article made unproven accusations against the mayor, the editors wouldn't print it for fear of being sued for ___.

    a. paradox   b. expulsion   c. empathy   d. libel

_____ 11. Janet's ___ fear of marriage surfaced when Elliot proposed, and she reacted by insisting that they end their previously happy relationship.

    a. benign   b. viable   c. latent   d. menial

(Continues on next page)

_____ 12. We were amazed to learn that gentle, soft-spoken Professor Geyer writes
horror novels under the ___ of Trent Paterson.

a. interim   b. pseudonym   c. consensus   d. expulsion

_____ 13. Heather was ___ when, after diving into the pool, she bounced back up to
the surface with the top of her bathing suit around her waist.

a. redundant   b. mortified   c. viable   d. credible

PART B
Write **C** if the italicized word is used **correctly**. Write **I** if the word is used **incorrectly**.

_____ 14. When I was a child, I hated broccoli, but now I'm quite *averse* to it.

_____ 15. Stage scenery often shows the *facades* of buildings, painted on a flat surface.

_____ 16. During meditation, heart rate slows as a person enters a state of calm *frenzy.*

_____ 17 Although Dad usually *shuns* sweets, he can't resist an occasional hot fudge sundae.

_____ 18. "That bow tie *detracts* from Alan's appearance," said Paloma. "He looks strangled and gift-wrapped."

_____ 19. Because pollution is *conducive* to rainfall, there is a great deal more rain in downtown New York
City than in nearby rural Long Island.

_____ 20. Despite his great success as a singer, Robert has remained as down-to-earth and *haughty* as ever.

_____ 21. The company president was so impressed with Greta's sales record that he honored her with
expulsion.

_____ 22. My sister didn't find her career *niche* until she took a computer course and discovered her talent
for programming.

_____ 23. By careful saving, I managed to *deplete* my bank account from $80 to almost $1,200 by the
summer's end.

_____ 24. Keith is an excellent mental-health counselor who feels genuine *empathy* for those who come to
him for help.

_____ 25. I expected my interview to last only twenty minutes or so, but the interviewer did such a *cursory*
job that I was there for over an hour.

Score   (Number correct) _____   x 4 = _____ %

Enter your score above and in the vocabulary performance chart on the inside back cover of the book.

UNIT FOUR: Test 2

PART A

Complete each item with a word from the box. Use each word once.

a. **commemorate**	b. **consensus**	c. **credible**	d. **designate**	e. **divulge**
f. **flaunt**	g. **gist**	h. **improvise**	i. **interim**	j. **paradox**
k. **secular**	l. **simulate**	m.**viable**		

_____ 1. It's a(n) ___ that we can sometimes be more generous by giving less.

_____ 2. Authors often state the ___ of an article in the introductory paragraph.

_____ 3. Alonso ___s his good voice by singing louder than anyone else in the choir.

_____ 4. More and more nuns are wearing ___ clothes rather than traditional religious dress.

_____ 5. On Presidents' Day, the nation ___s George Washington and Abraham Lincoln.

_____ 6. I think it's selfish of Dolly not to ___ the secret recipe for her wonderful salad dressing.

_____ 7. Films that ___ the experience of riding on a roller coaster give me a genuine feeling of nausea.

_____ 8. I don't mind speaking before a group if I have time to prepare, but I'd be scared to death if I had to ___ a speech on the spot.

_____ 9. The only ___ plan for making enough money to keep up the payments on the house is to rent out some of its rooms.

_____ 10. Although the businessman at first seemed to be a ___ witness, the police started doubting him once he began to change the details of his story.

_____ 11. The ___ among the city's sportswriters is that Bridgewater High will win the basketball championship this year.

_____ 12. When the church's pastor resigned, a retired minister stepped in for the ___ until a permanent replacement was found.

_____ 13. The boys ___(e)d my little brother the treasurer of their tree-house club because he's the only one who receives a regular allowance.

(Continues on next page)

PART B
Write **C** if the italicized word is used **correctly**. Write **I** if the word is used **incorrectly**.

_____ 14. Sharon is *endowed* with the gift of photographic memory.

_____ 15. I admire Frank's vivid, crisp, and *redundant* writing.

_____ 16. In a democracy, it's important for people to *waive* their right to vote.

_____ 17. The woods near our house *comprise* oak, maple, and beech trees.

_____ 18. This morning, Velma ate a *bizarre* breakfast of orange juice, cereal, and coffee.

_____ 19. In my nightmare, the evil monster's *benign* eyes frightened me to death.

_____ 20. The TV contract will be *nullified* if the star misses any more rehearsals.

_____ 21. Wayne has *transcended* his usual good grades by failing three out of his four classes this semester.

_____ 22. Because *menial* tasks require little thought, I was able to plan some of my essay while cleaning my apartment yesterday.

_____ 23. The *glib* street salesman smoothly claimed that the "gold" watch was just my style and that I'd find no better bargain anywhere else.

_____ 24. After working in a hospital one summer, Andy has great *disdain* for the hard-working nurses he feels serve the patients so well.

_____ 25. The host's famous sister remained in her room for most of the party, although she did *condescend* to come downstairs and say good night to the other guests before they left.

Score (Number correct) _____ x 4 = _____ %

Enter your score above and in the vocabulary performance chart on the inside back cover of the book.

UNIT FOUR: Test 3

PART A
Complete each sentence in a way that clearly shows you understand the meaning of the **boldfaced** word. Take a minute to plan your answer before you write.

Example: Sam **flaunted** his new convertible by *driving it back and forth past the school with its top down* .

1. My favorite **secular** holiday is _____

   _____.

2. An author might use a **pseudonym** because _____

   _____.

3. A stiff arm **hampers** _____

   _____.

4. My father showed his **elation** at the news by _____

   _____.

5. The children are so **blasé** about fireworks that _____

   _____.

6. In our office, the secretary's job includes such **menial** tasks as _____

   _____.

7. I find it **detracts** from a restaurant meal when _____

   _____.

8. Lamont is **averse** to city life because _____

   _____.

9. One of the most **bizarre** sights I've ever seen on campus is _____

   _____.

10. I was **mortified** when _____

    _____.

(Continues on next page)

PART B

After each **boldfaced** word are a *synonym* (a word that means the same as the boldfaced word), an *antonym* (a word that means the opposite of the boldfaced word), and a word that is neither. On the answer line, write the letter of the word that is the antonym.

	Example: __b__ divulge	a. reveal	b. conceal	c. defend
____	11. **haughty**	a. proud	b. humble	c. tall
____	12. **disdain**	a. loss	b. contempt	c. admiration
____	13. **benign**	a. cruel	b. broken	c. kindly
____	14. **shun**	a. owe	b. seek	c. avoid
____	15. **facade**	a. back	b. light	c. front

PART C

Use five of the following ten words in sentences. Make it clear that you know the meaning of the word you use. Feel free to use the past tense or plural form of a word.

a. **condescend**	b. **consensus**	c. **deplete**	d. **deviate**	e. **diligent**
f. **empathy**	g. **gist**	h. **interim**	i. **niche**	j. **waive**

16. _____

_____

17. _____

_____

18. _____

_____

19. _____

_____

20. _____

_____

Score (Number correct) _____ x 5 = _____%

UNIT FOUR: Test 4 (Word Parts)

PART A
Listed in the left-hand column below are ten common word parts, along with words in which the parts are used. In each blank, write in the letter of the correct definition on the right.

Word Parts	Examples	Definitions
____ 1. **aster-, astro-**	aster, astrologer	a. Someone who (does something)
____ 2. **contra-**	contrary, contraceptive	b. Star, outer space
____ 3. **-er, -or**	singer, visitor	c. All; everywhere
____ 4. **-gamy**	bigamy, polygamy	d. Straight
____ 5. **geo-**	geographic, geophysics	e. A god or God
____ 6. **mis-**	misbehave, misrepresent	f. Against; contrasting; opposite
____ 7. **omni-**	omnipotent, omnivorous	g. Marriage
____ 8. **pop**	populous, populate	h. Earth
____ 9. **rect**	directly, erect	i. People
____ 10. **the, theo-**	monotheism, theology	j. Wrong; badly

PART B
Using the answer line provided, complete each *italicized* word in the sentences below with the correct word part from the box. Not every word part will be used.

a. **aster-**	b. **contra-**	c. **-er**	d. **-gamy**	e. **geo-**
f. **mis-**	g. **omni-**	h. **pop**	i. **rect**	j. **theo-**

_____ 11. Vanilla ice cream is even more (. . . *ular*) ___ among Americans than chocolate is.

_____ 12. (. . . *ry*) ___ to what many suppose, Shakespeare made his living by acting as well as writing.

_____ 13. Circling the sun between the paths of Mars and Jupiter are thousands of (. . . *oids*) ___, or small planets.

_____ 14. In a society with twice as many women as men, or twice as many men as women, (*bi* . . .) ___ would be practical.

_____ 15. An interesting (. . . *graphic*) ___ fact is that Mount Everest, the highest mountain in the world, has grown a foot taller over the last century.

(Continues on next page)

PART C
Use your knowledge of word parts to determine the meaning of the **boldfaced** words. On the answer line, write the letter of each meaning.

_____ 16. Mr. Nolan is a man of many **misdeeds**.

     a. religious feelings   b. girlfriends   c. immoral acts

_____ 17. Houses are usually **rectilinear**; that is, they are characterized by

     a. opposing forces.   b. straight lines.   c. great cost.

_____ 18. There will be many **exhibitors** at the state fair this year.

     a. farm exhibits   b. people who exhibit   c. exhibit fees

_____ 19. Throughout history, a common form of government has been **theocracy**, in which the government is considered to be based on

     a. laws voted on by everyone.   b. immoral laws.   c. religious authority.

_____ 20. There's too much knowledge in the world today for any one person to claim **omniscience**.

     a. knowledge of biology   b. complete knowledge   c. partial knowledge

Score   (Number correct) _____ x 5 = _____%

Enter your score above and in the vocabulary performance chart on the inside back cover of the book.

Unit Five

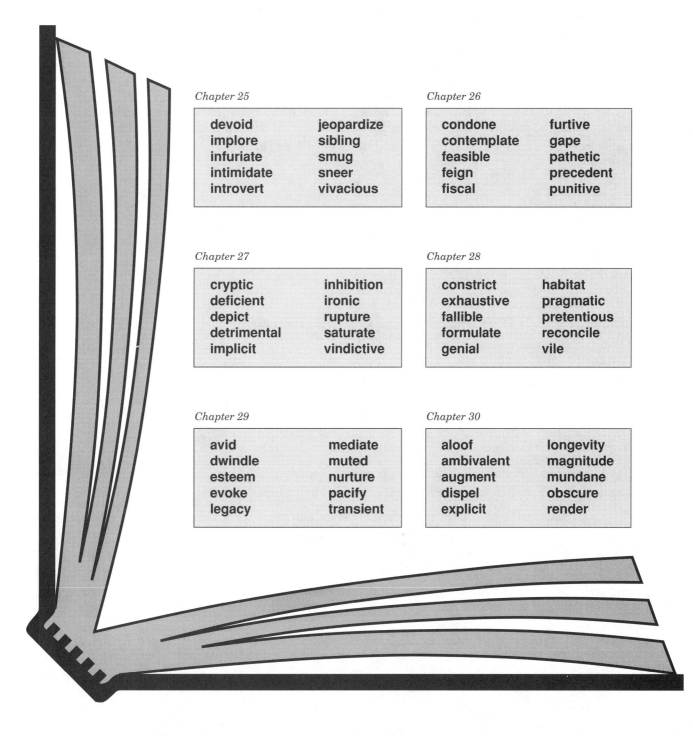

Chapter 25

devoid	jeopardize
implore	sibling
infuriate	smug
intimidate	sneer
introvert	vivacious

Chapter 26

condone	furtive
contemplate	gape
feasible	pathetic
feign	precedent
fiscal	punitive

Chapter 27

cryptic	inhibition
deficient	ironic
depict	rupture
detrimental	saturate
implicit	vindictive

Chapter 28

constrict	habitat
exhaustive	pragmatic
fallible	pretentious
formulate	reconcile
genial	vile

Chapter 29

avid	mediate
dwindle	muted
esteem	nurture
evoke	pacify
legacy	transient

Chapter 30

aloof	longevity
ambivalent	magnitude
augment	mundane
dispel	obscure
explicit	render

devoid	jeopardize
implore	sibling
infuriate	smug
intimidate	sneer
introvert	vivacious

Ten Words in Context

In the space provided, write the letter of the meaning closest to that of each **boldfaced** word. Use the context of the sentences to help you figure out each word's meaning.

1 devoid
(dǐ-void′)
-adjective

- The French fries were so thin, dry, and **devoid** of taste that they seemed like splinters of wood.
- Sometimes Carl is totally **devoid** of common sense. Once he went on vacation leaving his front door unlocked and the newspaper delivery service uncanceled.

___ *Devoid of* means   a. without.   b. equal to.   c. possessing.

2 implore
(ǐm-plôr′)
-verb

- Please hide those Hershey bars, and don't tell me where they are no matter how much I **implore** you.
- The princess **implored** the evil magician to spare the handsome prince's life.

___ *Implore* means   a. to educate.   b. to deny.   c. to urge.

3 infuriate
(ǐn-fyoor′ē-āt′)
-verb

- Peter so **infuriated** Sheila that she slammed down the phone while he was still talking.
- At the grocery store, it **infuriates** me when people with a cartload of food get in the express line.

___ *Infuriate* means   a. to anger.   b. to encourage.   c. to frighten.

4 intimidate
(ǐn-tǐm′ə-dāt′)
-verb

- Will's huge size **intimidates** strangers, but anyone who knows him realizes that he's a very gentle man.
- Public speaking so **intimidates** Charlene that she would rather write four term papers than give a single oral report.

___ *Intimidate* means   a. to calm.   b. to scare.   c. to annoy.

5 introvert
(ǐn′trə-vûrt′)
-noun

- Pearl is a very outgoing person, but her boyfriend Larry is such an **introvert** that he seldom socializes at all.
- It could be difficult for an **introvert** to succeed in sales, which involves considerable contact with the public.

___ *Introvert* means   a. a conceited person.   b. a shy person.   c. a busy person.

6 jeopardize
(jěp′ər-dīz′)
-verb

- Molly is so clumsy that she **jeopardizes** every fragile item she touches. Whatever she picks up is liable to get broken.
- Pregnant women who take drugs **jeopardize** their babies' health.

___ *Jeopardize* means   a. to play with.   b. to take into account.   c. to put in danger.

7 sibling
(sĭb′lĭng)
-*noun*

- Do you think twins are more similar in personality than other **siblings**?
- It's hard enough for children to move to foster homes; it's even worse when **siblings** have to be separated.

___ *Sibling* means
  a. a brother or sister.   b. a cousin.   c. a friend.

8 smug
(smŭg)
-*adjective*

- Self-confidence is a virtue, but being **smug** is carrying self-confidence too far.
- I avoid **smug** people. They are very generous in judging themselves while viewing others narrow-mindedly.

___ *Smug* means
  a. full of life.   b. dishonest.   c. too self-satisfied.

9 sneer
(snēr)
-*verb*

- Janice is terrific with little children. No matter how silly their questions are, she never **sneers** at them.
- Instead of encouraging us when we make a mistake, our biology teacher **sneers** at us with a scornful smile or a put-down.

___ *Sneer at* means
  a. to leave.   b. to mock.   c. to ignore.

10 vivacious
(vĭ-vā′shəs)
-*adjective*

- My father is such a **vivacious** host that he makes his guests feel bright and lively too.
- Between scenes, the actors might appear tired and dull, but they become **vivacious** once the camera is on.

___ *Vivacious* means
  a. good-looking.   b. peppy.   c. irritable.

Matching Words with Definitions

Following are definitions of the ten words. Clearly write or print each word next to its definition. The sentences above and on the previous page will help you decide on the meaning of each word.

1. _____ A shy or inwardly directed person

2. _____ Completely lacking

3. _____ A sister or brother

4. _____ To anger greatly

5. _____ Lively; full of life and enthusiasm

6. _____ To beg; plead

7. _____ To show or express contempt or ridicule

8. _____ To make timid or afraid; frighten

9. _____ Overly pleased with one's own cleverness, goodness, etc.; too self-satisfied

10. _____ To endanger; put at risk of loss or injury

CAUTION: Do not go any further until you are sure the above answers are correct. Then you can use the definitions to help you in the following practices. Your goal is eventually to know the words well enough so that you don't need to check the definitions at all.

➤ *Sentence Check 1*

Using the answer line provided, complete each item below with the correct word from the box. Use each word once.

a. **devoid**	b. **implore**	c. **infuriate**	d. **intimidate**	e. **introvert**
f. **jeopardize**	g. **sibling**	h. **smug**	i. **sneer**	j. **vivacious**

_____ 1. You may call Linda charming and ___, but to me, she's just an irritating chatterbox.

_____ 2. I ___ you not to mention the VCR to Hakim. I want to surprise him with it.

_____ 3. The genius who invents a chocolate ice cream that's ___ of calories should win a medal.

_____ 4. Working with computers all day suits my brother. He's too much of a(n) ___ to enjoy working much with other people.

_____ 5. I don't understand why Eileen enjoys activities that ___ her life, like skydiving and mountain climbing.

_____ 6. Christmas is the one time of year when my grandparents, parents, and three ___s are able to get together.

_____ 7. There used to be little that angered my father, but since he got laid off, it seems that everything we kids do ___s him.

_____ 8. When he found Art selling drugs near the elementary school, the police officer ___(e)d at him, snarling, "You scum."

_____ 9. It's better to get children's cooperation by setting shared goals than by trying to ___ them with threats of punishment.

_____ 10. Jenny would be more popular if she didn't get that ___ look on her face every time she answers the teacher's question correctly.

NOTE: Now check your answers to these questions by turning to page 177. Going over the answers carefully will help you prepare for the next two practices, for which answers are not given.

➤ *Sentence Check 2*

Using the answer lines provided, complete each item below with **two** words from the box. Use each word once.

_____
_____ 1–2. The people I love best can ___ me the most. No one can make me as angry as my parents and ___s can. I guess close relationships are conducive° to strong feelings, both positive and negative.

_____
_____ 3–4. It won't do any good to ___ me to help you with your term paper. Since you delayed working on it for so long, I'm ___ of sympathy. I don't mean to gloat°, but why should I give up my evening when I was diligent° about doing my paper on time and you were partying all week?

_____ 5–6. I think Marvin only pretends to look down on the weight lifters in school. He ___s at them to hide the fact that they ___ him.

_____

_____ 7–8. Among her close friends, my sister is known as a really ___ woman, energetic and bubbly. But she often seems like a(n) ___ around people she doesn't know well.

_____

_____ 9–10. I told Seth he would ___ his chances of getting a date for the dance if he waited until the last minute to ask someone. But he was ___ enough to think that any girl he asked would be happy to break a date with someone else to go to the dance with him.

_____

➤ _Final Check:_ Cal and His Sisters

Here is a final opportunity for you to strengthen your knowledge of the ten words. First read the following selection carefully. Then fill in each blank with a word from the box at the top of the previous page. (Context clues will help you figure out which word goes in which blank.) Use each word once.

I've never met (1)_____s who are less alike than Cal and his sisters,

Margo and Tina. Cal is smart, but he isn't very popular. He thinks he's right about everything and

isn't afraid to say so. It's hard to like someone who is so (2)_____ about his

intelligence. It is especially hard for Margo and Tina at report-card time, when Cal flaunts° his

straight A's. On the other hand, everybody loves Margo, a true extrovert° who's the life of any

party. She's so (3)_____ that she's always fun to be with, and her

charisma° always draws people to her, even complete strangers. Tina is just the opposite. She is

such a(n) (4)_____ that you hardly know she's around. When she does

speak up to voice an opinion, Cal (5)_____s at her ideas, dismissing them

as "ridiculous." Of course, such comments devastate° Tina, often bringing her to tears. Margo is

too confident for Cal to (6)_____. Even when they were little, he couldn't

frighten her. But it (7)_____s her when he is mean to Tina. She's afraid he

will (8)_____ Tina's chance of ever gaining confidence. Margo constantly

(9)_____s Cal to be more benevolent° toward Tina, but he seems

(10)_____ of sympathy for his shy sister.

_____
| **Scores**   Sentence Check 2 _____%   Final Check _____% |
_____

Enter your scores above and in the vocabulary performance chart on the inside back cover of the book.

CHAPTER

26

condone	furtive
contemplate	gape
feasible	pathetic
feign	precedent
fiscal	punitive

Ten Words in Context

In the space provided, write the letter of the meaning closest to that of each **boldfaced** word. Use the context of the sentences to help you figure out each word's meaning.

1 condone
(kən-dōn')
-verb

- I cannot **condone** Barb's smoking in public It threatens other people's health.
- I can overlook it when you're five minutes late. But how can I **condone** your walking in to work an hour late?

___ *Condone* means   a. to excuse.   b. to recall.   c. to punish.

2 contemplate
(kŏn'təm-plāt')
-verb

- Because Ben hadn't studied for the test, he **contemplated** cheating. He quickly realized, however, that the eagle-eyed teacher would spot him.
- Whenever Anne's husband drank too much, she would **contemplate** divorce, but then she would feel guilty for thinking about leaving a sick man.

___ *Contemplate* means   a. to consider.   b. to pretend.   c. to avoid.

3 feasible
(fē'zə-bəl)
-adjective

- It isn't **feasible** for me to work full time and keep the house clean unless my spouse shares the cleaning chores.
- Marilyn told her supervisor, "It just isn't **feasible** for this staff to do the work of the two people who were fired. You need to hire more people."

___ *Feasible* means   a. wrong.   b. legal.   c. possible.

4 feign
(fān)
-verb

- Since I had heard about my surprise party, I had to **feign** shock when everyone yelled, "Surprise!"
- You can **feign** a head cold by pretending you're too stuffed up to pronounce an *l*, *n*, or *m*. Try it by saying, "I have a code id by dose."

___ *Feign* means   a. to wish for.   b. to prove.   c. to fake.

5 fiscal
(fĭs'kəl)
-adjective

- The gift shop closed because of **fiscal** problems. It simply didn't make enough money to cover costs.
- Some states have passed laws allowing child-support payments to be taken directly from the paychecks of divorced parents who ignore their **fiscal** responsibility to their children.

___ *Fiscal* means   a. emotional.   b. financial.   c. unfair.

6 furtive
(fûr'tĭv)
-adjective

- The detective noticed the **furtive** movement of the thief's hand toward a man's pocket.
- According to experts, teenagers who are **furtive** about where they are going and with whom may be involved with drugs.

___ *Furtive* means   a. secret.   b. dependable.   c. serious.

7 gape
(gāp)
-verb

- Everyone stopped to **gape** at the odd-looking sculpture in front of the library.
- Because drivers slowed down to **gape** at an accident in the southbound lanes, northbound traffic was backed up for miles.

___ *Gape* means   a. to yell.   b. to appreciate.   c. to stare.

8 pathetic
(pə-thĕt′ĭk)
-adjective

- That plumber's work was **pathetic**. Not only does the faucet still drip, but now the pipe is leaking.
- Health care in some areas of the world is **pathetic**. People are dying of diseases that are easily treatable with modern medicine.

___ *Pathetic* means   a. ordinary.   b. miserable.   c. expensive.

9 precedent
(prĕs′ĭ-dĕnt)
-noun

- When Jean's employer gave her three months off after her baby was born, a **precedent** was set for any other woman in the firm who became pregnant.
- To set a **precedent**, the teacher gave the student who stole an exam an F for the entire course. "Others will think twice before they do the same," he explained.

___ *Precedent* means   a. a question.   b. a delay.   c. a model.

10 punitive
(pyōō′nĭ-tĭv)
-adjective

- Judge Starn is especially **punitive** with drunken drivers, giving every one of them a jail term.
- Many parents find that reward is a better basis for teaching children than **punitive** action is.

___ *Punitive* means   a. punishing.   b. forgiving.   c. uneven.

Matching Words with Definitions

Following are definitions of the ten words. Clearly write or print each word next to its definition. The sentences above and on the previous page will help you decide on the meaning of each word.

1. _____   Possible; able to be done

2. _____   Done or behaving so as not to be noticed; secret; sneaky

3. _____   To stare in wonder or amazement, often with one's mouth wide open

4. _____   Anything that may serve as an example in dealing with later similar circumstances

5. _____   To forgive or overlook

6. _____   Giving or involving punishment; punishing

7. _____   Financial

8. _____   To think about seriously

9. _____   Pitifully inadequate or unsuccessful

10. _____   To pretend; give a false show of

CAUTION: Do not go any further until you are sure the above answers are correct. Then you can use the definitions to help you in the following practices. Your goal is eventually to know the words well enough so that you don't need to check the definitions at all.

➤ *Sentence Check 1*

Using the answer line provided, complete each item below with the correct word from the box. Use each word once.

a. condone	b. contemplate	c. feasible	d. feign	e. fiscal
f. furtive	g. gape	h. pathetic	i. precedent	j. punitive

_____ 1. Handicapped people don't like others to ___ at them. Instead of a stare, a simple smile would be appreciated.

_____ 2. From time to time, I ___ attending business school, but so far I've made no firm decision.

_____ 3. Lawyers can strengthen a case by finding a useful ___ among previous similar cases.

_____ 4. It's not ___ for me to attend two weddings in the same afternoon, so I'll have to choose between them.

_____ 5. The principal does not ___ hitting students. He believes that every problem has a nonviolent solution.

_____ 6. At the low-cost clinic, Clayton had to give evidence of his ___ situation, such as a tax form or current pay stub, before he could receive treatment.

_____ 7. The people on the elevator didn't want to stare at the patch on my eye, but several took ___ glances.

_____ 8. Mr. Hall's living conditions were ___. There was no heat or electricity in his apartment, and the walls were crumbling.

_____ 9. When I gave my oral report in class, I tried to ___ confidence, but my shaking legs revealed my nervousness.

_____ 10. My mother wasn't usually ___, but one day I pushed her too far, and she said, "If you do that one more time, I will send you to your room for the rest of your adolescence."

NOTE: Now check your answers to these questions by turning to page 177. Going over the answers carefully will help you prepare for the next two practices, for which answers are not given.

➤ *Sentence Check 2*

Using the answer lines provided, complete each item below with **two** words from the box. Use each word once.

_____
_____ 1–2. "Would it be ___ for us to buy a new copy machine?" I asked at the office budget meeting. My boss replied, "Unfortunately, our ___ situation too tight. That purchase would create a deficit° in our budget."

_____
_____ 3–4. Some parents take only ___ measures when children misbehave. They never take time to ___ the benefits of a gentler approach. However, benign° encouragement is often more effective than punishment.

_____   5–6. Several passersby stopped to ___ at the homeless man and his ___
_____   shelter, made of cardboard and a torn blanket. The poignant° sight
                               moved one woman to go to a restaurant and buy a meal for the man.

_____   7–8. The fourth-grade teacher said, "I will not ___ any ___ behavior in my
_____   class. Rita, please read out loud the note you secretly passed to Ellen."

_____   9–10. The ___ was set many years ago: When the winner of a beauty contest
_____   is announced, the runner-up ___s happiness for the winner, despite the
                                fact that she is quite devoid° of happiness at the moment.

➤ _Final Check:_ **Shoplifter**

Here is a final opportunity for you to strengthen your knowledge of the ten words. First read the following selection carefully. Then fill in each blank with a word from the box at the top of the previous page. (Context clues will help you figure out which word goes in which blank.) Use each word once.

Valerie took a (1)_____ glance around her. When it seemed that no one was watching, she stuffed a blue shirt into the bottom of her purse and darted out of the women's department. She walked slowly around the shoe department for a while and then left the store. "Stop! You! Stop!" shouted a guard who seemed to appear from nowhere. Then another man in street clothes grabbed her purse and pulled out the shirt.

"But . . . but . . . It's not mine. I don't know how it got there," Valerie cried.

The two men just looked at each other and laughed at the blatant° lie. The guard said, "That's what all shoplifters say. People steal without taking time to (2)_____ the possible results. Then when they're caught, they loudly (3)_____ innocence."

As the guard began to phone the police, Valerie implored° the men, "Please don't press charges. Please. This is the first time I've ever done anything like this, and I'll never do it again."

The men laughed again. "Your argument is (4)_____," the man in street clothes said. "It's everyone's first time. Our store has a policy on shoplifters: It's mandatory° for us to press charges, even if it's the first offense. We can't set a bad (5)_____ by letting a shoplifter go, as if we (6)_____(e)d such crimes."

"That's right," said the guard. "Shoplifting is all too prevalent° in our store. This shirt costs only twenty dollars, but the twenties add up. Our (7)_____ officer has reported a loss of about $150,000 worth of merchandise to shoplifters last year. So it simply isn't (8)_____ to let you walk away. Unfortunately, we have no choice but to take (9)_____ action."

Soon Valerie was led to the police car. She covered her face as other shoppers stopped to (10)_____ at the lovely young woman, an unlikely-looking criminal.

Scores	Sentence Check 2 _____%	Final Check _____%

Enter your scores above and in the vocabulary performance chart on the inside back cover of the book.

cryptic	inhibition
deficient	ironic
depict	rupture
detrimental	saturate
implicit	vindictive

Ten Words in Context

In the space provided, write the letter of the meaning closest to that of each **boldfaced** word. Use the context of the sentences to help you figure out each word's meaning.

1 cryptic
(krĭp′tĭk)
-adjective

- I begged Tony to tell me the big secret, but he always gave the same **cryptic** reply: "It's a green world, my friend."
- Next to the dead woman's body was a **cryptic** note that said, "Not now."

__ *Cryptic* means   a. cruel.   b. mystifying.   c. humorous.

2 deficient
(dĭ-fĭsh′ənt)
-adjective

- When people have too little iron in their blood, it sometimes means that their diet is also **deficient** in iron.
- Gil's manners are **deficient**. For example, I've never heard him thank anyone for anything.

__ *Deficient* means   a. insufficient.   b. sensitive.   c. increasing.

3 depict
(dĭ-pĭkt′)
-verb

- The painting **depicts** a typical nineteenth-century summer day in the park.
- Harriet Beecher Stowe's novel *Uncle Tom's Cabin* **depicted** the cruelty of slavery so forcefully that the book helped to begin the Civil War.

__ *Depict* means   a. to hide.   b. to show.   c. to predict.

4 detrimental
(dĕ′trə-mĕn′təl)
-adjective

- Do you think all television is **detrimental** to children, or are some programs a positive influence on them?
- The gases from automobiles and factories have been so **detrimental** to the environment that some of the damage may be permanent.

__ *Detrimental* means   a. useful.   b. new.   c. damaging.

5 implicit
(ĭm-plĭs′ĭt)
-adjective

- When the gangster growled, "I'm sure you want your family to stay healthy," Harris understood the **implicit** threat.
- Although it's never been said, there's an **implicit** understanding that Carla will be promoted when Earl finally retires.

__ *Implicit* means   a. playful.   b. modern.   c. unspoken.

6 inhibition
(ĭn′hə-bĭsh′ən)
-noun

- A two-year-old has no **inhibitions** about running around naked.
- Sarah's family is openly affectionate, with no **inhibitions** about hugging or kissing in public.

__ *Inhibition* means   a. an inner block.   b. a habit.   c. a purpose.

7 ironic
(ī-rŏn′ĭk)
-adjective

- It's **ironic** that Loretta is such a strict mother, because she was certainly wild in her youth.
- "The Gift of the Magi" is a short story with an **ironic** twist: A woman sells her long hair to buy a chain for her husband's watch, while her husband sells his watch to buy ornaments for her hair.

___ *Ironic* means   a. unexpected.   b. inadequate.   c. reasonable.

8 rupture
(rŭp′chər)
-verb

- If the dam were to **rupture**, the town would disappear under many feet of water.
- The bulge in the baby's stomach was caused by a muscle wall that **ruptured** and would have to be repaired.

___ *Rupture* means   a. to heal.   b. to exist.   c. to come apart.

9 saturate
(săch′ə-rāt′)
-verb

- Most people like their cereal crunchy, but Teresa lets hers sit until the milk has **saturated** every piece.
- Studying history for three hours **saturated** my brain—I couldn't have absorbed one more bit of information.

___ *Saturate* means   a. to protect.   b. to empty.   c. to fill.

10 vindictive
(vĭn-dĭk′tĭv)
-adjective

- If a woman refuses to date Leon, he becomes **vindictive**. One way he takes revenge is to insult the woman in public.
- After she was given two weeks' notice, the **vindictive** employee intentionally jumbled the company's files.

___ *Vindictive* means   a. sympathetic.   b. spiteful.   c. puzzling.

Matching Words with Definitions

Following are definitions of the ten words. Clearly write or print each word next to its definition. The sentences above and on the previous page will help you decide on the meaning of each word.

1. _____ A holding back or blocking of some action, feeling, or thought

2. _____ Having a vague or hidden meaning; puzzling

3. _____ Suggested but not directly expressed; unstated, but able to be understood

4. _____ Inclined to seek revenge; vengeful

5. _____ To represent in pictures or words; describe

6. _____ To burst or break apart

7. _____ Lacking something essential; inadequate

8. _____ To soak or fill as much as possible

9. _____ Harmful

10. _____ Opposite to what might be expected

CAUTION: Do not go any further until you are sure the above answers are correct. Then you can use the definitions to help you in the following practices. Your goal is eventually to know the words well enough so that you don't need to check the definitions at all.

➣ *Sentence Check 1*

Using the answer line provided, complete each item below with the correct word from the box. Use each word once.

a. **cryptic**	b. **deficient**	c. **depict**	d. **detrimental**	e. **implicit**
f. **inhibition**	g. **ironic**	h. **rupture**	i. **saturate**	j. **vindictive**

_____ 1. A person can be intelligent and yet be ___ in common sense.

_____ 2. When the pressure in the gas pipe became too great, the pipe ___(e)d.

_____ 3. Isn't it ___ that the richest man in town won the million-dollar lottery?

_____ 4. Even something as healthful as vitamins can be ___ to your health when taken in very large amounts.

_____ 5. Becky's customary lack of ___ was evident the day she came to class barefoot.

_____ 6. In the novel *Oliver Twist*, Charles Dickens ___s life in an English orphanage as truly pitiful.

_____ 7. Street gangs are ___. If anyone harms a member of a gang, the other members will take full revenge.

_____ 8. The fifth-grade assignment was written in double talk. Everyone laughed as the students tried to make out the teacher's ___ message.

_____ 9. The aroma of Gretchen's perfume so ___(e)d the air in the car that Steve coughed and rolled down a window.

_____ 10. While it's not written in teachers' contracts, there is a(n) ___ understanding that teachers will spend time preparing lessons and responding to students' work.

NOTE: Now check your answers to these questions by turning to page 177. Going over the answers carefully will help you prepare for the next two practices, for which answers are not given.

➣ *Sentence Check 2*

Using the answer lines provided, complete each item below with **two** words from the box. Use each word once.

_____
_____ 1–2. Water-balloon fights are fun until a balloon ___s against your clothes, and they get ___(e)d with cold water.

_____
_____ 3–4. Most viewers find the painting, with its dozens of dots on a white background, to be ___. However, it's possible to figure out what the painting ___s by mentally connecting the dots.

_____ 5–6. I feel it's a waste of energy to retaliate° when someone has injured me, but my sister is always trying to get even with people. Her ___ attitude is ___ to her relationships with family and friends.

_____   7–8. It's ___ that the book _Live Simply on Little Money_ has made the author
_____   wealthy, since a(n) ___ message of the book is that the author himself
                                    requires little money.

_____   9–10. Gerry feels people should "lose their ___s" and do whatever they feel
_____   like doing, but I think people who are altogether ___ in self-control
                                    have poor manners.

➤ _Final Check:_ **A Nutty Newspaper Office**

Here is a final opportunity for you to strengthen your knowledge of the ten words. First read the following
selection carefully. Then fill in each blank with a word from the box at the top of the previous page.
(Context clues will help you figure out which word goes in which blank.) Use each word once.

My therapist says it's (1)_____ to my mental health to keep my

thoughts bottled up inside of me, so I'll drop all (2)_____s and tell you

about the newspaper office where I work.

Let me describe my editor first. It's sort of (3)_____ that Ed is in

communications because I've never met anyone harder to talk to. Although he's a proponent° of

clear expression, Ed communicates as unclearly as anyone I know. For example, if I say, "How are

you doing today, Ed?" he'll give me some (4)_____ response such as "The

tidal pools of time are catching up with me." I used to think there might be some deep wisdom

(5)_____ in Ed's statements, but now I just think he's a little bizarre°.

Then there's Seymour, our sportswriter. Seymour is perfectly normal except that he has

unexplained fits of crying two or three times a week. In the middle of a conversation about the

baseball playoffs or the next heavyweight title fight, Seymour suddenly goes into a frenzy° of

crying and (6)_____s handfuls of Kleenex with his tears.

Now, I don't mean to (7)_____ our office as a totally depressing place.

It is not entirely (8)_____ in excitement, but even our excitement is a little

weird. It is usually provided by Jan, a (9)_____ typesetter who, whenever she

feels injured by Ed, takes revenge in some horrible but entertaining way. One of her favorite types

of reprisal° is sneaking fictional items about him into the society column. I'll never forget the time

Ed was in the hospital after his appendix (10)_____(e)d. He almost broke

his stitches when he read that he was taking a vacation at a nudist colony. The article infuriated°

him so that he probably would have sued the newspaper for libel° if he didn't work there himself.

Scores	Sentence Check 2 _____%	Final Check _____%

constrict	habitat
exhaustive	pragmatic
fallible	pretentious
formulate	reconcile
genial	vile

Ten Words in Context

In the space provided, write the letter of the meaning closest to that of each **boldfaced** word. Use the context of the sentences to help you figure out each word's meaning.

1 constrict
(kən-strĭkt')
-verb

- The summer highway construction will **constrict** traffic by confining it to only two lanes.
- For centuries in China, girls' feet were **constricted** with binding to keep them from growing to normal size. Women's feet were considered most attractive if they were under four inches long.

___ *Constrict* means   a. to expand.   b. to repair.   c. to squeeze.

2 exhaustive
(ĭg-zô'stĭv)
-adjective

- Don't buy a used car without putting it through an **exhaustive** inspection. Check every detail, from hood to trunk.
- My teacher recommended an **exhaustive** thousand-page biography of Freud, but who has time to read such a thorough account?

___ *Exhaustive* means   a. smooth.   b. detailed.   c. narrow.

3 fallible
(făl'ə-bəl)
-adjective

- "I know we all are **fallible**," the boss told his workers. "But do you have to make so many of your mistakes on company time?"
- When they are little, kids think their parents can do no wrong, but when they become teenagers, their parents suddenly seem **fallible**.

___ *Fallible* means   a. optimistic.   b. friendly.   c. imperfect.

4 formulate
(fôr'myə-lāt')
-verb

- The author first **formulated** an outline of his plot and then began writing his mystery.
- Before stepping into his boss's office, Hank had carefully **formulated** his case for a raise.

___ *Formulate* means   a. to develop.   b. to question.   c. to accept.

5 genial
(jēn'yəl)
-adjective

- I was worried that my grandmother's treatment at the nursing home might be harsh, so I was relieved when the nurses and aides turned out to be very **genial**.
- Libby found her first dance instructor so harsh and unpleasant that she changed to a more **genial** one.

___ *Genial* means   a. good-looking.   b. practical.   c. good-natured.

6 habitat
(hăb'ĭ-tăt)
-noun

- Many people believe that wild animals should be allowed to remain in their natural **habitats** and not be captured and put in zoos.
- Mosses can live in a large variety of humid **habitats**, from very cold to very hot.

___ *Habitat* means   a. a pattern.   b. a plan.   c. a territory.

7 **pragmatic**
(prăg-măt′ĭk)
-adjective

- We always called my sister "Practical Polly" because she was the most **pragmatic** member of the family.
- When I was single, I spent most of my money on travel. Now that I have a family to support, I must spend my money in more **pragmatic** ways.

___ *Pragmatic* means   a. sensible.   b. patient.   c. pleasant.

8 **pretentious**
(prē-tĕn′shəs)
-adjective

- Dana's classmates don't like her because she's so **pretentious**. It's hard to like someone who acts as if she knows it all.
- My aunt marked her husband's grave with a large, **pretentious** monument, as though he were a member of a royal family.

___ *Pretentious* means   a. overly imaginative.   b. important-seeming.   c. cruel.

9 **reconcile**
(rĕk′ən-sīl′)
-verb

- When my grandfather died, we worked hard to **reconcile** Grandmother to the fact that he was really gone.
- After his third wreck in six months, Tony **reconciled** himself to living somewhere along a bus line and doing without a car.

___ *Reconcile to* means   a. to bring to accept.   b. to frighten about.   c. to hide from.

10 **vile**
(vīl)
-adjective

- My sister loves a certain cheese that has the **vile** odor of something that fell off a garbage truck.
- When I finally get around to cleaning out my refrigerator, I always find some **vile** moldy food at the back of a shelf.

___ *Vile* means   a. threatening.   b. natural.   c. nasty.

Matching Words with Definitions

Following are definitions of the ten words. Clearly write or print each word next to its definition. The sentences above and on the previous page will help you decide on the meaning of each word.

1. _____ To bring (oneself or someone else) to accept

2. _____ The natural environment of an animal or plant

3. _____ Making a show of excellence or importance, especially when undeserved

4. _____ Capable of making an error

5. _____ To make smaller or narrower, as by squeezing or shrinking

6. _____ Covering all possible details; complete; thorough

7. _____ Friendly, pleasant, and kindly

8. _____ Offensive to the senses, feelings, or thoughts; disgusting

9. _____ To plan or express in an orderly way

10. _____ Practical

CAUTION: Do not go any further until you are sure the above answers are correct. Then you can use the definitions to help you in the following practices. Your goal is eventually to know the words well enough so that you don't need to check the definitions at all.

➤ *Sentence Check 1*

Using the answer line provided, complete each item below with the correct word from the box. Use each word once.

a. **constrict**	b. **exhaustive**	c. **fallible**	d. **formulate**	e. **genial**
f. **habitat**	g. **pragmatic**	h. **pretentious**	i. **reconcile**	j. **vile**

_____ 1. Our cafeteria serves the world's most ___ beef stew, full of big globs of fat.

_____ 2. Why is Debra acting so unfriendly today? She's usually so ___.

_____ 3. My mother was forced to ___ herself to my independence when I moved into my own apartment.

_____ 4. Bright light ___s the pupils of our eyes, letting in less light. Darkness makes them wider, letting in more light.

_____ 5. My supervisor told me that if I wished to work on an independent project, I should first ___ a detailed plan of my idea.

_____ 6. For her term paper on orchids, Wilma did ___ research, covering every aspect of the flower's growth and marketing.

_____ 7. ___ about his intelligence, Norm tries to impress people with a lot of big words.

_____ 8. Children's stories sometimes mistakenly show penguins at the North Pole. The birds' ___ is actually near the South Pole.

_____ 9. "It would be more ___," my daughter said, "if you went to the grocery once a week for a larger order rather than going daily for just a few items."

_____ 10. When the auto mechanic said, "Well, I'm ___ like everyone else," I responded, "Yes, but your mistake almost got me flattened by a truck."

NOTE: Now check your answers to these questions by turning to page 177. Going over the answers carefully will help you prepare for the next two practices, for which answers are not given.

➤ *Sentence Check 2*

Using the answer lines provided, complete each item below with **two** words from the box. Use each word once.

_____
_____ 1–2. "You want me to be perfect, but that's impossible!" my daughter cried. "___ yourself to the fact that every one of us is ___." It wasn't until then that I realized how detrimental° my criticism had been to our relationship.

_____
_____ 3–4. Wildlife experts ___(e)d a plan to preserve what little remains of the gorilla's natural ___. Continued loss of that territory would jeopardize° the survival of the species.

_____
_____ 5–6. My roommate was not at all ___ about fiscal° matters. He would spend our household money on videotapes and ___-smelling cigars and leave us without food.

_____   7–8. When our pet python escaped, we quickly made a(n) ___ search
_____   throughout the house and grounds. We found him wrapped around our
                                  dog, about to ___ the poor mutt to death.

_____   9–10. At the sales seminar, we were taught to be ___ with customers and
_____   never to be ___, no matter how much we know. Customers like warm,
                                  amiable° salespeople, not ones who show off.

➤ *Final Check:* **Roughing It**

Here is a final opportunity for you to strengthen your knowledge of the ten words. First read the following
selection carefully. Then fill in each blank with a word from the box at the top of the previous page.
(Context clues will help you figure out which word goes in which blank.) Use each word once.

"Whose brilliant idea was this anyway?" Sara asked. "If people were intended to sleep on the

ground and cook over a fire, we wouldn't have beds and microwave ovens."

"Stop complaining," Emily said. "At least *you've* got on dry clothes. You didn't end up

walking through some (1)_____ mud because your canoe overturned. And

you didn't have a (2)_____ partner who claimed to know everything about

canoeing but actually didn't know enough to steer around a rock."

"So I made a mistake," George said. "We're all (3)_____."

"Well," Emily responded, "your mistake has lost us our tent. And our sleeping bags and

clothes are saturated° with muddy water."

Then Doug spoke up. "It's no big deal. Sara and I will lend you clothes, and you two can

squeeze into our tent."

"Squeeze is right, " said Emily. "Four in one tent will (4)_____ us so

much that we won't be able to exhale."

"It's your choice," said Doug. "Decide if you want to be in a crowded tent or sleep out in this

wild-animal (5)_____."

Sara couldn't resist adding, "If you had listened to me and were more

(6)_____ when planning for this trip, we wouldn't be in such a mess. You

would have written a(n) (7)_____ list of what we would need, from A to Z.

Then you would have (8)_____(e)d a clear plan for who would take what.

Then we wouldn't be out here with two corkscrews but no plastic to wrap our belongings in."

"Let's just stop complaining before this degenerates° into a shouting match. We should be a

little more (9)_____ with one another," said Doug. "We need to

(10)_____ ourselves to our imperfect situation and not let it detract° so

much from our vacation that we forget to have a good time."

Scores	Sentence Check 2 _____%	Final Check _____%

Enter your scores above and in the vocabulary performance chart on the inside back cover of the book.

avid	mediate
dwindle	muted
esteem	nurture
evoke	pacify
legacy	transient

Ten Words in Context

In the space provided, write the letter of the meaning closest to that of each **boldfaced** word. Use the context of the sentences to help you figure out each word's meaning.

1 avid
(ăv′ĭd)
-adjective

- Ramia, an **avid** reader, enjoys nothing more than a good science-fiction novel.
- Artie is such an **avid** sports fan that he has two televisions tuned to different sporting events so he doesn't miss any action.

___ *Avid* means   a. likable.   b. devoted.   c. helpful.

2 dwindle
(dwĭn′dəl)
-verb

- As the number of leaves on the tree **dwindled**, the number on the ground increased.
- Chewing nicotine gum helped Doreen's craving for cigarettes to **dwindle**. She smoked fewer and fewer cigarettes each day until she quit altogether.

___ *Dwindle* means   a. to make sense.   b. to drop suddenly.   c. to decrease.

3 esteem
(ĕ-stēm′)
-noun

- When Mr. Bauer retired after coaching basketball for thirty years, his admiring students gave him a gold whistle as a sign of their **esteem**.
- The critics had such **esteem** for the play that they voted it "Best Drama of the Year."

___ *Esteem* means   a. concern.   b. appreciation.   c. curiosity.

4 evoke
(ē-vōk′)
-verb

- Strangely enough, seeing my son's high-school graduation picture **evoked** memories of his infancy.
- The smells of cider and pumpkin pie **evoke** thoughts of autumn.

___ *Evoke* means   a. to bring out.   b. to shelter.   c. to follow.

5 legacy
(lĕg′ə-sē)
-noun

- Ana's great-grandfather, grandmother, and mother were all musicians. She must have inherited their **legacy** of musical talent because she's an excellent piano and guitar player.
- One of the richest **legacies** that my mother handed down to me is the love of nature. I've inherited her interests in growing flowers and in hiking.

___ *Legacy* means   a. memory.   b. high hope.   c. inherited gift.

6 mediate
(mē′dē-āt′)
-verb

- My father refused to **mediate** quarrels between my sister and me. He would say, "Settle your own fights."
- Each of the farmers claimed the stream was part of his property. Finally, they agreed to let the town council **mediate** their conflict.

___ *Mediate* means   a. to participate in.   b. to settle.   c. to observe.

7 muted
(myo͞o′təd)
-*adjective*

- When I put in my earplugs, the yelling from the next apartment becomes **muted** enough so that it no longer disturbs me.
- The artist used **muted** rather than bright colors, giving the painting a quiet, peaceful tone.

___ *Muted* means   a. soft.   b. temporary.   c. boring.

8 nurture
(nûr′chər)
-*verb*

- Although I often forget to water or feed my plants, my sister carefully **nurtures** her many ferns and violets.
- Many animals feed and protect their babies, but female fish, in general, do not **nurture** their young. The female only lays the eggs, which are guarded by the male until they hatch.

___ *Nurture* means   a. to inspect.   b. to seek out.   c. to care for.

9 pacify
(păs′ə-fī′)
-*verb*

- When I'm feeling nervous or upset, I often **pacify** myself with a soothing cup of mint tea.
- Not only did I anger Roberta by calling her boyfriend "a creep," but I failed to **pacify** her with my note of apology: "I'm sorry I called Mel a creep. It's not always wise to tell the truth."

___ *Pacify* means   a. to amuse.   b. to encourage.   c. to soothe.

10 transient
(trăn′shənt)
-*adjective*

- The drug's dangers include both permanent brain damage and **transient** side effects, such as temporarily blurred vision.
- Julie wants a lasting relationship, but Carlos seems interested in only a **transient** one.

___ *Transient* means   a. dull.   b. short-lived.   c. hard to notice.

Matching Words with Definitions

Following are definitions of the ten words. Clearly write or print each word next to its definition. The sentences above and on the previous page will help you decide on the meaning of each word.

1. _____   Softened; toned down; made less intense

2. _____   Temporary; passing soon or quickly

3. _____   Enthusiastic and devoted

4. _____   To make calm or peaceful

5. _____   To draw forth, as a mental image or a feeling

6. _____   To gradually lessen or shrink

7. _____   To settle (a conflict) by acting as a go-between

8. _____   High regard; respect; favorable opinion

9. _____   To promote development by providing nourishment, support, and protection

10. _____   Something handed down from people who have come before

CAUTION: Do not go any further until you are sure the above answers are correct. Then you can use the definitions to help you in the following practices. Your goal is eventually to know the words well enough so that you don't need to check the definitions at all.

➣ Sentence Check 1

Using the answer line provided, complete each item below with the correct word from the box. Use each word once.

a. **avid**	b. **dwindle**	c. **esteem**	d. **evoke**	e. **legacy**
f. **mediate**	g. **muted**	h. **nurture**	i. **pacify**	j. **transient**

_____ 1. When my newborn nephew starts to scream, we ___ him by rocking him and singing softly.

_____ 2. The photos in my album ___ many fond memories of my high-school friends.

_____ 3. If you study too long at one sitting, your concentration will eventually begin to ___.

_____ 4. At the party, Yoko and I kept our conversation ___ so that no one would overhear us.

_____ 5. You must ___ a child with love and respect as well as with food and shelter.

_____ 6. Part of the charm of spring is that it's ___. It comes and goes so quickly that I can't wait for its return.

_____ 7. To show his ___ for her singing, the talent agent sent Mary flowers after she performed in a local theater.

_____ 8. My cousin Bobby is the most ___ collector I know. He collects almost anything, from baseball cards to beer cans.

_____ 9. Shakespeare's work, a priceless ___ from the sixteenth and seventeenth centuries, has been enjoyed by generation after generation.

_____10. Rather than go to court, Mr. Hillman and the owner of the gas station agreed to have a lawyer ___ their disagreement.

NOTE: Now check your answers to these questions by turning to page 177. Going over the answers carefully will help you prepare for the next two practices, for which answers are not given.

➣ Sentence Check 2

Using the answer lines provided, complete each item below with **two** words from the box. Use each word once.

_____
_____   1–2. Becky's ___ for Gerald turned out to be ___. She discovered that he used drugs and could not condone° his habit, so she broke up with him.

_____
_____   3–4. Leo is such a(n) ___ chef that his enthusiasm for cooking never ___s. He's been known to cook with great zeal° for ten straight hours.

_____
_____   5–6. Loud music upsets our canary, but ___ tones ___ her.

_____ 7–8. It is necessary to ___ a human infant because it is the biological ___ of

_____ newborn mammals to be unable to survive on their own. Parental care is indispensable°.

_____ 9–10. In the Bible, King Solomon ___s a dispute between two women, each

_____ of whom claims the same child as her own. Pretending that the child will be cut in two, he sees the horror that this thought ___s in one of the women. He then knows that she is the true mother.

➤ *Final Check:* Getting Scared

Here is a final opportunity for you to strengthen your knowledge of the ten words. First read the following selection carefully. Then fill in each blank with a word from the box at the top of the previous page. (Context clues will help you figure out which word goes in which blank.) Use each word once.

Do you remember trying to scare yourself and everybody else when you were a kid? For instance, maybe you were a(n) (1)_____ roller-coaster rider, closing your eyes and screaming and loving it all. Afterward, you would (2)_____ your still nervous stomach by quietly sipping an ice-cold Coke. If a short roller-coaster ride gave you too (3)_____ a thrill, there was always the long-term fear of a horror movie. If the horrors it depicted° were vile° enough, you might be scared about going to bed for the next three months.

And remember popping out from behind corners yelling "Boo!" at your brother? The fight that followed ("You didn't scare me one bit." "Did too." "Did not." "Did too.") would go on until a grown-up (4)_____(e)d the conflict. (Parents always seemed to be there to settle disputes among siblings° or to (5)_____ and reassure you at times when you needed support.)

At other times, you and your friends probably sat around a campfire late at night, engaging in your favorite nocturnal° activity—telling ghost stories. Thrilled with the horror of it all, you spoke in voices so (6)_____ they were almost whispers. The storyteller who gained the most (7)_____ was the one who could (8)_____ the greatest terror in others. If anybody's fear started to (9)_____, this expert would build it up again with the most effective story in the campfire repertoire°, the story of the ghost in the outhouse, a (10)_____ handed down from older brothers and sisters to younger ones. The story always made you so scared that you needed to go to the outhouse. But fearing the ghost there, how could you?

Scores	Sentence Check 2 _____%	Final Check _____%

Enter your scores above and in the vocabulary performance chart on the inside back cover of the book.

aloof	longevity
ambivalent	magnitude
augment	mundane
dispel	obscure
explicit	render

Ten Words in Context

In the space provided, write the letter of the meaning closest to that of each **boldfaced** word. Use the context of the sentences to help you figure out each word's meaning.

1 aloof
(ə-lōof′)
-adjective

___ *Aloof* means

- Some people say that the English are **aloof**, but the English people I've met seem warm and open.
- I knew that Taylor was upset with me about something because he was **aloof** even when I tried to be friendly.

   a. motivated.   b. lazy.   c. cold.

2 ambivalent
(ăm-bĭv′ə-lənt)
-adjective

___ *Ambivalent* means

- "Because I'm **ambivalent** about marriage," Earl said, "I keep swinging back and forth between wanting to set the date and wanting to break off my engagement."
- I'm **ambivalent** about my mother-in-law. I appreciate her desire to be helpful, but I dislike her efforts to run our lives.

   a. meaning well.   b. having mixed feelings.   c. experienced.

3 augment
(ôg-mĕnt′)
-verb

___ *Augment* means

- Why are women willing to **augment** their height when high heels harm their feet so much?
- Because Jenna needed additional money, she **augmented** her salary by typing term papers for college students.

   a. to add to.   b. to risk.   c. to cover up.

4 dispel
(dĭ-spĕl′)
-verb

___ *Dispel* means

- Vickie's sweet note of apology was enough to **dispel** the slight anger Rex still felt toward her.
- I tried to **dispel** my friend's fears about her blind date that evening by telling her that my parents met on a blind date.

   a. to cause.   b. to eliminate.   c. to communicate.

5 explicit
(ĕks-plĭs′ĭt)
-adjective

___ *Explicit* means

- The novel's sex scene was **explicit**, leaving nothing to the imagination.
- My parents were very **explicit** about what I could and could not do during their three-day absence. They presented me with a detailed list!

   a. brief.   b. mysterious.   c. specific.

6 longevity
(lŏn-jĕv′ĭ-tē)
-noun

___ *Longevity* means

- Volvos and Hondas are known for their **longevity**, often outlasting more expensive cars.
- The animal with the greatest **longevity** is the giant land tortoise, which can live several hundred years.

   a. form.   b. life span.   c. size.

7 magnitude
(măg′nĭ-tōōd′)
-noun

- Numbers in the billions and trillions are of too great a **magnitude** for most people to grasp.
- When the bank teller realized the **magnitude** of his error, he panicked at the thought of being held responsible for the loss of so large a sum of money.

___ *Magnitude* means   a. amount.   b. time.   c. length.

8 mundane
(mŭn-dān′)
-adjective

- Because Usha teaches belly dancing every day, it is simply one more **mundane** activity to her.
- The most **mundane** activities can turn into extraordinary events. For instance, I met my best friend while washing my clothes at the laundromat.

___ *Mundane* means   a. exciting.   b. painful.   c. commonplace.

9 obscure
(ŏb-skyōōr′)
-adjective

- The chemist didn't express his theory clearly, so it remained **obscure** to all but a few scientists.
- The police easily discovered who committed the murder, but even to the best psychiatrists, the killer's motives remained **obscure**.

___ *Obscure* means   a. unimportant.   b. unclear.   c. known.

10 render
(rĕn-dər′)
-verb

- Don't let the baby near your term paper with that crayon, or she will **render** it unreadable.
- Phyllis added so much red pepper to the chili that she **rendered** it too hot for anyone to eat.

___ *Render* means   a. to remember.   b. to make.   c. to wish.

Matching Words with Definitions

Following are definitions of the ten words. Clearly write or print each word next to its definition. The sentences above and on the previous page will help you decide on the meaning of each word.

1. _____   To drive away as if by scattering; cause to vanish

2. _____   Size

3. _____   Ordinary; everyday

4. _____   Stated or shown clearly and exactly

5. _____   Having conflicting feelings about someone or something

6. _____   To cause (something) to become; make

7. _____   Not easily understood; not clearly expressed

8. _____   Cool and reserved; distant in personal relations

9. _____   To increase; make greater, as in strength or quantity

10. _____   Length of life

CAUTION: Do not go any further until you are sure the above answers are correct. Then you can use the definitions to help you in the following practices. Your goal is eventually to know the words well enough so that you don't need to check the definitions at all.

➤ *Sentence Check 1*

Using the answer line provided, complete each item below with the correct word from the box. Use each word once.

a. **aloof**	b. **ambivalent**	c. **augment**	d. **dispel**	e. **explicit**
f. **longevity**	g. **magnitude**	h. **mundane**	i. **obscure**	j. **render**

_____ 1. The best writers can describe something ___ so that it doesn't seem ordinary at all.

_____ 2. The architect decided to add another pillar to the building to ___ its support.

_____ 3. "Russell seems ___ toward me," Janice said, "as if he both likes and dislikes me."

_____ 4. Recent research suggests that our parents' ___ doesn't necessarily affect how long we will live.

_____ 5. When I'm frightened, I try to appear ___ because looking cool and distant helps me feel in control.

_____ 6. The essence of my science teacher's genius is that he is able to make complicated, ___ ideas clear to students.

_____ 7. "If you keep walking on the backs of your shoes like that, you will ___ them as flat as the floor," Annie's mother said.

_____ 8. If Claude proposes marriage to Jean, he will ___ any doubts she may still have as to whether or not he really loves her.

_____ 9. "I try to make my test questions as ___ as possible," said Mr. Baines, "so that my students will know exactly what answers I'm looking for."

_____ 10. I began to realize the ___ of the insect population when I read that there are more kinds of insects living today than all other kinds of animals in the world.

NOTE: Now check your answers to these questions by turning to page 177. Going over the answers carefully will help you prepare for the next two practices, for which answers are not given.

➤ *Sentence Check 2*

Using the answer lines provided, complete each item below with **two** words from the box. Use each word once.

_____
_____ 1–2. When asked about his ___, ninety-year-old Mr. Greene gives an ___ recipe for a long life: eat well, exercise, and stay away from hospitals. "It's ironic°," he explains, "that I got the worst infection of my life at a hospital."

_____
_____ 3–4. Harried was able to ___ the family income by working overtime, but her problems with her husband and children increased in ___.

_____   5–6. I'm ___ about playing with our rock band. The music is a source of
_____   elation° for me, but I'm afraid it will ___ me deaf one of these days.

_____   7–8. Gail sometimes appears cold and conceited, but she is ___ only toward
_____   people she strongly dislikes. With all others, her usual genial° and modest
                                  manner soon ___s any impression that she is haughty°.

_____   9–10. "Does the idea that we don't always see things as they really are seem
_____   ___ to you?" the teacher asked. "If so, it will become clearer if you
                                   relate it to the ___ experience of looking down a road. Doesn't it look
                                   narrower in the distance than it really is?"

➤ _Final Check:_ My Sister's Date

Here is a final opportunity for you to strengthen your knowledge of the ten words. First read the following selection carefully. Then fill in each blank with a word from the box at the top of the previous page. (Context clues will help you figure out which word goes in which blank.) Use each word once.

I watched as my older sister, Ruth, removed the last spiked curler from her hair. We gaped° at the result. She somehow had (1)_____(e)d her hair limp as spaghetti. When Ruth started to cry, I tried to pacify° her with my usual gentleness: "Why are you such a crybaby about some stupid guy?"

The guy was Steven Meyer. He and Ruth were going to a high school dance. She'd had a crush on him for years, for reasons that were (2)_____ to me. (I never had been able to discern° what she saw in him.)

When Ruth began to (3)_____ her makeup by applying some more powder, she gave a terrifying scream that probably reduced my (4)_____ by at least a year. She informed me between sobs that a pimple had just appeared on her nose, making her "look like a vile° witch." I studied her face, expecting a pimple of truly amazing (5)_____. Instead, I spotted a tiny speck. I tried to (6)_____ Ruth's worries: "So, it makes you look like a witch. Don't you want to look bewitching?" But she just began to cry again. I took this opportunity to go downstairs and wait for Steven Meyer.

He arrived a half hour before Ruth was ready. Observing him through my thick glasses, I tried to figure out exactly what Ruth saw in him. We talked until she appeared at the top of the stairs. Trying to look (7)_____, she came down very slowly, wearing a cool, distant expression.

When Ruth returned home later that night, her comment about the evening was (8)_____: "Totally rotten." She said that Steven, far from being extraordinary, had turned out to be "the most (9)_____ sort of person in the world." It seemed Ruth had bypassed feeling (10)_____ about Steven and gone straight from love to hate.

It's just as well, since I've been married to Steven for ten years now.

Scores	Sentence Check 2 _____%	Final Check _____%

Enter your scores above and in the vocabulary performance chart on the inside back cover of the book.

UNIT FIVE: *Review*

The box at the right lists twenty-five words from Unit Five. Using the clues at the bottom of the page, fill in these words to complete the puzzle that follows.

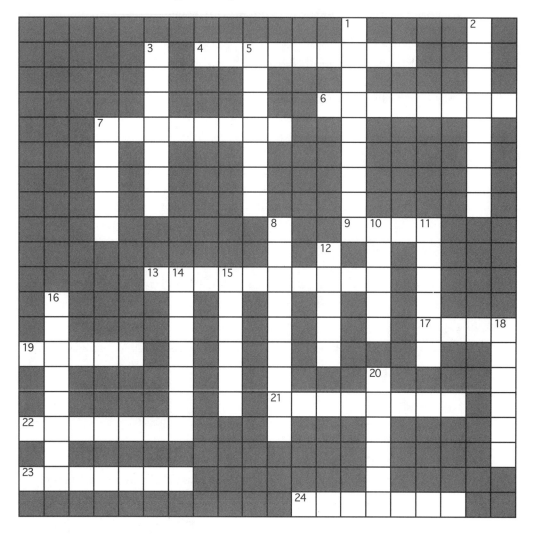

aloof
ambivalent
avid
constrict
depict
dispel
fallible
feign
furtive
genial
implicit
ironic
mediate
mundane
muted
nurture
obscure
pathetic
pragmatic
punitive
saturate
sibling
smug
sneer
vivacious

ACROSS

4. To make smaller or narrower, as by squeezing or shrinking
6. Pitifully inadequate or unsuccessful
7. To soak or fill as much as possible
9. Overly pleased with one's own cleverness, goodness, etc.; self-satisfied
13. Having conflicting feelings about someone or something
17. Enthusiastic and devoted
19. Cool and reserved
21. Suggested but not directly expressed

22. Not easily understood or clearly expressed
23. To settle (a conflict) by acting as a go-between
24. A sister or brother

DOWN

1. Lively; full of enthusiasm
2. Giving or involving punishment; punishing
3. Done or behaving so as not to be noticed; secret; sneaky
5. To promote the development of by providing nourishment, support, and protection

7. To show or express contempt or ridicule
8. Practical
10. Softened; toned down; made less intense
11. Friendly, pleasant, and kindly
12. To pretend; give a false show of
14. Ordinary; everyday
15. Opposite to what might be expected
16. Capable of making an error
18. To represent in pictures or words; describe
20. To drive away as if scattering; cause to vanish

UNIT FIVE: Test 1

PART A

Choose the word that best completes each item and write it in the space provided.

_____ 1. Dean is so ___ that he refers to his position of hamburger cook at a fast-food restaurant as "chef."

    a. punitive   b. transient   c. pretentious   d. muted

_____ 2. Endangered species won't survive unless their ___ are preserved.

    a. inhibitions   b. habitats   c. precedents   d. siblings

_____ 3. Peter hasn't been ___ about quitting his job, but he's hinted at it.

    a. explicit   b. avid   c. fallible   d. punitive

_____ 4. In talking with the social worker, the abused child ___ a life of horror.

    a. depicted   b. implored   c. intimidated   d. nurtured

_____ 5. I didn't let the kids stay up late last night because I didn't want to set a(n) ___ for future nights.

    a. longevity   b. sibling   c. inhibition   d. precedent

_____ 6. When my brother complained of a shortage of cash, his ___ message was "Can you lend me some money?"

    a. smug   b. avid   c. implicit   d. vivacious

_____ 7. Rosa has ___ her son's temper tantrums for so long that he thinks they're acceptable behavior.

    a. infuriated   b. jeopardized   c. dwindled   d. condoned

_____ 8. The poker gang laughed when Mom asked to join their game, but their ___ for her rose as she won the first four hands.

    a. esteem   b. longevity   c. legacy   d. magnitude

_____ 9. While driving home three hours after her curfew, Lucille ___ an excuse she hoped her parents would believe.

    a. formulated   b. dispelled   c. ruptured   d. intimidated

_____ 10. After a(n) ___ search during which I crawled around my entire apartment, my "missing" contact lens fell out of my eye.

    a. exhaustive   b. fiscal   c. pretentious   d. vindictive

_____ 11. Jerome deserves his excellent grades, but he doesn't have to be ___ and say, "Naturally, I got straight A's again."

    a. obscure   b. deficient   c. smug   d. muted

(Continues on next page)

_____ 12. It's ___ that my rich uncle is so stingy and my parents, who aren't rich, are always lending money to family members.

   a. exhaustive   b. ironic   c. furtive   d. pragmatic

_____ 13. Although he had heard about his grandmother's aches and pains a million times, Dennis ___(e)d interest whenever she complained to him.

   a. implore   b. feign   c. mediate   d. pacify

PART B
Write **C** if the italicized word is used **correctly**. Write **I** if the word is used **incorrectly**.

____ 14. *Saturate* the washcloth by wringing it out.

____ 15. I don't consider cooking an entire meal a *mundane* task because I do it so rarely.

____ 16. The poem is *obscure* because it jumps from one complicated image to another.

____ 17. Joel is such an *introvert* that he often strikes up conversations with total strangers.

____ 18. After our truck ran over a sharp rock, a tire *ruptured*. Luckily, we had a spare in the trunk.

____ 19. Mort's back talk *pacified* his father, who then denied him the use of the car for a month.

____ 20. The suspect had such a *furtive* expression that he appeared to be hiding something.

____ 21. I think I'm coming down with the flu. I've been feeling weak and *vivacious* all morning.

____ 22. Liz has a great sense of humor. Her jokes can *infuriate* me when nothing else can make me smile.

____ 23. My Great Dane *intimidates* visitors with her loud bark and large size, but she's really very friendly.

____ 24. I have to ignore Jesse completely now to *dispel* any idea he may have that I'm romantically interested in him.

____ 25. In the package, pantyhose look so small that it's hard to believe they'll *constrict* enough to fit over a woman's legs and hips.

Score   (Number correct) _____ x 4 = _____ %

Enter your score above and in the vocabulary performance chart on the inside back cover of the book.

UNIT FIVE: Test 2

PART A
Complete each item with a word from the box. Use each word once.

a. **ambivalent**	b. **contemplate**	c. **detrimental**	d. **evoke**	e. **feasible**
f. **fiscal**	g. **inhibition**	h. **jeopardize**	i. **legacy**	j. **magnitude**
k. **muted**	l. **reconcile**	m. **sibling**		

_____ 1. To make the bright green a more ___ shade, the painter added a few drops of black.

_____ 2. Music in a minor key often ___s sad feelings in the listener.

_____ 3. Eating sticky dried fruits can be as ___ to your teeth as eating candy.

_____ 4. No one realized the ___ of Nora's depression until she tried to kill herself.

_____ 5. Isabel has ___ feelings about her job. She loves the work but hates her boss.

_____ 6. Why ___ dropping out of school when you've got only two semesters to go?

_____ 7. It isn't ___ to grow roses in our back yard. There's too much shade back there for roses.

_____ 8. My love of the outdoors is a(n) ___ from my grandfather, who often hiked in the mountains.

_____ 9. The company is in such bad ___ shape that over half the employees will soon be laid off.

_____ 10. Dick ___(e)d his chances of getting the job when he addressed the interviewer by the wrong name.

_____ 11. My ___s will be coming from California and Arkansas to celebrate our parents' thirtieth anniversary.

_____ 12. At first, Tiffany was reluctant to sit in Santa Claus's lap, but she overcame her ___s when she saw that he was handing out candy canes.

_____ 13. As the wedding drew near, Brenda had to ___ herself to the fact that her son would marry a woman she disliked.

(Continues on next page)

PART B

Write **C** if the italicized word is used **correctly**. Write **I** if the word is used **incorrectly**.

_____ 14. Karen found the chicken salad *vile*. One small taste made her gag.

_____ 15. I asked Sal to *augment* the stereo because it was giving me a headache.

_____ 16. Some spiders have surprising *longevity,* living as long as twenty years.

_____ 17. I enjoy watching championship boxing matches because they are so *devoid* of violence.

_____ 18. When the *vindictive* tenant moved out, he broke all the windows in his apartment.

_____ 19. The Changs' *transient* marriage has already lasted over fifty years.

_____ 20. Paul *sneered* at the rock star who was his idol and asked her to autograph his record album.

_____ 21. Being a *pragmatic* person, my brother values music and poetry more than practical things.

_____ 22. An *avid* reader, Judy spends much of her time enjoying newspapers, magazines and books.

_____ 23. My liking for my supervisor *dwindled* as his temper grew shorter and his list of "don'ts" grew longer.

_____ 24. Fascinated by the cartoon on TV, the little boy *gaped* at his mother as she left for work.

_____ 25. When a friend broke her expensive china bowl, Harriet remained *genial*, saying, "Don't worry about it. I almost dropped it once myself."

Score (Number correct) _____ x 4 = _____ %

Enter your score above and in the vocabulary performance chart on the inside back cover of the book.

UNIT FIVE: Test 3

PART A
Complete each sentence in a way that clearly shows you understand the meaning of the **boldfaced** word. Take a minute to plan your answer before you write.

Example: To increase your **longevity**, *exercise frequently and avoid alcohol, tobacco, and high-fat foods* .

1. One thing the nursery-school teacher did to **nurture** each child each day was _____

   _____.

2. **Pragmatic** Ramona spends her money on such things as _____

   _____.

3. The critic summed up how **pathetic** the actor's performance was with this comment: " _____

   _____."

4. Lionel **implored** his parents to _____

   _____.

5. The **magnitude** of Carol's musical talent became clear to us when _____

   _____.

6. A student **deficient** in study skills might _____

   _____.

7. We learned how **fallible** the house builder was when _____

   _____.

8. To **mediate** the argument between my sister and me, _____

   _____.

9. Enrique was **rendered** helpless when _____

   _____.

10. When Mary Lou asked the fortuneteller, "What will my career be?" the **cryptic** reply was " _____

    _____."

(Continues on next page)

PART B

After each **boldfaced** word are a *synonym* (a word that means the same as the boldfaced word), an *antonym* (a word that means the opposite of the boldfaced word), and a word that is neither. On the answer line, write the letter of the word that is the antonym.

Example: __b__ **dwindle**   a. lessen   b. increase   c. turn

____ 11. **aloof**   a. angry   b. friendly   c. reserved

____ 12. **detrimental**   a. harmful   b. orderly   c. beneficial

____ 13. **intimidate**   a. delay   b. frighten   c. encourage

____ 14. **genial**   a. unpleasant   b. kindly   c. inborn

____ 15. **punitive**   a. rewarding   b. requiring   c. punishing

PART C

Use five of the following ten words in sentences. Make it clear that you know the meaning of the word you use. Feel free to use the past tense or plural form of a word.

a. **condone**	b. **esteem**	c. **feign**	d. **habitat**	e. **implore**
f. **inhibition**	g. **pacify**	h. **sibling**	i. **smug**	j. **vindictive**

16. _____

_____

17. _____

_____

18. _____

_____

19. _____

_____

20. _____

_____

Score   (Number correct) _____ x 5 = _____ %

Enter your score above and in the vocabulary performance chart on the inside back cover of the book.

A. Limited Answer Key

Important Note: Be sure to use this answer key as a learning tool only. You should not turn to this key until you have considered carefully the sentence in which a given word appears.

Used properly, the key will help you to learn words and to prepare for the activities and tests for which answers are not given. For ease of reference, the title of the "Final Check" passage in each chapter appears in parentheses.

Chapter 1 (Joseph Palmer)
Sentence Check 1
1. adamant
2. encounter
3. malign
4. amiable
5. amoral
6. epitome
7. absolve
8. antagonist
9. animosity
10. eccentric

Chapter 2 (Telephone Salespeople)
Sentence Check 1
1. dilemma
2. wary
3. inclination
4. curt
5. sabotage
6. demoralize
7. subsequent
8. irate
9. zeal
10. retort

Chapter 3 (A Cruel Sport)
Sentence Check 1
1. tangible
2. obsolete
3. acclaim
4. adjacent
5. escalate
6. engross
7. exploit
8. methodical
9. terminate
10. elicit

Chapter 4 (Bald Is Beautiful)
Sentence Check 1
1. infirmity
2. implication
3. infringe
4. succinct
5. sparse
6. innovation
7. revitalize
8. subjective
9. inequity
10. deter

Chapter 5 (No Luck with Women)
Sentence Check 1
1. mercenary
2. allusion
3. altruistic
4. assail
5. euphemism
6. taint
7. appease
8. syndrome
9. arbitrary
10. banal

Chapter 6 (A Taste of Parenthood)
Sentence Check 1
1. audience
2. sympathetic
3. childhood
4. pendant
5. quartet
6. nonessential
7. happily
8. unicycle
9. annually
10. hypertension

Chapter 7 (Accident and Recovery)
Sentence Check 1
1. calamity
2. ponder
3. flagrant
4. comprehensive
5. conventional
6. persevere
7. rehabilitate
8. turmoil
9. fluctuate
10. venture

Chapter 8 (Animal Senses)
Sentence Check 1
1. enhance
2. attest
3. dispatch
4. exemplify
5. enigma
6. nocturnal
7. discern
8. orient
9. mobile
10. attribute

Chapter 9 (Money Problems)

Sentence Check 1

1. predominant
2. concurrent
3. constitute
4. prerequisite
5. nominal
6. decipher
7. recession
8. default
9. confiscate
10. hypothetical

Chapter 10 (The New French Employee)

Sentence Check 1

1. suffice
2. sinister
3. vulnerable
4. intricate
5. implausible
6. sanctuary
7. incoherent
8. scrutiny
9. degenerate
10. intercede

Chapter 11 (A Cruel Teacher)

Sentence Check 1

1. immaculate
2. blight
3. gloat
4. blatant
5. contrive
6. garble
7. retaliate
8. gaunt
9. qualm
10. plagiarism

Chapter 12 (It's Never Too Late)

Sentence Check 1

1. exclaimed
2. biorhythm
3. patricide
4. homeward
5. inflexible
6. forceful
7. semiprivate
8. finalists
9. humanitarian
10. humiliated

Chapter 13 (Learning to Study)

Sentence Check 1

1. Intermittent
2. devastate
3. incorporate
4. indispensable
5. incentive
6. rigor
7. squander
8. curtail
9. digress
10. succumb

Chapter 14 (The Mad Monk)

Sentence Check 1

1. intrinsic
2. alleviate
3. virile
4. cynic
5. infamous
6. covert
7. revulsion
8. speculate
9. benefactor
10. demise

Chapter 15 (Conflict Over Holidays)

Sentence Check 1

1. aspire
2. benevolent
3. diversion
4. mandatory
5. abstain
6. deficit
7. dissent
8. affiliate
9. agnostic
10. lucrative

Chapter 16 (Dr. Martin Luther King, Jr.)

Sentence Check 1

1. Conversely
2. extrovert
3. poignant
4. prevalent
5. contend
6. proponent
7. charisma
8. contemporary
9. traumatic
10. quest

Chapter 17 (Relating to Parents)

Sentence Check 1

1. prone
2. congenial
3. flippant
4. prompt
5. rapport
6. impasse
7. relentless
8. perception
9. reprisal
10. rationale

Chapter 18 (Held Back by Fears)

Sentence Check 1

1. boyish
2. Wisdom
3. discouraged
4. immobile
5. produced
6. magnified
7. duplicate
8. psychoanalyst
9. intensify
10. claustrophobia

Chapter 19 (Interview with a Rude Star)

Sentence Check 1

1. comprise
2. redundant
3. haughty
4. libel
5. glib
6. benign
7. blasé
8. facade
9. condescend
10. pseudonym

Chapter 20 (The Nightmare of Gym)

Sentence Check 1

1. detract
2. ominous
3. averse
4. elation
5. nullified
6. endow
7. expulsion
8. disdain
9. divulge
10. mortified

Chapter 21 (Skipping Church)

Sentence Check 1

1. latent
2. designate
3. deviate
4. credible
5. interim
6. cursory
7. secular
8. improvise
9. shun
10. simulate

Chapter 22 (A Model Teacher)

Sentence Check 1

1. waive
2. commemorate
3. deplete
4. transcend
5. complacent
6. niche
7. menial
8. diligent
9. consensus
10. empathy

Chapter 23 (My Talented Roommate)

Sentence Check 1

1. bizarre
2. repertoire
3. falter
4. conducive
5. gist
6. hamper
7. viable
8. paradox
9. frenzy
10. flaunt

Chapter 24 (Fascinating Courses)

Sentence Check 1

1. actor
2. geochemistry
3. omnipresent
4. asterisk
5. director
6. theologian
7. misplace
8. contradicts
9. Monogamy
10. populated

Chapter 25 (Cal and His Sisters)

Sentence Check 1

1. vivacious
2. implore
3. devoid
4. introvert
5. jeopardize
6. sibling
7. infuriate
8. sneer
9. intimidate
10. smug

Chapter 26 (Shoplifter)

Sentence Check 1

1. gape
2. contemplate
3. precedent
4. feasible
5. condone
6. fiscal
7. furtive
8. pathetic
9. feign
10. punitive

Chapter 27 (A Nutty Newspaper Office)

Sentence Check 1

1. deficient
2. rupture
3. ironic
4. detrimental
5. inhibition
6. depict
7. vindictive
8. cryptic
9. saturate
10. implicit

Chapter 28 (Roughing It)

Sentence Check 1

1. vile
2. genial
3. reconcile
4. constrict
5. formulate
6. exhaustive
7. Pretentious
8. habitat
9. pragmatic
10. fallible

Chapter 29 (Getting Scared)

Sentence Check 1

1. pacify
2. evoke
3. dwindle
4. muted
5. nurture
6. transient
7. esteem
8. avid
9. legacy
10. mediate

Chapter 30 (My Sister's Date)

Sentence Check 1

1. mundane
2. augment
3. ambivalent
4. longevity
5. aloof
6. obscure
7. render
8. dispel
9. explicit
10. magnitude

B. Dictionary Use

It isn't always possible to figure out the meaning of a word from its context, and that's where a dictionary comes in. Following is some basic information to help you use a dictionary.

HOW TO FIND A WORD

A dictionary contains so many words that it can take a while to find the one you're looking for. But if you know how to use guide words, you can find a word rather quickly. *Guide words* are the two words at the top of each dictionary page. The first guide word tells what the first word is on the page. The second guide word tells what the last word is on that page. The other words on a page fall alphabetically between the two guide words. So when you look up a word, find the two guide words that alphabetically surround the word you're looking for.

- Which of the following pair of guide words would be on a page with the word *skirmish*?

     skimp / **skyscraper**   **skyward** / **slave**   **sixty** / **skimming**

The answer to this question and the questions that follow are given on the next page.

HOW TO USE A DICTIONARY LISTING

A dictionary listing includes many pieces of information. For example, here is a typical listing. Note that it includes much more than just a definition.

> **driz•zle** (drĭz′əl), *v.*, **-zled, -zling,** *n.* — *v.* To rain gently and steadily in fine drops.
> — *n.* A very light rain. —**driz′zly,** *adj.*

Key parts of a dictionary entry are listed and explained below.

Syllables. Dots separate dictionary entry words into syllables. Note that *drizzle* has one dot, which breaks the word into two syllables.

- To practice seeing the syllable breakdown in a dictionary entry, write the number of syllables in each word below.

     gla•mour _____   **mic•ro•wave** _____   **in•de•scrib•a•ble** _____

Pronunciation guide. The information within parentheses after the entry word shows how to pronounce the entry word. This pronunciation guide includes two types of symbols: pronunciation symbols and accent marks.

Pronunciation symbols represent the consonant and vowel sounds in a word. The consonant sounds are probably very familiar to you, but you may find it helpful to review some of the sounds of the vowels—*a, e, i, o,* and *u.* Every dictionary has a key explaining the sounds of its pronunciation symbols, including the long and short sounds of vowels.

Long vowels have the sound of their own names. For example, the *a* in *pay* and the *o* in *no* both have long vowel sounds. Long vowel sounds are shown by a straight line above the vowel.

In many dictionaries, the *short vowels* are shown by a curved line above the vowel. Thus the *i* in the first syllable of *drizzle* is a short *i.* The pronunciation chart on the inside front cover of this book indicates that the short *i* has the sound of *i* in *sit.* It also indicates that the short *a* has the sound of *a* in *hat,* that the short *e* has the sound of *e* in *ten,* and so on.

- Which of the words below have a short vowel sound? Which has a long vowel sound?

     drug _____   **night** _____   **sand** _____

Another pronunciation symbol is the *schwa* (ə), which looks like an upside-down *e*. It stands for certain rapidly spoken, unaccented vowel sounds, such as the *a* in *above*, the *e* in *item*, the *i* in *easily*, the *o* in *gallop*, and the *u* in *circus*. More generally, it has an "uh" sound, like the "uh" a speaker makes when hesitating. Here are three words that include the schwa sound:

in•fant (ĭn′fənt)   **bum•ble** (bŭm′bəl)   **de•liv•er** (dĭ-lĭv′ər)

- Which syllable in *drizzle* contains the schwa sound, the first or the second? _____

Accent marks are small black marks that tell you which syllable to emphasize, or stress, as you say a word. An accent mark follows *driz* in the pronunciation guide for *drizzle,* which tells you to stress the first syllable of *drizzle.* Syllables with no accent mark are not stressed. Some syllables are in between, and they are marked with a lighter accent mark.

- Which syllable has the stronger accent in *sentimental*? _____

sen•ti•men•tal (sĕn′tə-mĕn′tl)

Parts of speech.   After the pronunciation key and before each set of definitions, the entry word's parts of speech are given. The parts of speech are abbreviated as follows:

noun—*n.*   pronoun—*pron.*   adjective—*adj.*   adverb—*adv.*   verb—*v.*

- The listing for *drizzle* shows that it can be two parts of speech. Write them below:

_____   _____

Definitions.   Words often have more than one meaning. When they do, each meaning is usually numbered in the dictionary. You can tell which definition of a word fits a given sentence by the meaning of the sentence. For example, the word *charge* has several definitions, including these two: **1.** To ask as a price. **2.** To accuse or blame.

- Show with a check which definition (1 or 2) applies in each sentence below:

The store charged me less for the blouse because it was missing a button.   1 ___   2 ___

My neighbor has been charged with shoplifting.   1 ___   2 ___

Other information.   After the definitions in a listing in a hardbound dictionary, you may get information about the *origin* of a word. Such information about origins, also known as *etymology,* is usually given in brackets. And you may sometimes be given one or more synonyms or antonyms for the entry word. *Synonyms* are words that are similar in meaning to the entry word; *antonyms* are words that are opposite in meaning.

WHICH DICTIONARIES TO OWN

You will find it useful to own two recent dictionaries: a small paperback dictionary to carry to class and a hardbound dictionary, which contains more information than a small paperback version. Among the good dictionaries strongly recommended are both the paperback and the hardcover editions of the following:

The American Heritage Dictionary
The Random House College Dictionary
Webster's New World Dictionary

ANSWERS TO THE DICTIONARY QUESTIONS

Guide words: *skimp/skyscraper*   Accent: stronger accent on third syllable *(men)*
Number of syllables: 2, 3, 5   Parts of speech: noun and verb
Vowels: *drug, sand* (short); *night* (long)   Definitions: 1; 2
Schwa: second syllable of *drizzle*

C. List of Words and Word Parts

Note: Word parts are in *italics*.

absolve, 8
abstain, 84
acclaim, 16
adamant, 8
adjacent, 16
affiliate, 84
agnostic, 84
alleviate, 80
allusion, 24
aloof, 164
altruistic, 24
ambivalent, 164
amiable, 8
amoral, 8
animosity, 8
ann, enn, 28
antagonist, 8
appease, 24
arbitrary, 24
aspire, 84
assail, 24
aster-, astro-, 130
-ate, 62
attest, 46
attribute, 46
audi, audio-, 28
augment, 164
averse, 114
avid, 160
banal, 24
benefactor, 80
benevolent, 84
benign, 110
bio-, 62
bizarre, 126
blasé, 110
blatant, 58
blight, 58
calamity, 42
charisma, 88
claim, clam, 62
commemorate, 122
complacent, 122
comprehensive, 42

comprise, 110
concurrent, 50
condescend, 110
condone, 148
conducive, 126
confiscate, 50
congenial, 92
consensus, 122
constitute, 50
constrict, 156
contemplate, 148
contemporary, 88
contend, 88
contra-, 130
contrive, 58
conventional, 42
conversely, 88
cor, cour, 96
covert, 80
credible, 118
cryptic, 152
cursory, 118
curt, 12
curtail, 76
cycl, cyclo-, 28
cynic, 80
decipher, 50
default, 50
deficient, 152
deficit, 84
degenerate, 54
demise, 80
demoralize, 12
depict, 152
deplete, 122
designate, 118
deter, 20
detract, 114
detrimental, 152
devastate, 76
deviate, 118
devoid, 144
di-, du-, 96
digress, 76

dilemma, 12
diligent, 122
discern, 46
disdain, 114
dispatch, 46
dispel, 164
dissent, 84
diversion, 84
divulge, 114
-dom, 96
dwindle, 160
eccentric, 8
elation, 114
elicit, 16
empathy, 122
encounter, 8
endow, 114
engross, 16
enhance, 46
enigma, 46
epitome, 8
-er, -or, 130
escalate, 16
esteem, 160
euphemism, 24
evoke, 160
exemplify, 46
exhaustive, 156
explicit, 164
exploit, 16
expulsion, 114
extrovert, 88
facade, 110
fallible, 156
falter, 126
feasible, 148
feign, 148
fin, 62
fiscal, 148
flagrant, 42
flaunt, 126
flex, flect, 62
flippant, 92
fluctuate, 42